WARP/WEFT/SETT
A Reference Manual for Handweavers

June H. Beveridge

One of the most frequent problems faced by weavers is the selection of a warp, a weft and a sett to achieve a satisfactory weft-faced fabric. Now author June Beveridge gives weavers an easy-to-use guide for selecting the best warp/weft/sett combinations without having to go through the time-consuming and often expensive process of weaving samples.

This manual gives the weaver 944 photographs of actual-size samples, each using the most common reed sizes and the most popular cotton and linen warps and each one woven with the same sequence of weft yarns. Information on warp and weft selection, yarn systems, yarn calculations and metric conversions, as well as a suppliers' lists giving yarn manufacturers, retail outlets and mail order firms assist the weaver in achieving the best possible results.

Regardless of the type of loom used, **Warp/Weft/Sett: A Reference Manual for Handweavers** allows the teacher, the beginning or advanced student, or professional to utilize their time and skills to the best advantage.

WARP/WEFT/SETT

A Reference Manual for Handweavers

June H. Beveridge

Photography by
Steven E. Beveridge

 VAN NOSTRAND REINHOLD COMPANY
New York Cincinnati Toronto London Melbourne

Dedication

To my daughter, Lauren, with love.

Acknowledgments

I wish to thank all those companies who so graciously participated in this book for their kind assistance.

Undoubtedly and regrettably, there are omissions. The criteria for selecting yarns to be used in the text were based on national availability and on those yarns that are routinely and consistently manufactured, so that there is a degree of continuity.

To Lucille Landis and Klara Cherepov who checked the text and made suggestions, to the many weavers who gave encouragement, and in particular, to Rita Weiss—thank you.

Copyright © 1980 by June H. Beveridge
Library of Congress Catalog Card Number 80-11619
ISBN 0-442-26129-2

Printed in United States of America

Published in 1980 by Van Nostrand Reinhold Company
A division of Litton Educational Publishing, Inc.
135 West 50th Street, New York, NY 10020, U.S.A.

Van Nostrand Reinhold Limited
1410 Birchmount Road
Scarborough, Ontario M1P 2E7, Canada

Van Nostrand Reinhold Australia Pty. Ltd.
17 Queen Street
Mitcham, Victoria 3132, Australia

Van Nostrand Reinhold Company Limited
Molly Millars Lane
Wokingham, Berkshire, England

16 15 14 13 12 11 10 9 8 7 6 5 4 3 2 1

Library of Congress Cataloging in Publication Data

Beveridge, June, H.
    Warp/weft/sett.

    Includes index.
    1. Hand weaving. I. Title
TT848.B45   746.1'4   80-11619
ISBN 0-442-26129-2

CONTENTS

INTRODUCTION

One of the most frequent problems a weaver has before embarking on a project is selecting a warp, a weft and a sett to achieve a satisfactory weft-faced fabric. With so many thousands of possible combinations from which to choose, many weavers determine which warp/weft/sett to use by sampling, a time consuming, expensive and frequently boring procedure. If the first sample is not satisfactory, adjustments must be made, either in the choice of sett if a specific weft and/or warp are to be used or in the warp or weft yarns if limited by the number of reeds available.

The samples illustrated in this book are intended to be a guideline to eliminate, if possible, sampling time and expense by giving you an immediate point of comparison between particular sizes of cotton and linen warp yarns, each used with a variety of possible weft yarns and setts. Shown are the most popular cotton and linen warps, each woven with the same sequence of weft yarns, and each using the most common reed sizes, or numbers of ends per inch. You should keep in mind that individual techniques, equipment and styles vary and that these factors might make it necessary to make some alterations to achieve the desired results.

COTTON WARP: 10/2   **Weft E**

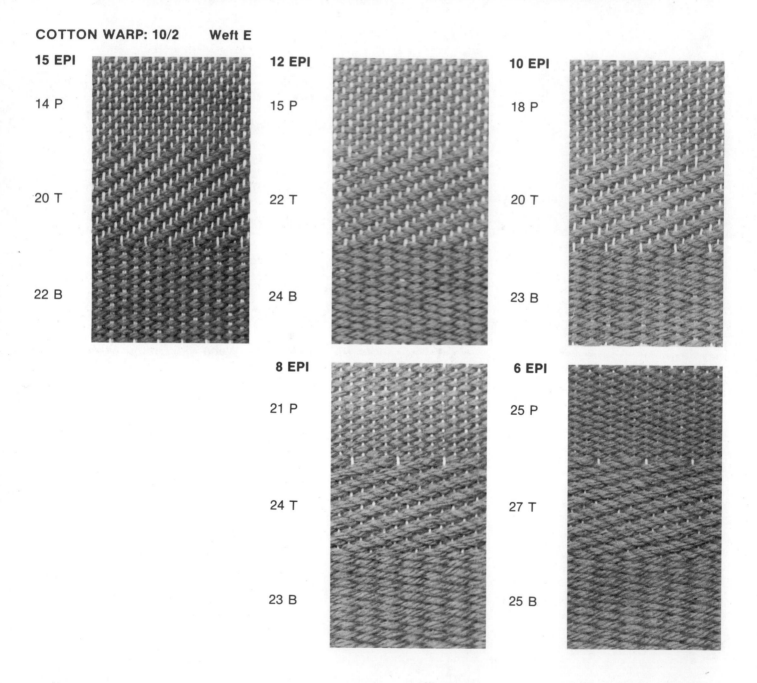

15 EPI

14 P

20 T

22 B

12 EPI

15 P

22 T

24 B

10 EPI

18 P

20 T

23 B

8 EPI

21 P

24 T

23 B

6 EPI

25 P

27 T

25 B

The Warp And The Weft

A fiber's characteristics determine the system and equipment used to spin it. Long staple wool fibers make a smooth, hard-twisted yarn when spun parallel on the worsted system. Short staple wools, from sheep as well as other animals, are spun on the woolen system and usually result in softer, loftier yarns. Cotton has its own methods and equipment.

When considering commercially spun yarns, it is very important to understand how they are described. The various terminologies may be confusing to the handweaver, but many efforts, such as the Tex system, have been made to universalize yarn sizing, and standardization has become common in many aspects of the textile industry.

Each system—woolen, worsted, lea, cotton, etc.—has its own *count,* defined as *yarn size in length per unit of mass.* When we talk of *yarn size,* we are referring to the denominator that states how many yards of a single (unplied) yarn is required to make one pound of that yarn. Each system (see Table I) has its own numerical *constant* to express the basic number of yards (unplied) per pound upon which the entire system depends. So when we speak, for example, of a 20/3 cotton, we are referring to a cotton *count* of 20 times the *constant* (840 yards per pound, singles) divided by the number of *ply* (3), which equals 5600 yards per pound. In calculating the yardage of a yarn, **always be sure to use the correct system for that yarn.**

It is important to understand how yarns are described so that you know what type of yarn you are purchasing and how much might be required. Most of the yarns used in this book have their yardages stated on the package by the manufacturer so there is little difficulty in calculating how much is needed for a specific project. But when a yarn is described only by count and ply (and perhaps fiber content), you must be able to compute that system in order to insure that you have enough yardage for your project. In the finer grades of yarn, using a 20/2 worsted as an example, a few yards here and there will make little difference since you are dealing with a yarn that has about 5000 yards per pound. However, when a heavier yarn is considered, say one with only 350 yards to the pound, a twenty yard, or 6 percent, difference might throw the calculations off to the point where you might not have enough to complete a project. Therefore, if you have a supply of warp on hand, the major purchasing consideration has to be given to the weft yarns, with final adjustment being made in the sett. On the other hand, if you have the weft yarn, selection of the warp yarn has to be worked "backwards," as it were, with the final adjustment again being made by the choice of sett.

If in doubt as to which system a yarn belongs, the *hand* (feel of the yarn) will frequently indicate whether it is woolen system (soft finish, like handspun) or the worsted system (hard finish and very uniform). With the aid of a magnifying glass, you can select a fiber from the yarn (move several inches away from the cut end of the strand so you pick an entire fiber) and, still using the glass, check the length of the fiber. The worsted system uses fibers that are longer than 1½ inches; in the woolen system, the fibers are shorter.

If you spin your own yarn, the rules of industry scarcely apply; if you run out of yarn, you can spin some more, and, since the major charm of handspun is its lack of perfection, the variations in weight or color may not matter. But if you are short of a commercially spun yarn and have to buy some more, the results could be disastrous, especially if there is a difference in dye lot. Another important point to consider is that, if the loom is dressed with a wide warp and it becomes necessary to change the reed, there is additional stress upon the warp plus the strong possibility of using too much warp to re-dress the loom, thus shorting the final yardage.

Table I lists the standard yarn systems, as used by most commercial spinners in the United States and abroad. Keep in mind that various production yarn winders vary from package to package so that one cone or skein may have more or less yarn than another of the same lot. The formulas given for computing yarn systems are accurate; the handweaver is advised to use them as offered, rounding off the fractions or decimals, and remembering that, although most manufacturers exercise strict quality control, the yarns sold do not always match the theory to the letter. There are also many imported yarns currently on the market that are described in metric terms, not all of whose manufacturers give yardage and weights in U.S. terms. *Table II* gives a useful conversion chart.

The Sett

Some yarns are more elastic, or have a softer hand or a less hard finish than yarns with the same given count or yardage per pound and therefore compress more in the woven cloth and take more picks per inch than one might expect. The sett becomes a factor in this compaction when given a specific size warp.

When we talk about *sett,* we are describing the density of the fabric produced by the number of ends per inch. Another term frequently used is sley, that is the number of ends of warp threaded through the reed. Do not confuse sett or sley with reed size; a reed of ten dents per inch*, for example, can be sleyed many ways; one end per dent (10 EPI), two ends per dent (20 EPI), two ends every other dent with a single end between (15 EPI), three ends per dent (30 EPI), etc.

If you take the same warp yarn and the same weft yarn and weave them at five different setts, as illustrated on page 4, you will see how, as the warp ends are spaced farther apart and the weft is more readily meshed within them rather than being pushed over and under the warp yarns, the angles of the twill diagonals change. Note also how the plain and basket weaves are compacted in the samples having fewer ends per inch.

So, a general rule is that the fewer the ends per inch, the closer packed all the filling yarns will be when the warp is woven off with the same yarn throughout. With a *heavy* beat, the warp ends can, for the most part, be completely covered, regardless of the sett. As the ends per inch lessen, the weft is compressed more.

The "hairiness" of a yarn is also often a factor in this compaction. A smooth, fuzzless yarn will compact more within a warp than a yarn that is fuzzy or hairy.

Occasionally, when a warp is set too close, a pick will not "stay put" after beating and continue to slide around within the fell; for example, the basket weave section shown in Figure 372.

---

* Reeds are historically calibrated in dents per inch; however, if you have a reed that has dents per centimeter, see Table II for equivalents. The differences in the number of ends per inch versus the number of ends per centimeter becomes important when you are following a draft in which the threading directions are given in one terminology, and your equipment is made in another; the conversion *must* be made or else you will miscalculate the width of the fabric. If your reeds are stated in centimeters, you must first convert to inches before using the calculations for the samples in this book.

The Samples

All of the samples in the book have been woven on a four-harness floor loom and threaded in a straight draw. The treadling order in each sample is:

> *Plain* weave (or tabby): 13, 24
> *Twill* weave: 12, 23, 34, 41
> *Basket* weave: 12, 34

The weaves are presented by warp size beginning with the finest, those with the most yards per pound, and continuing in order of increased weight, or fewer yards per pound. Figures 1-502 and 796-873 illustrate cotton warps. Figures 503-795 and 874-939 show the linen warps. The samples are grouped by the number of ends per inch (EPI). For example, to find a sample woven on a 5/2 cotton warp, with 15 EPI, look under the heading *5/2 Cotton* and then find the sub-group showing the 15 EPI samples.

The cotton and linen warps selected for the samples in this book have been chosen because of their strength, uniformity and popularity. When selecting a warp, remember that, during the course of weaving it off the loom, the yarn is subjected to much stress, tension and abrasion, and therefore should be constructed of sufficiently long fibers, well twisted together, to withstand the strain imposed upon it. For these reasons, yarns spun on the woolen system are usually not suitable for warps. It is recommended that the warp yarns be used singlefold only; otherwise the tension within the dents will not be uniform. If a heavier yarn is required, select a plied yarn that is more appropriate to the size needed.

All of the wefts in Figures 1 through 795, which have been used *singlefold,* have been presented in the same sequence throughout the entire series of warps and are shown actual size. *Table III* and *Table IV* give the data on these wefts yarns. For example, Figure 45 shows that the warp is a 24/3 cotton, and the weft is B, described in Table III as Cum worsted 20/2. The plain (P) weave section has 22 picks per inch, the twill (T) section has 40 picks, and the basket (B) section has 64 picks, all sleyed at 20 EPI.

Where a sample has been omitted, it is either because the warp is too fine (a 20/2 cotton will not support a heavy 4 ply berber) or too heavy (an 8/5 linen is not suitable for a 20/2 worsted) and is therefore an improbable combination. 8/5 and 8/4 linen warps are too heavy to be sleyed in a 15 or 12 dent reed and have been omitted entirely.

The wefts used in the *Supplemental* section (Figures 796-939) reflect just a part of the tremendous variety of yarns now on the market, and a few examples are included to offer a more complete range of comparison and possibility. The warp sizes (both cotton and linen) as well as the EPI selected in this section were a calculated guess based on the size of the weft yarn. Many of these examples have been woven on more than one sett to offer a variety of results or to indicate better suitability. The data on these yarns can be found in *Appendix III.*

All samples were woven to three inches, allowing one inch each for the plain, the twill and the basket weave sections. Please note that if the web is measured while the warp is under tension, the heavier the weft used, the more it will "shrink" when the beam is released. When weaving, measurements should be made while the warp is *not* under tension. Again, individual weavers vary in the number of picks per inch used, so the information given for the samples is intended as a guide only.

The *beat* of the fell in the samples is as consistent throughout all the weavings as I was able to make it. In the cotton warps, the beat is very gentle on the theory that one soft beat will produce a satisfactory result. *All cotton warp samples have one beat after the shot and before the shed is changed.* You can beat more than once and/or as firmly as your particular habit is. The linen warp samples have a heavy beat since linen is usually used as a warp for rugs or heavy fabrics. *All linen warp samples have one heavy beat after the shot and before the shed is changed.*

All samples in this book are "loom state." No fulling, finishing or pressing has been done. Neither has an effort been made to make any sample "look good." The weaving was done with a steady rhythm and shows what each combination actually looks like. It is left to you to make aesthetic judgments.

The yarns selected for the samples are readily available either in weaving supply outlets and art needlework stores, or via mail order. Only quality yarns of 100% wool have been used for all the wefts. Only yarns that are uniform in spin (no slubs, novelties, etc.) have been used. Continuity, or the consistent year in and year out production of a yarn by its manufacturer, was also a requirement for the yarns chosen.

To the less experienced weaver it should be pointed out that, in selecting a sample from this book to use as a guide for a larger project, the wider the warp used, the greater the need to change either the number of ends per inch or the size of the weft yarn. The tension on a weft pick from selvage to selvage will be less on a narrow weaving (20 inches or less) than it will be on a weaving that is wider than 20 inches. It is often suggested that a sample done on a narrow width (as those in this book have been done) can safely be used above 24 inches of weaving width by reducing the number of EPI by one or two, *or* by using a slightly thinner yarn in the weft.

Also, the beat on the narrow warp usually has more pressure against the fell than it does on a wider warp. Therefore, the fell will frequently not pack on the wider cloth as it does on the narrow sample, and, even with the use of temples or stretchers, the weft will sometimes pull in at the selvages or not beat as compactly as desired.

Another aspect in going from a narrow width of warp to a wider width is that the tension between the front and back beams may have to be lessened so that the pick will beat in as desired. The tighter the tension between the beams, the less the weft will compress. This is where style of weaving and equipment become deciding factors.

The *Appendixes* alphabetically list yarn manufacturers and their addresses, selling procedures and product data, with Figure numbers if their product has been illustrated.

The *Indexes* give a summary of all the information needed for each sample: warp type and size, weft, EPI and picks per inch. The wefts used are identified in Table III (for cotton warp), Table IV (for linen warp) and in Appendix III (for supplemental yarns). *A note of caution:* be sure to refer to the appropriate Table/Appendix when identifying the weft yarns used in the samples. The Indexes can also be used in reverse to find a sample that most closely approximates the materials you have on hand or plan to use.

Table I: Yarn Systems

System	Constant	Unit of Count
Cotton	840 yards/pound	1 count
Linen	300 yards/pound	1 lea, or 1 cut
Worsted	560 yards/pound	1 count
Woolen	1600 yards/pound	1 run

Size given multiplied by the constant for each system divided by ply equals yards per pound
Example: 3/2 cotton = 3 (single size) X 840 (constant) ÷
            2 (ply) = 1260 yards/pound

• If a yarn has been plied more than once, it is written with the number of the final ply, then the previous one, and finally the yarn size.
• To find the yarn size, if given the number of yards per pound, multiply the yardage figure by the number of ply and then divide that number by the system constant.
• U.S. spinners usually put the size of the yarn first, followed by the number of ply. European spinners usually put the ply first followed by the yarn size. When ordering by mail, it is safe to stipulate what ply and yardage you wish. If the yarn is on hand, merely count the number of strands to ascertain which number refers to size and which to ply.

Table II: Metric Conversions

1 gram = .0022 pounds
1 ounce = 28.34 grams
1 kilo = 1000 grams = 2.2049 pounds = 35.28 ounces
1 pound = 28.34 X 16 = 453.44 grams

1 meter = 1.093 yards = 39.35 inches
1 yard = .9144 meters

YARN CALCULATION

To determine the *meters per kilo* if a yarn is given in yards per pound, use this method:
Multiply yards per pound by .9 = meters per pound multiplied by 2.2 = meters per kilo
Example: 1260 yards/pound X .9 = 1134 meters/pound X 2.2
            = 2494.8 meters/kilo

To determine *yards per pound* if a yarn is given in meters per kilo, use this method:
Divide meters per kilo by .9 = yards per kilo divided by 2.2 = yards per pound
Example: 2494.8 meters/kilo ÷ .9 = 2772 yards/kilo ÷ 2.2
            = 1260 yards/pound
Note: multipliers in the formulas have been rounded.

REED SIZES

The chart below shows the dents per inch equivalent to dents per centimeters.

Dents per Inch	Dents per Centimeter
5	2
8	3
10	4
12	5
15	6
18	7
20	8

Table III: Cotton Warps

Figure	Warp	Ends per Inch	Mfg	YDS/LB	YDS/K	M/LB	M/K
1-43	20/2	20, 15, 12, 10	Kolme	8400	18480	7681	16898
44-89	24/3	20, 15, 12, 10, 8	Lily	6720	14784	6145	13518
90-134	20/3	20, 15, 12, 10, 8	Lily	5600	12320	5121	11265
135-196	10/2	20, 15, 12, 10, 8, 7½	Lily	4200	9340	3840	8448
197-281	16/4	15, 12, 10, 8, 7½, 6, 5, 4	Lily	3360	7392	3072	6759
282-346	10/3	15, 12, 10, 8, 7½, 6, 5	Lily	2800	6160	2560	5633
347-435	5/2	15, 12, 10, 8, 7½, 6, 5, 4	Lily	2100	4620	1920	4225
436-502	3/2	15, 12, 10, 8, 7½, 6, 5, 4	Kolme	1260	2772	1152	2535

Wefts Used With Cotton Warps

Weft	Yarn	Manufacturer	YDS/LB	YDS/K	M/LB	M/K
A	Same as warp					
B	20/2 Worsted	Cum	4990	10978	4565	10043
C	6/2 Filtgarn	Bergå	1508	3318	1495	3140
D	Tapestry	Appleton	1280	2816	1171	2576
E	Sesame Worsted	Bernat	1080	2376	988	2174
F	Knitting Worsted	Brunswick	1000	2200	915	2011
G	Persian	Columbia Minerva	800	1760	732	1610
H	Mattgarn	Cum	620	1364	567	1247
I	Asbo Rya	Cum	570	1254	521	1146
J	Shag Rug	Paternayan	360	792	329	724
K	Rug Yarn	Paternayan	250	550	229	504
L	4-Ply Heavy Berber	Wilde	160	352	146	321

- All fractions are rounded.
- All samples with 20 EPI have used a 10 dent reed, sleyed 2 ends per inch.
- All samples using 7½ EPI have used a 15 dent reed, sleyed every other dent.
- All other samples use reeds the same size as the ends per inch.

Table IV: Linen Warps

Figure #	Warp	Ends per Inch	Mfg	YDS/LB	YDS/K	M/LB	M/K
503-585	8/2	12, 10, 9, 8, 6, 5, 4	Bockens	1200	2640	1097	2414
586-668	8/3	12, 10, 9, 8, 6, 5, 4	Bockens	800	1760	732	1609
669-737	8/4	10, 9, 8, 6, 5, 4	Bockens	600	1320	549	1207
738-795	8/5	10, 9, 8, 6, 5, 4	Bockens	480	1056	439	966

Wefts Used With Linen Warps

Weft	Yarn	Manufacturer	YDS/LB	YDS/K	M/LB	M/K
M	Persian	Columbia Minerva	800	1760	732	1610
N	Mattgarn	Cum	620	1364	567	1247
O	Asbo Rya	Cum	570	1254	521	1146
P	Lightweight Rug	Wells	640	1408	586	1289
Q	Designer Yarn	Harrisville	500	1100	457	895
R	4-Ply Natural Berber	Wilde	432	950	395	869
S	Mediumweight Rug	Wells	400	880	366	805
T	Shag Rug	Paternayan	360	792	329	724
U	Rug Yarn	Paternayan	250	550	229	504
V	Berber	Scott's Woolen Mills	210	462	192	422
W	4-Ply Heavy Berber	Wilde	160	353	146	321
X	Mule Spun	Henry's Attic	150	330	137	301

Warps used as wefts are illustrated at the end of each chapter.

Abbreviations
YDS = yards
LB = pound
K = kilo
M = meter

THE SAMPLES

Cotton Warps

Figures 1-502

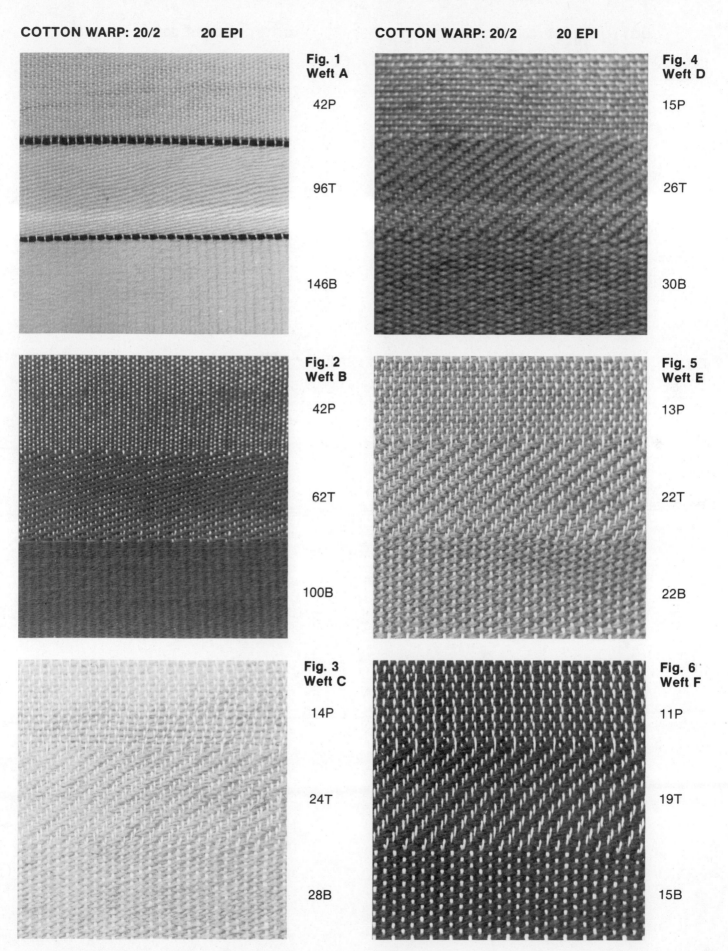

COTTON WARP: 20/2   20 EPI

Fig. 1
Weft A

42P

96T

146B

COTTON WARP: 20/2   20 EPI

Fig. 4
Weft D

15P

26T

30B

Fig. 2
Weft B

42P

62T

100B

Fig. 5
Weft E

13P

22T

22B

Fig. 3
Weft C

14P

24T

28B

Fig. 6
Weft F

11P

19T

15B

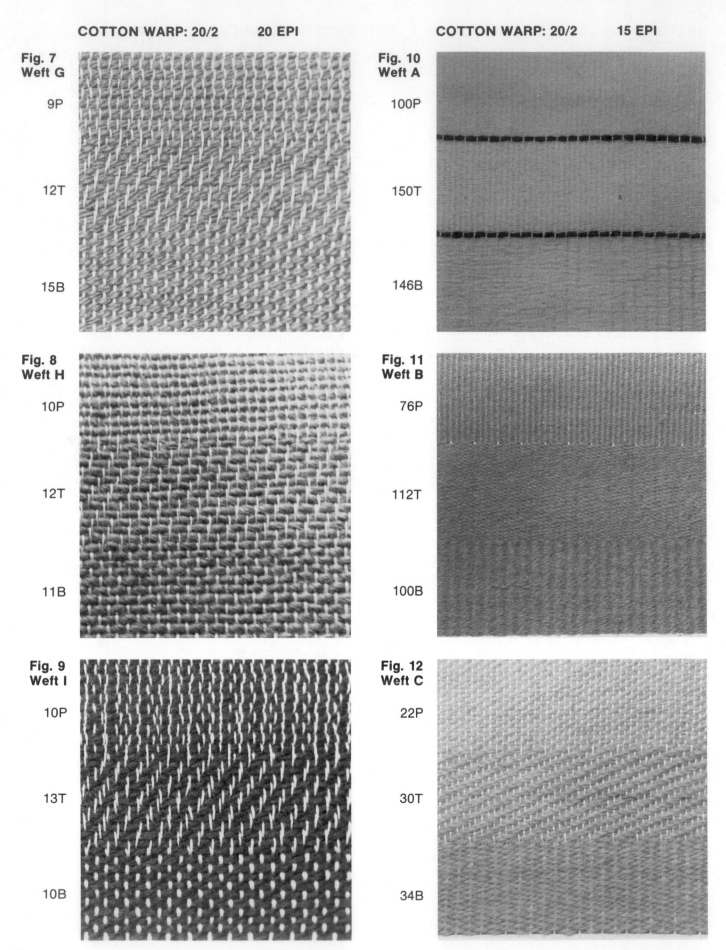

COTTON WARP: 20/2   20 EPI   COTTON WARP: 20/2   15 EPI

Fig. 7
Weft G

9P

12T

15B

Fig. 8
Weft H

10P

12T

11B

Fig. 9
Weft I

10P

13T

10B

Fig. 10
Weft A

100P

150T

146B

Fig. 11
Weft B

76P

112T

100B

Fig. 12
Weft C

22P

30T

34B

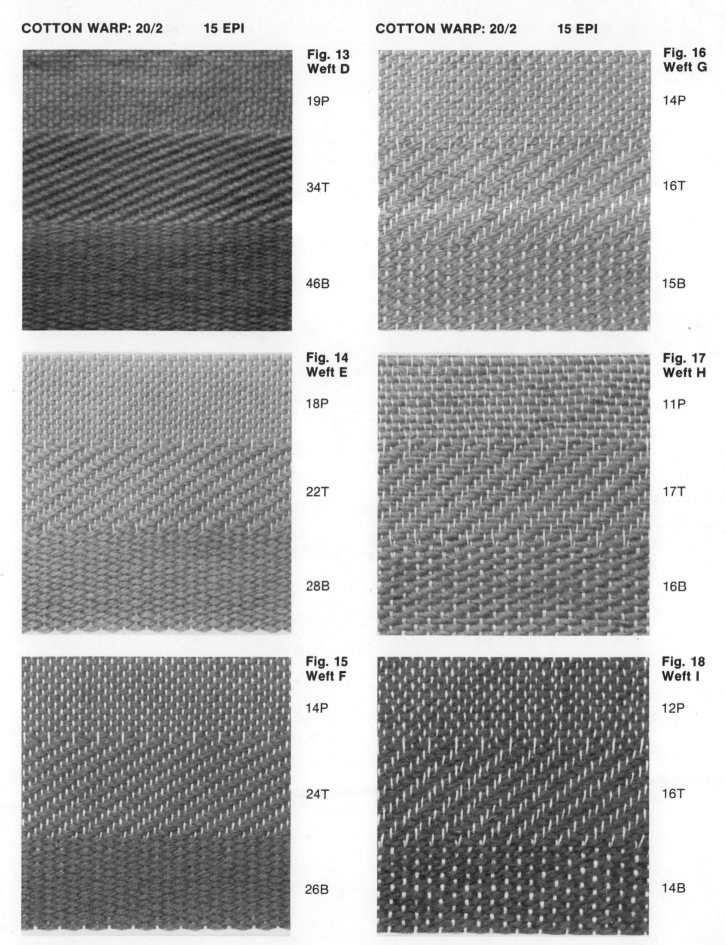

Fig. 13
Weft D

19P

34T

46B

Fig. 16
Weft G

14P

16T

15B

Fig. 14
Weft E

18P

22T

28B

Fig. 17
Weft H

11P

17T

16B

Fig. 15
Weft F

14P

24T

26B

Fig. 18
Weft I

12P

16T

14B

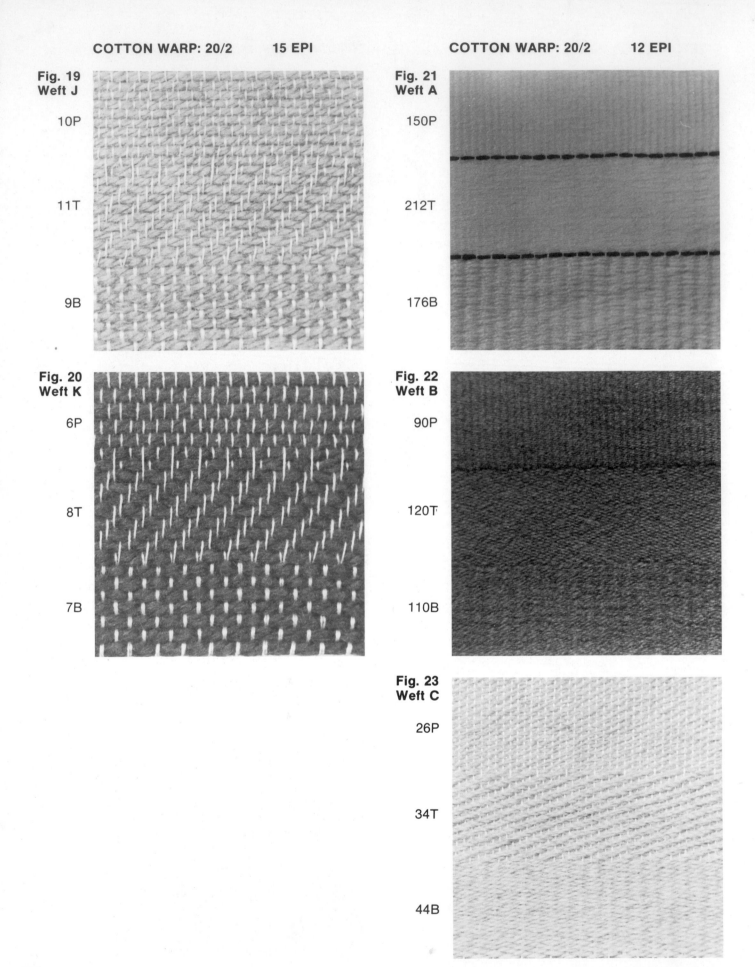

COTTON WARP: 20/2   15 EPI

COTTON WARP: 20/2   12 EPI

Fig. 19
Weft J

10P

11T

9B

Fig. 20
Weft K

6P

8T

7B

Fig. 21
Weft A

150P

212T

176B

Fig. 22
Weft B

90P

120T

110B

Fig. 23
Weft C

26P

34T

44B

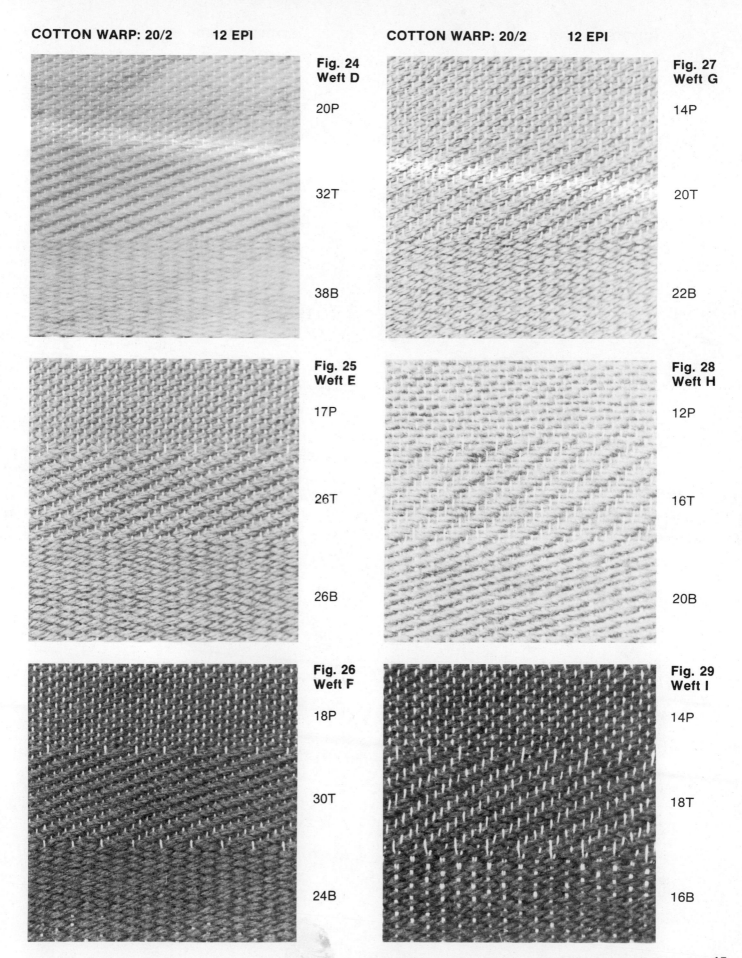

COTTON WARP: 20/2   12 EPI

COTTON WARP: 20/2   12 EPI

Fig. 24
Weft D

20P

32T

38B

Fig. 25
Weft E

17P

26T

26B

Fig. 26
Weft F

18P

30T

24B

Fig. 27
Weft G

14P

20T

22B

Fig. 28
Weft H

12P

16T

20B

Fig. 29
Weft I

14P

18T

16B

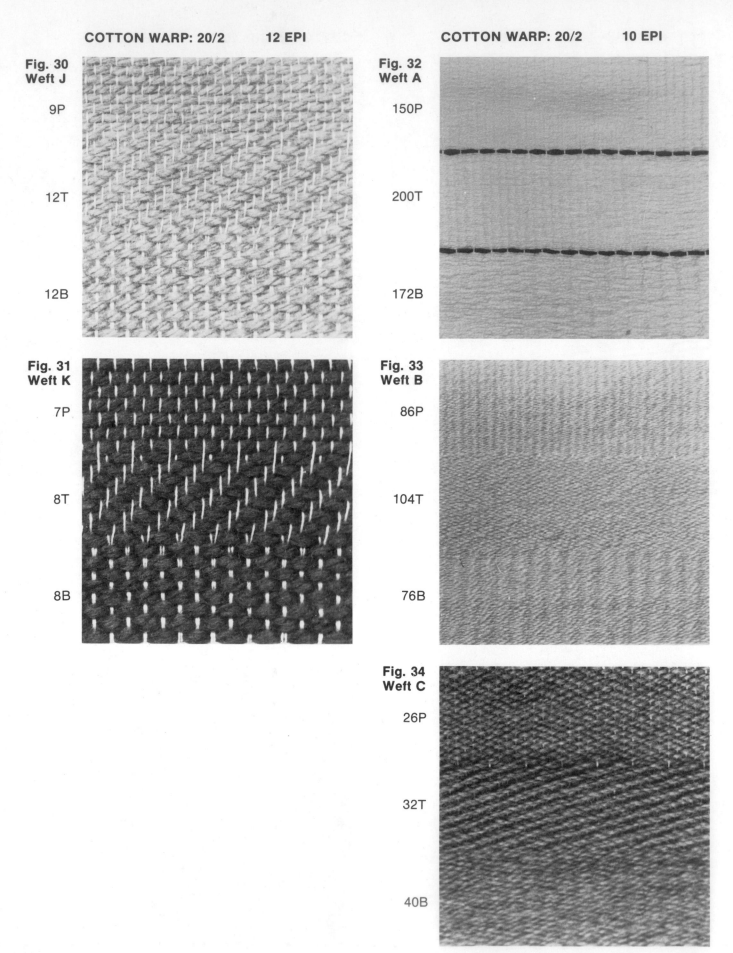

COTTON WARP: 20/2   12 EPI

Fig. 30
Weft J

9P

12T

12B

Fig. 31
Weft K

7P

8T

8B

COTTON WARP: 20/2   10 EPI

Fig. 32
Weft A

150P

200T

172B

Fig. 33
Weft B

86P

104T

76B

Fig. 34
Weft C

26P

32T

40B

16

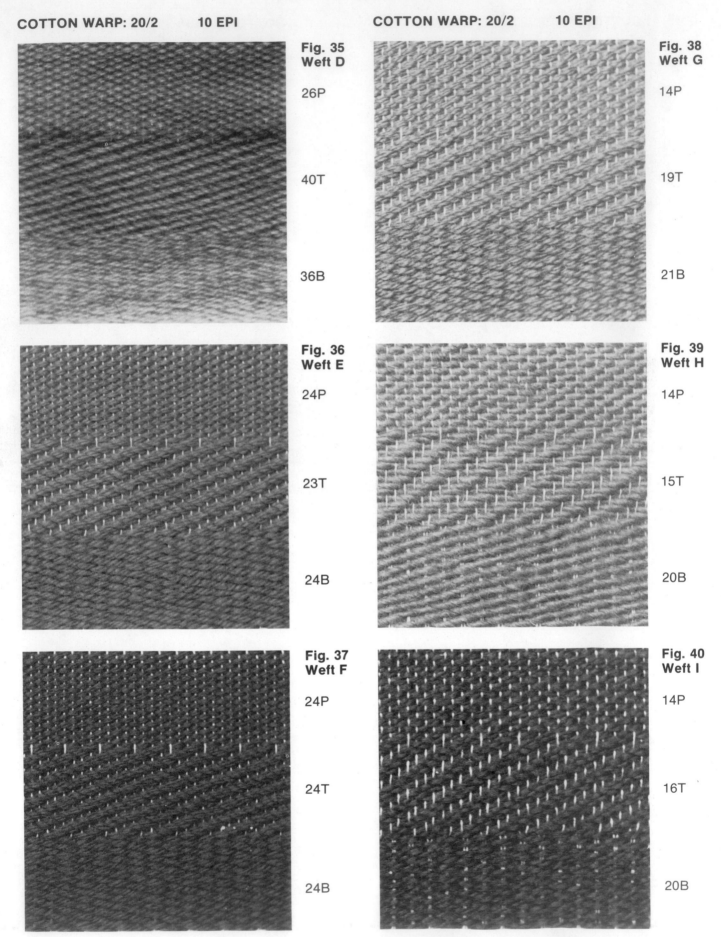

**Fig. 35
Weft D**

26P

40T

36B

**Fig. 38
Weft G**

14P

19T

21B

**Fig. 36
Weft E**

24P

23T

24B

**Fig. 39
Weft H**

14P

15T

20B

**Fig. 37
Weft F**

24P

24T

24B

**Fig. 40
Weft I**

14P

16T

20B

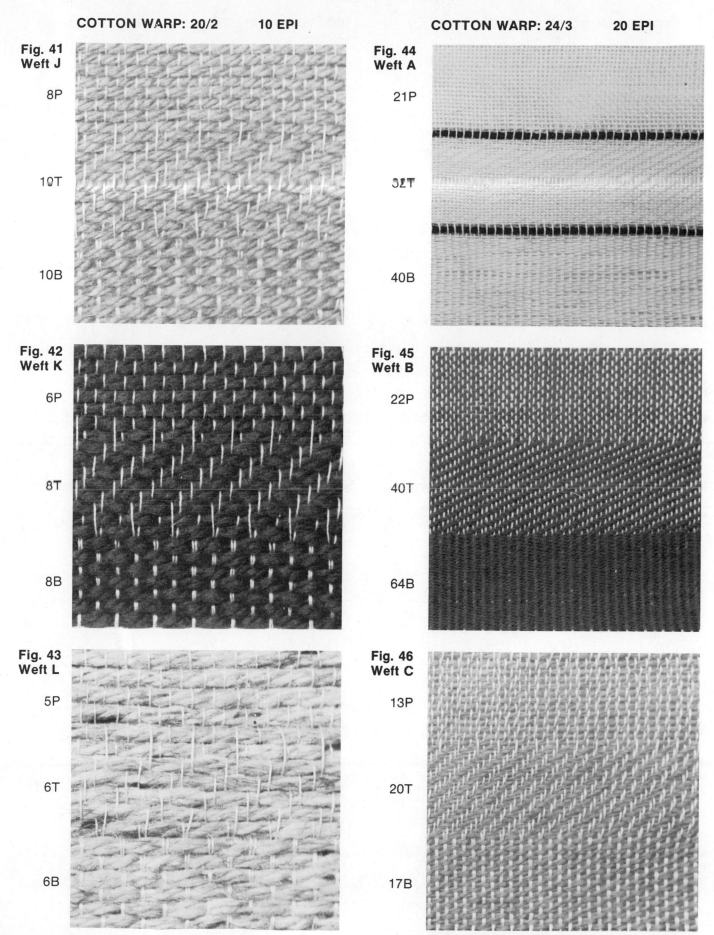

COTTON WARP: 20/2   10 EPI

Fig. 41
Weft J

8P

10T

10B

COTTON WARP: 24/3   20 EPI

Fig. 44
Weft A

21P

32T

40B

Fig. 42
Weft K

6P

8T

8B

Fig. 45
Weft B

22P

40T

64B

Fig. 43
Weft L

5P

6T

6B

Fig. 46
Weft C

13P

20T

17B

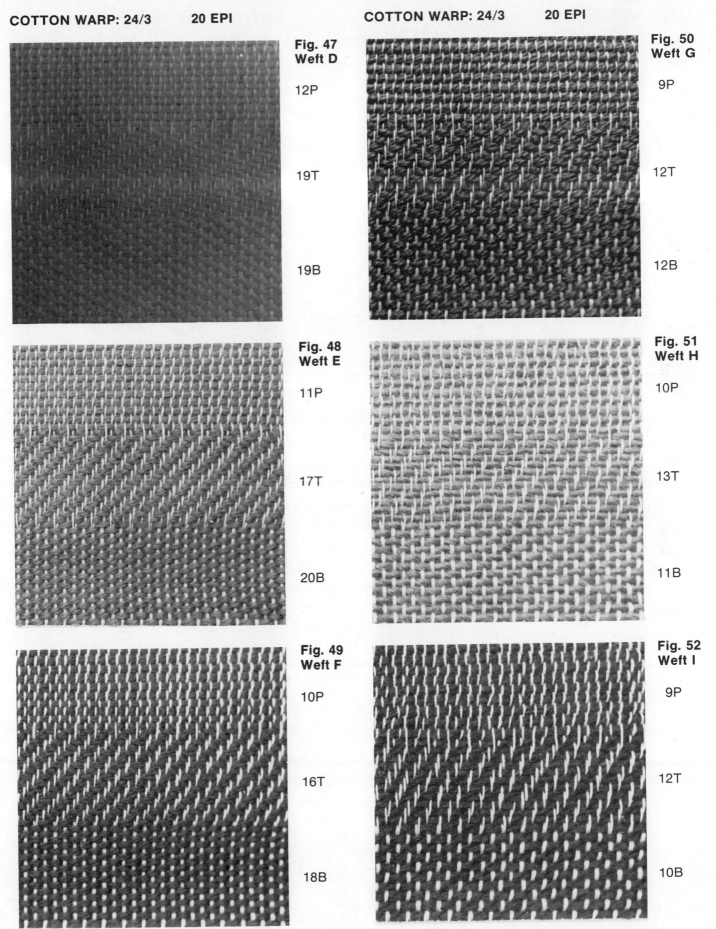

Fig. 47
Weft D

12P

19T

19B

Fig. 50
Weft G

9P

12T

12B

Fig. 48
Weft E

11P

17T

20B

Fig. 51
Weft H

10P

13T

11B

Fig. 49
Weft F

10P

16T

18B

Fig. 52
Weft I

9P

12T

10B

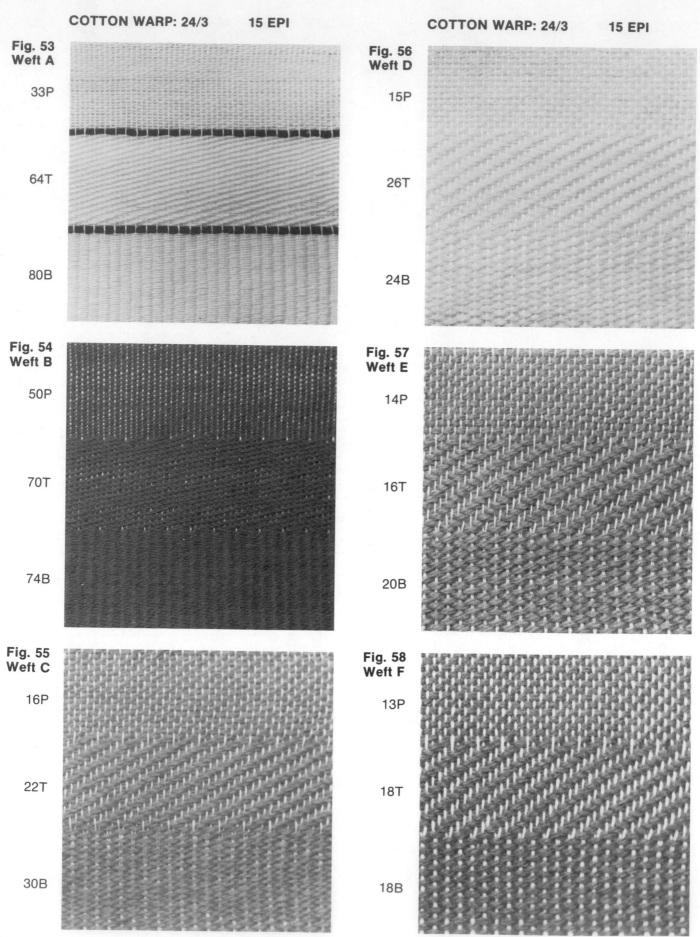

Fig. 53
Weft A

33P

64T

80B

Fig. 56
Weft D

15P

26T

24B

Fig. 54
Weft B

50P

70T

74B

Fig. 57
Weft E

14P

16T

20B

Fig. 55
Weft C

16P

22T

30B

Fig. 58
Weft F

13P

18T

18B

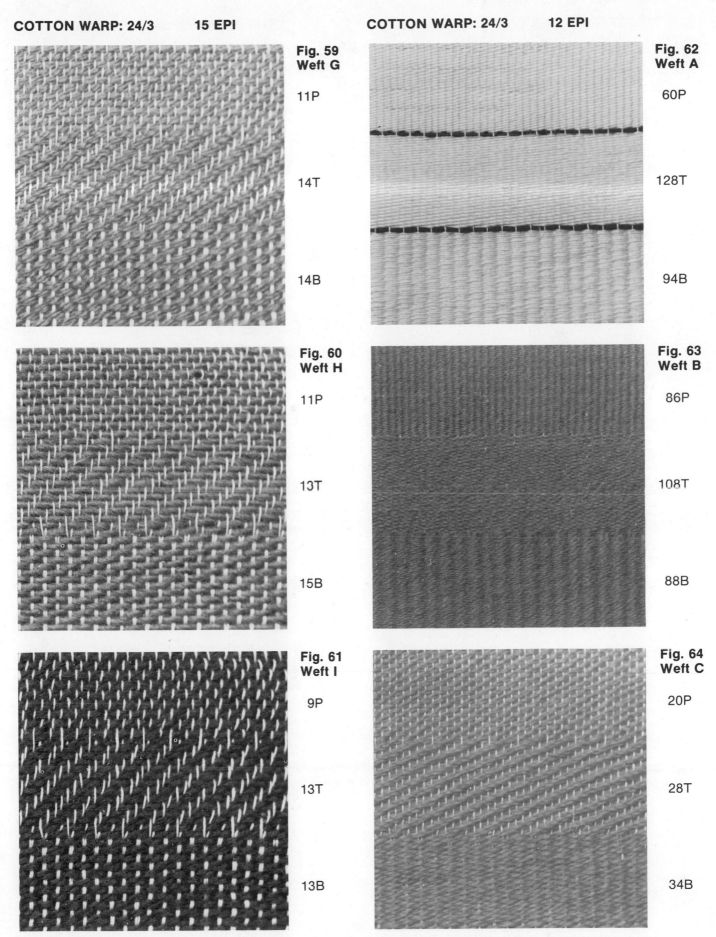

Fig. 59
Weft G

11P

14T

14B

Fig. 62
Weft A

60P

128T

94B

Fig. 60
Weft H

11P

13T

15B

Fig. 63
Weft B

86P

108T

88B

Fig. 61
Weft I

9P

13T

13B

Fig. 64
Weft C

20P

28T

34B

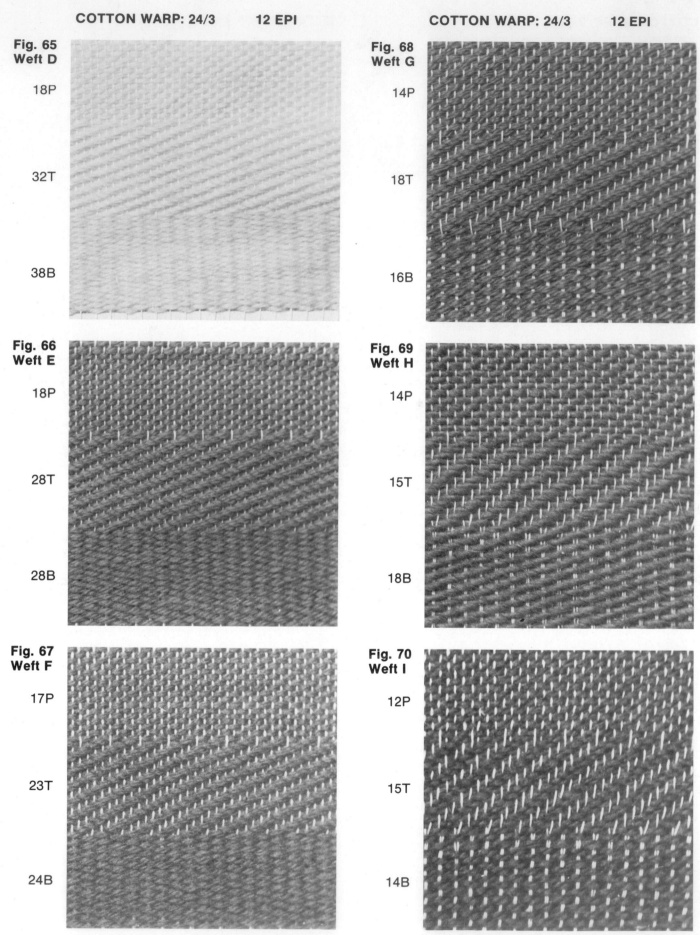

Fig. 65
Weft D

18P

32T

38B

Fig. 68
Weft G

14P

18T

16B

Fig. 66
Weft E

18P

28T

28B

Fig. 69
Weft H

14P

15T

18B

Fig. 67
Weft F

17P

23T

24B

Fig. 70
Weft I

12P

15T

14B

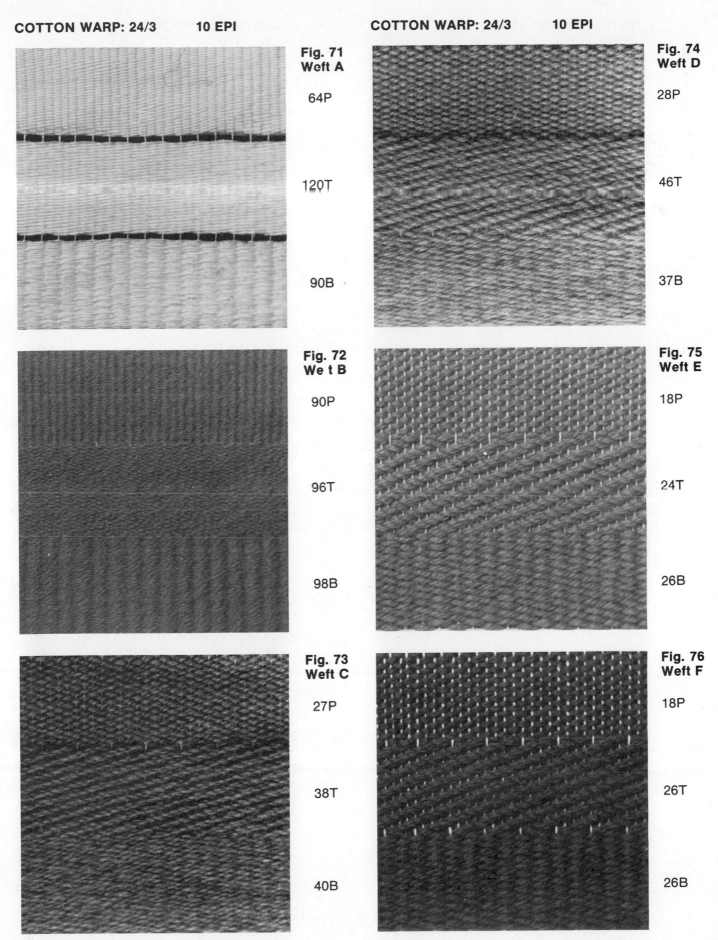

Fig. 71
Weft A

64P

120T

90B

Fig. 72
We t B

90P

96T

98B

Fig. 73
Weft C

27P

38T

40B

Fig. 74
Weft D

28P

46T

37B

Fig. 75
Weft E

18P

24T

26B

Fig. 76
Weft F

18P

26T

26B

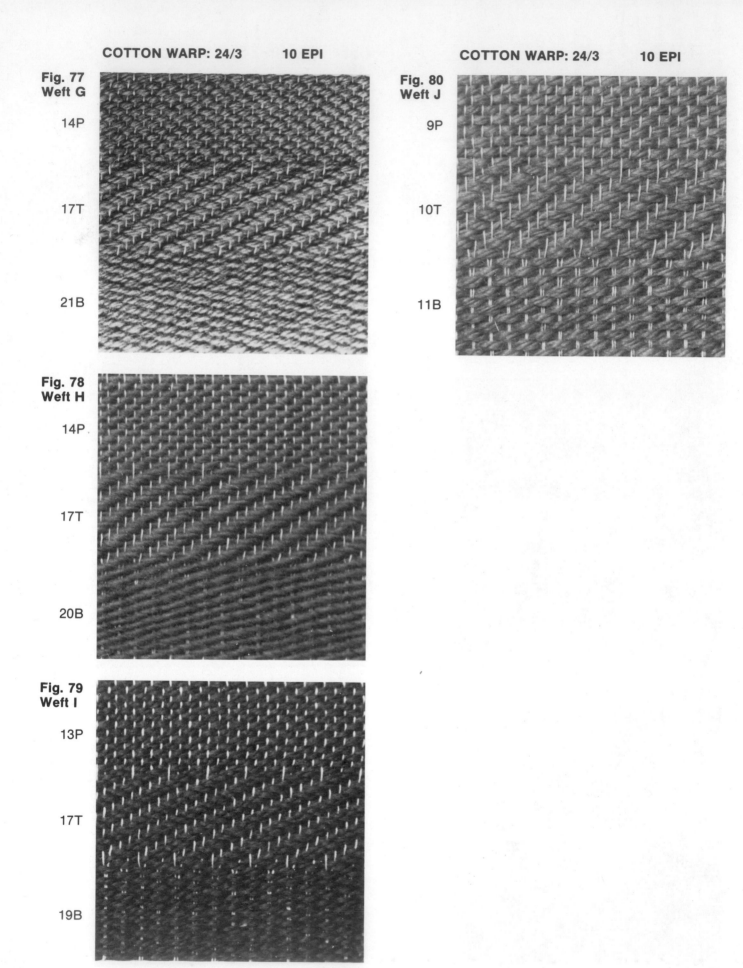

Fig. 77
Weft G

14P

17T

21B

Fig. 78
Weft H

14P

17T

20B

Fig. 79
Weft I

13P

17T

19B

Fig. 80
Weft J

9P

10T

11B

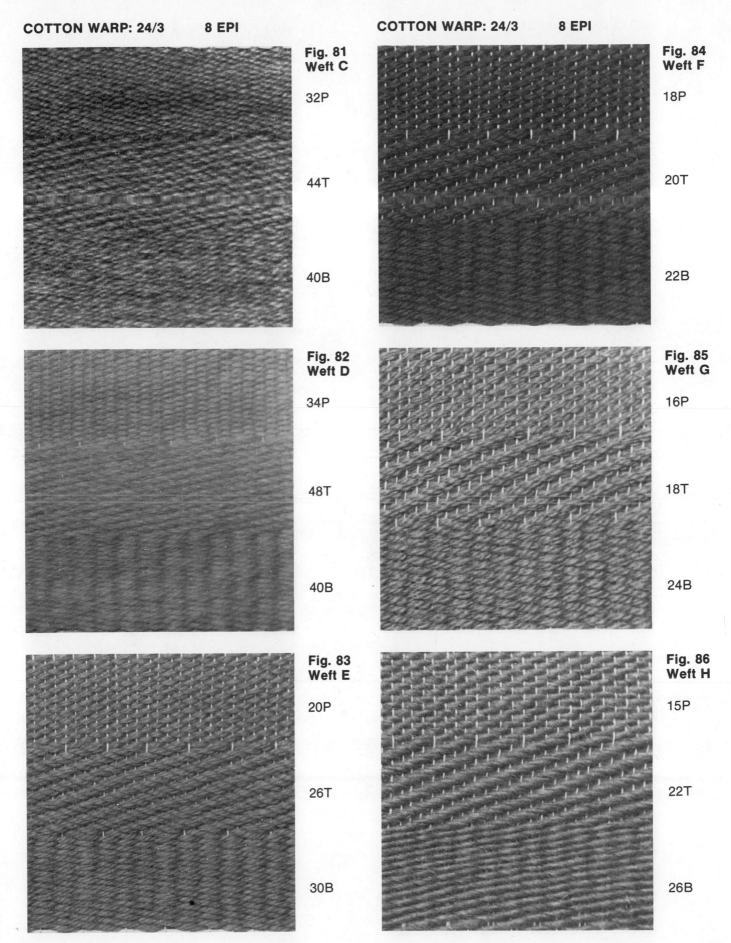

**Fig. 81
Weft C**

32P

44T

40B

**Fig. 84
Weft F**

18P

20T

22B

**Fig. 82
Weft D**

34P

48T

40B

**Fig. 85
Weft G**

16P

18T

24B

**Fig. 83
Weft E**

20P

26T

30B

**Fig. 86
Weft H**

15P

22T

26B

25

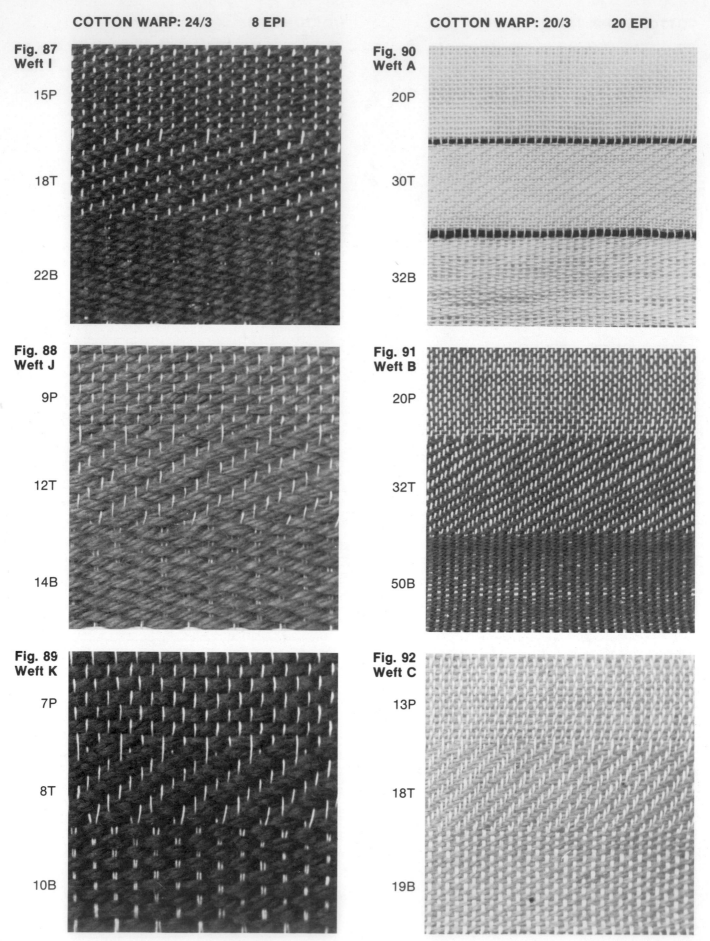

**Fig. 87
Weft I**

15P

18T

22B

**Fig. 88
Weft J**

9P

12T

14B

**Fig. 89
Weft K**

7P

8T

10B

**Fig. 90
Weft A**

20P

30T

32B

**Fig. 91
Weft B**

20P

32T

50B

**Fig. 92
Weft C**

13P

18T

19B

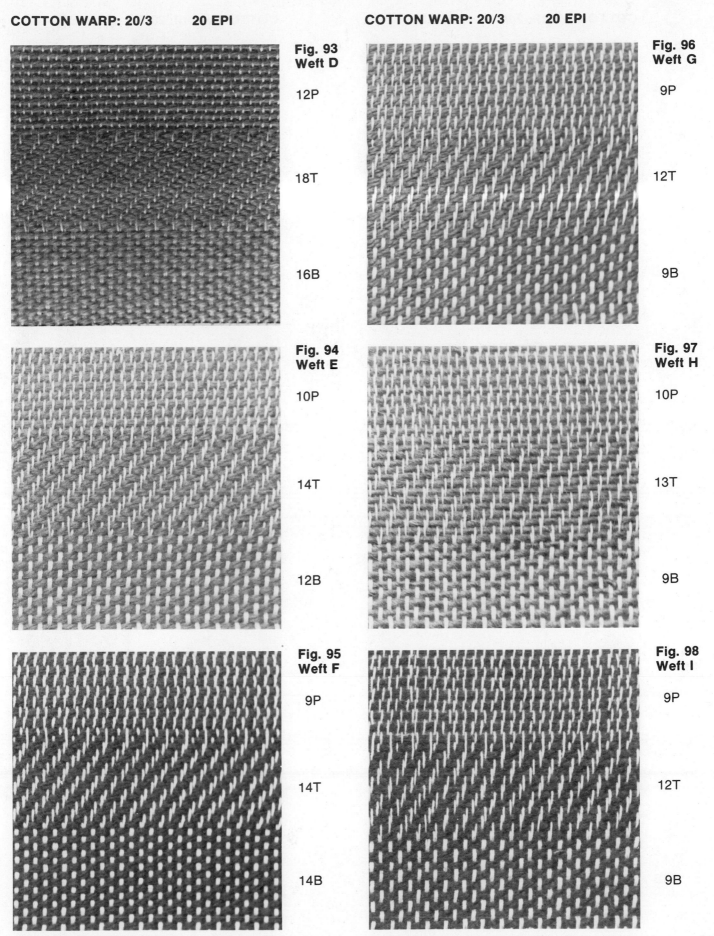

**Fig. 93
Weft D**

12P

18T

16B

**Fig. 96
Weft G**

9P

12T

9B

**Fig. 94
Weft E**

10P

14T

12B

**Fig. 97
Weft H**

10P

13T

9B

**Fig. 95
Weft F**

9P

14T

14B

**Fig. 98
Weft I**

9P

12T

9B

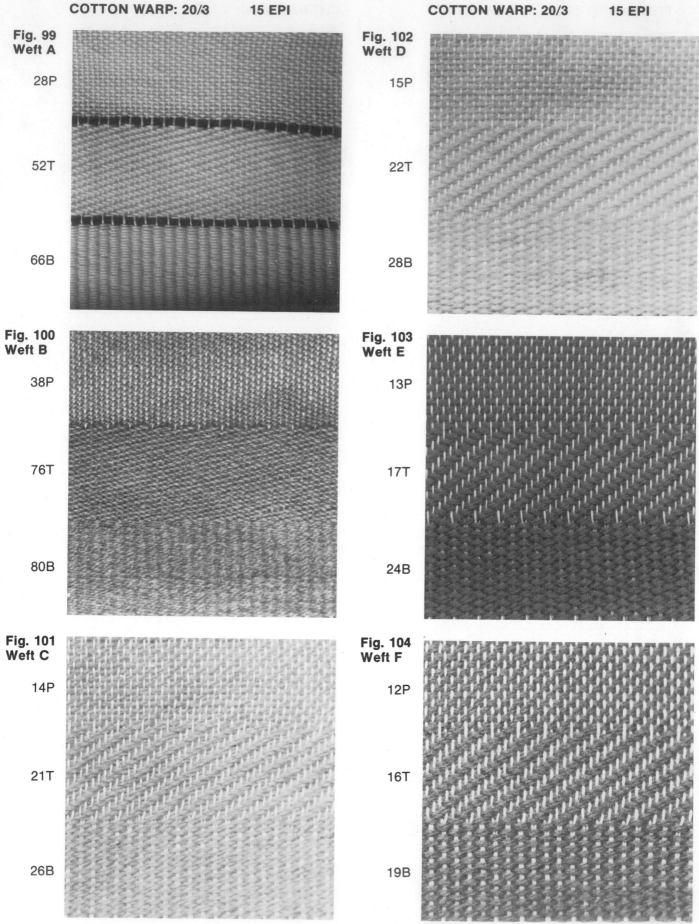

Fig. 99
Weft A

28P

52T

66B

Fig. 102
Weft D

15P

22T

28B

Fig. 100
Weft B

38P

76T

80B

Fig. 103
Weft E

13P

17T

24B

Fig. 101
Weft C

14P

21T

26B

Fig. 104
Weft F

12P

16T

19B

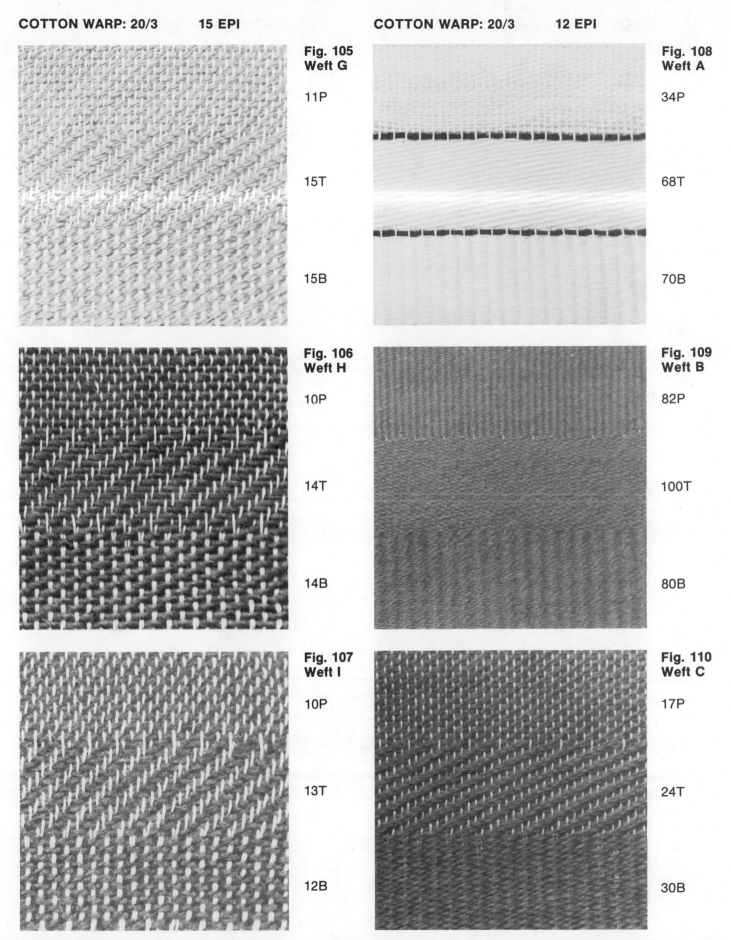

COTTON WARP: 20/3   15 EPI

COTTON WARP: 20/3   12 EPI

Fig. 105
Weft G

11P

15T

15B

Fig. 108
Weft A

34P

68T

70B

Fig. 106
Weft H

10P

14T

14B

Fig. 109
Weft B

82P

100T

80B

Fig. 107
Weft I

10P

13T

12B

Fig. 110
Weft C

17P

24T

30B

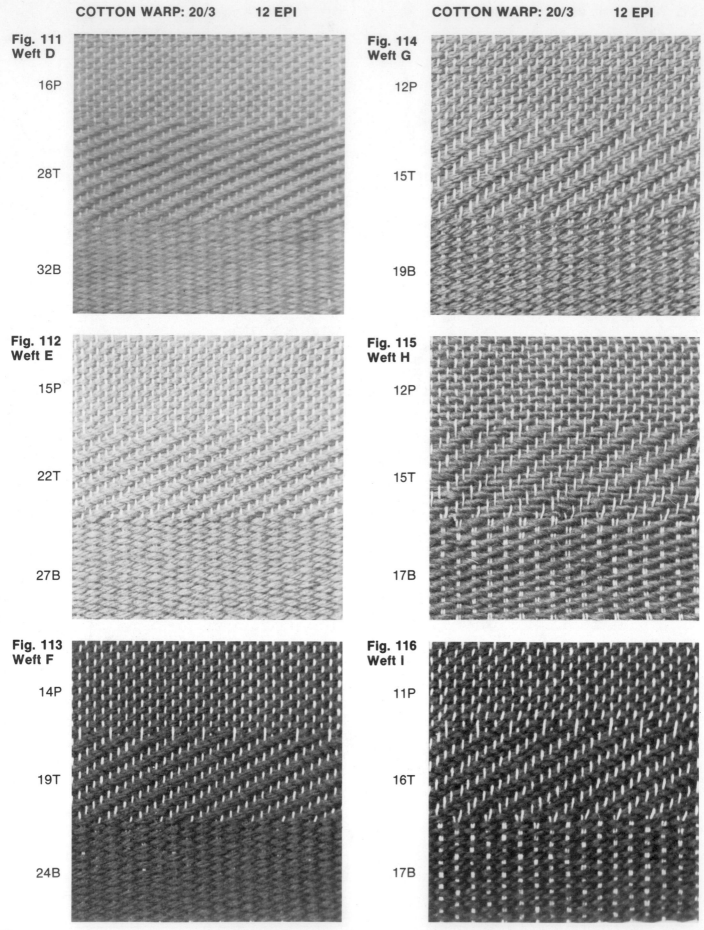

**Fig. 111
Weft D**

16P

28T

32B

**Fig. 114
Weft G**

12P

15T

19B

**Fig. 112
Weft E**

15P

22T

27B

**Fig. 115
Weft H**

12P

15T

17B

**Fig. 113
Weft F**

14P

19T

24B

**Fig. 116
Weft I**

11P

16T

17B

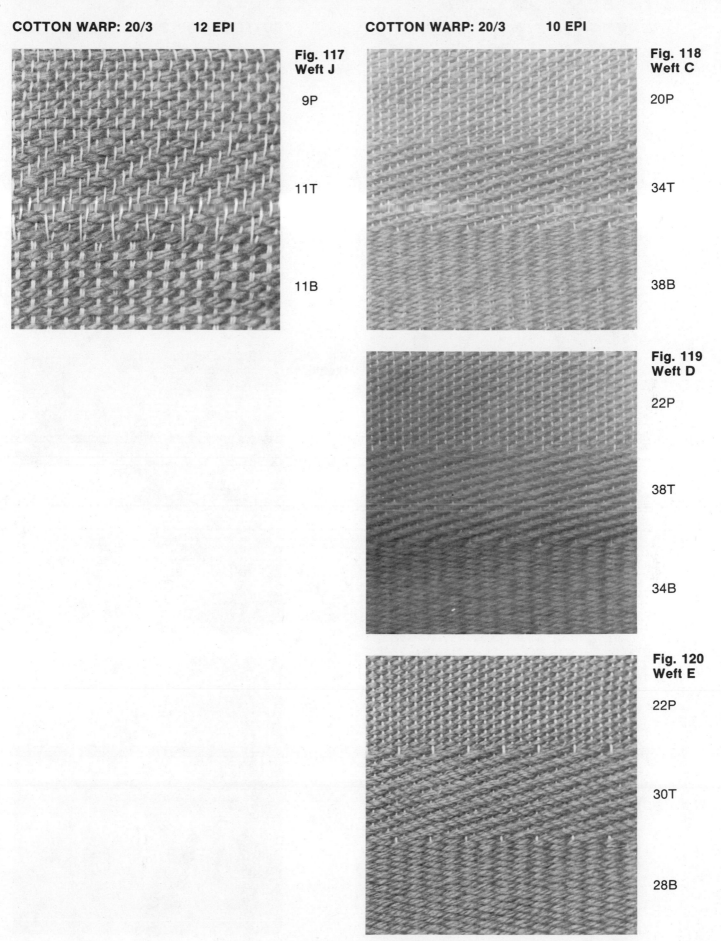

Fig. 117
Weft J

9P

11T

11B

Fig. 118
Weft C

20P

34T

38B

Fig. 119
Weft D

22P

38T

34B

Fig. 120
Weft E

22P

30T

28B

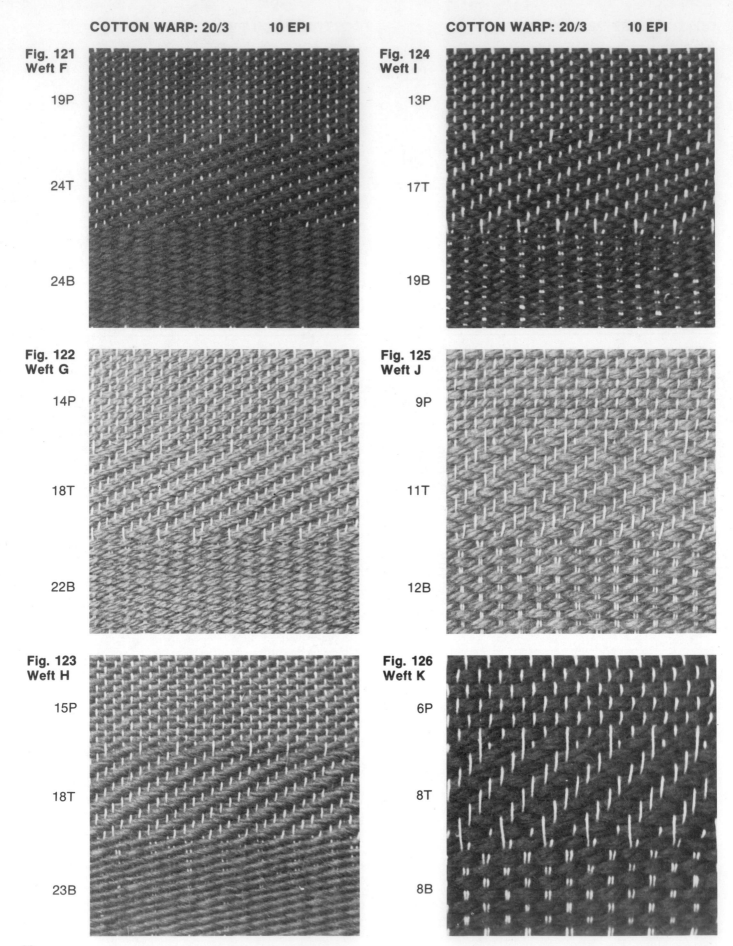

Fig. 121
Weft F

19P

24T

24B

Fig. 124
Weft I

13P

17T

19B

Fig. 122
Weft G

14P

18T

22B

Fig. 125
Weft J

9P

11T

12B

Fig. 123
Weft H

15P

18T

23B

Fig. 126
Weft K

6P

8T

8B

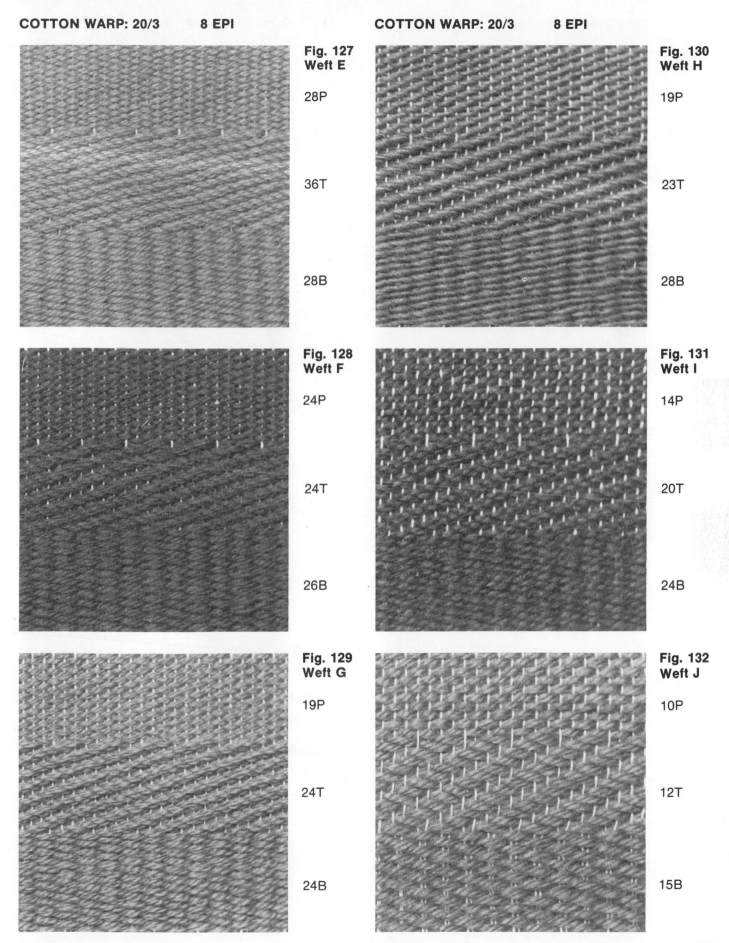

Fig. 127
Weft E

28P

36T

28B

Fig. 130
Weft H

19P

23T

28B

Fig. 128
Weft F

24P

24T

26B

Fig. 131
Weft I

14P

20T

24B

Fig. 129
Weft G

19P

24T

24B

Fig. 132
Weft J

10P

12T

15B

33

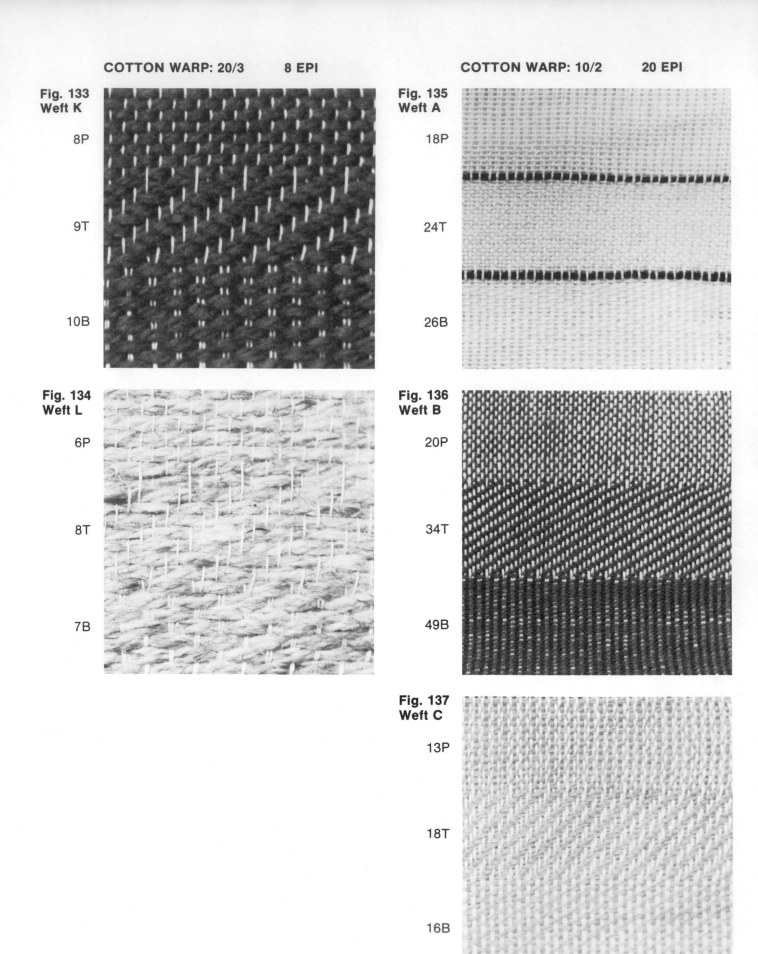

Fig. 133
Weft K

8P

9T

10B

Fig. 134
Weft L

6P

8T

7B

Fig. 135
Weft A

18P

24T

26B

Fig. 136
Weft B

20P

34T

49B

Fig. 137
Weft C

13P

18T

16B

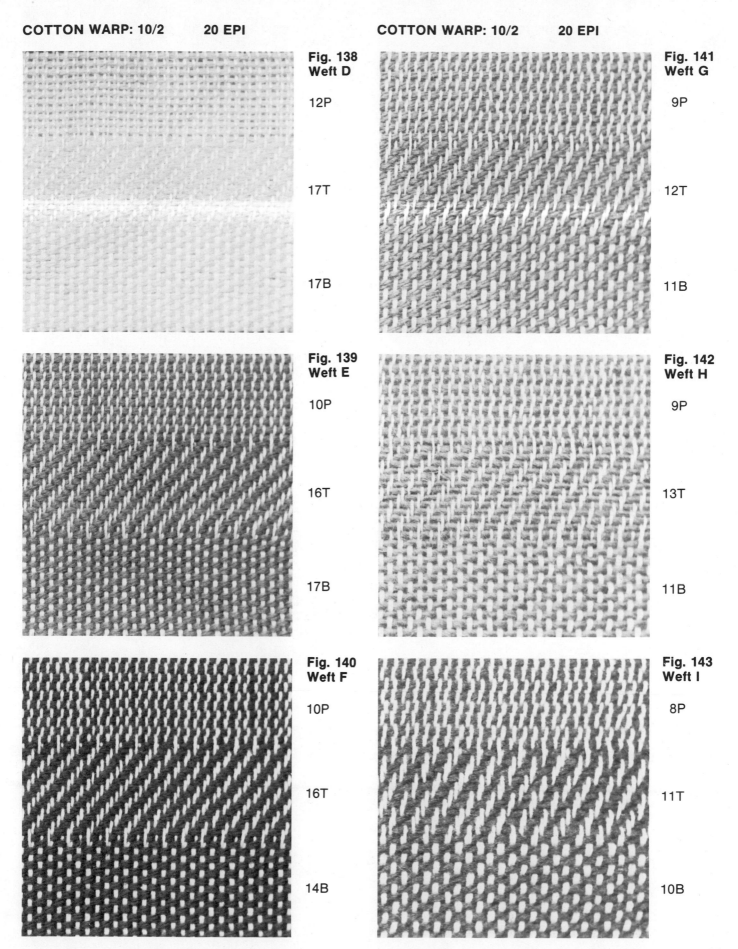

Fig. 138
Weft D

12P

17T

17B

Fig. 141
Weft G

9P

12T

11B

Fig. 139
Weft E

10P

16T

17B

Fig. 142
Weft H

9P

13T

11B

Fig. 140
Weft F

10P

16T

14B

Fig. 143
Weft I

8P

11T

10B

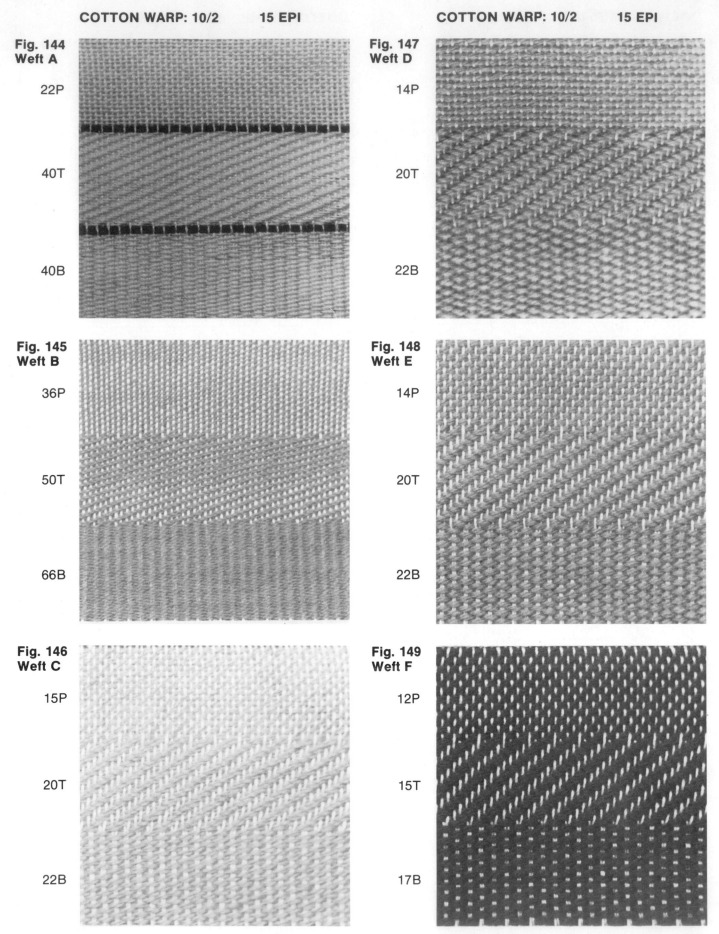

COTTON WARP: 10/2   15 EPI

COTTON WARP: 10/2   15 EPI

Fig. 144
Weft A

22P

40T

40B

Fig. 147
Weft D

14P

20T

22B

Fig. 145
Weft B

36P

50T

66B

Fig. 148
Weft E

14P

20T

22B

Fig. 146
Weft C

15P

20T

22B

Fig. 149
Weft F

12P

15T

17B

36

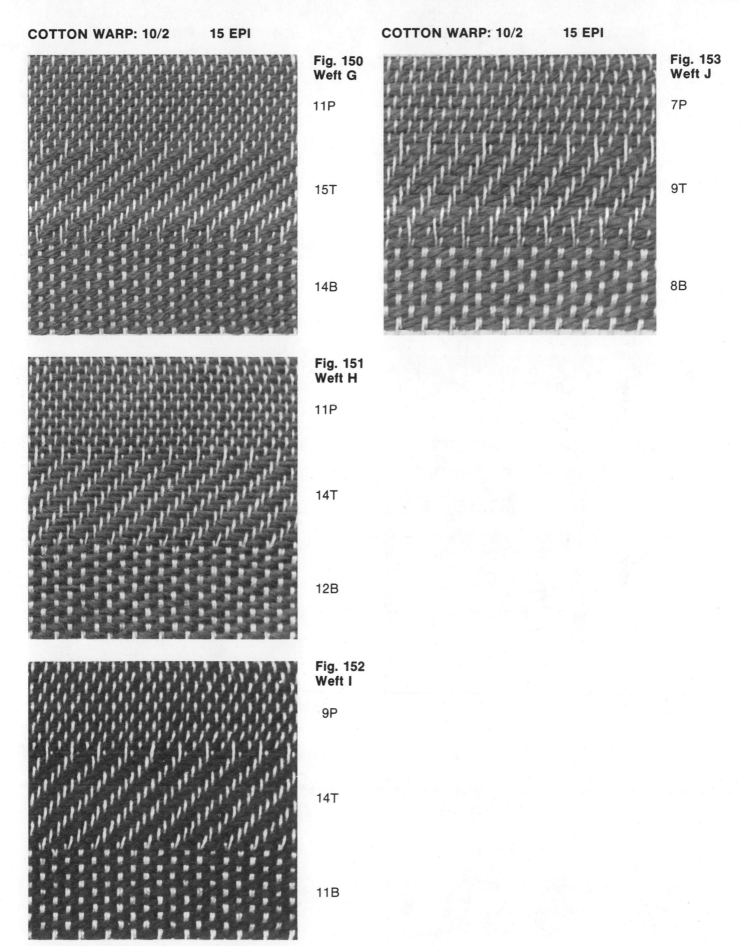

Fig. 150
Weft G

11P

15T

14B

Fig. 153
Weft J

7P

9T

8B

Fig. 151
Weft H

11P

14T

12B

Fig. 152
Weft I

9P

14T

11B

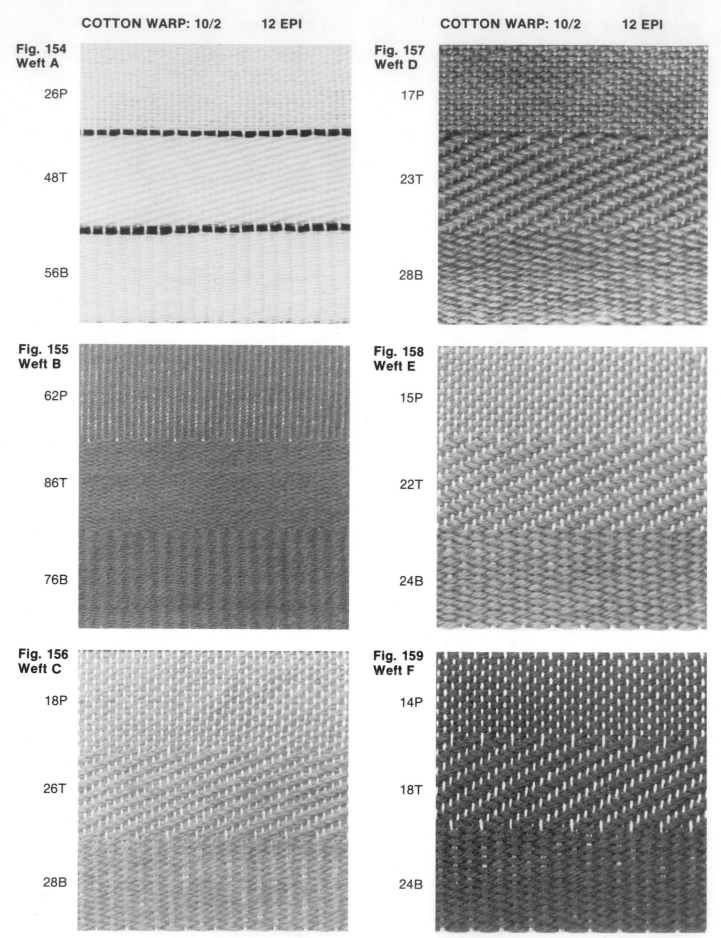

Fig. 154
Weft A

26P

48T

56B

Fig. 157
Weft D

17P

23T

28B

Fig. 155
Weft B

62P

86T

76B

Fig. 158
Weft E

15P

22T

24B

Fig. 156
Weft C

18P

26T

28B

Fig. 159
Weft F

14P

18T

24B

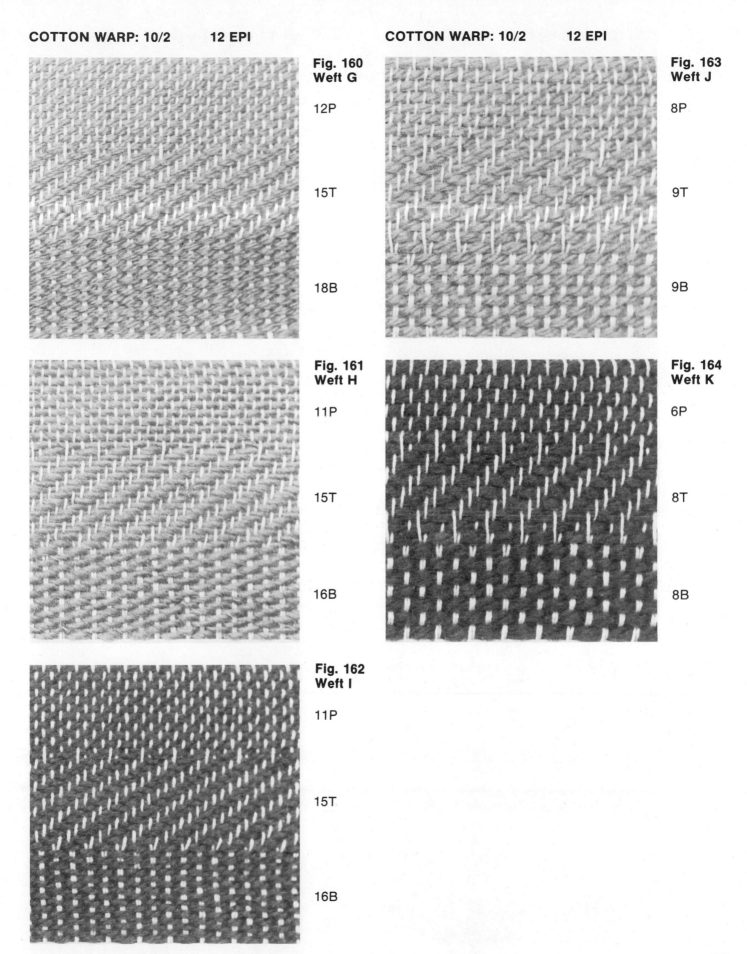

Fig. 160
Weft G

12P

15T

18B

Fig. 161
Weft H

11P

15T

16B

Fig. 162
Weft I

11P

15T

16B

Fig. 163
Weft J

8P

9T

9B

Fig. 164
Weft K

6P

8T

8B

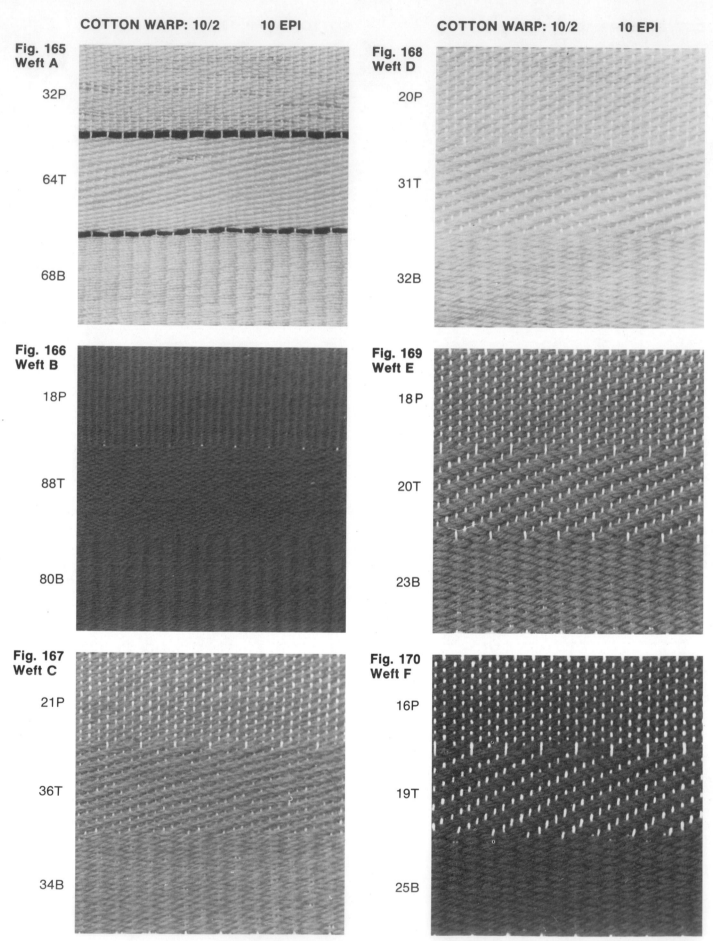

Fig. 165
Weft A

32P

64T

68B

Fig. 168
Weft D

20P

31T

32B

Fig. 166
Weft B

18P

88T

80B

Fig. 169
Weft E

18 P

20T

23B

Fig. 167
Weft C

21P

36T

34B

Fig. 170
Weft F

16P

19T

25B

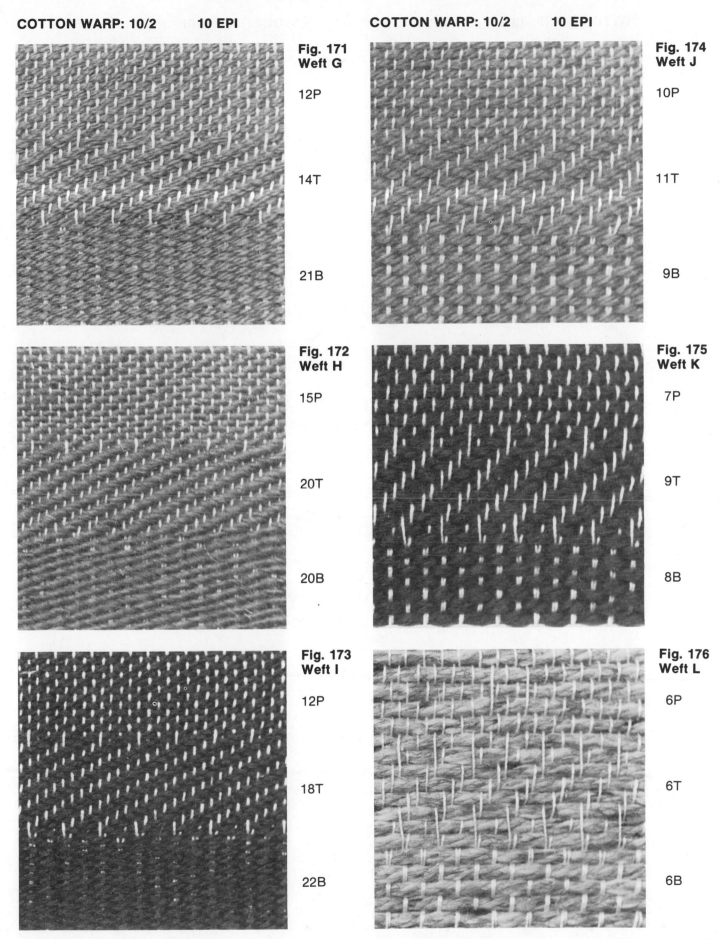

Fig. 171
Weft G

12P

14T

21B

Fig. 174
Weft J

10P

11T

9B

Fig. 172
Weft H

15P

20T

20B

Fig. 175
Weft K

7P

9T

8B

Fig. 173
Weft I

12P

18T

22B

Fig. 176
Weft L

6P

6T

6B

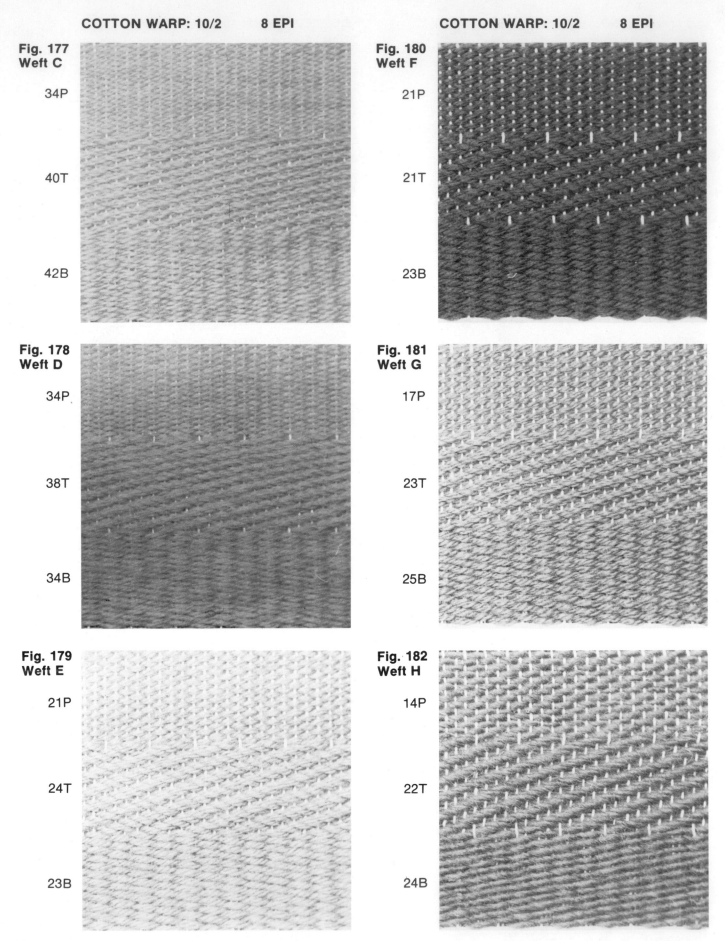

Fig. 177
Weft C

34P

40T

42B

Fig. 180
Weft F

21P

21T

23B

Fig. 178
Weft D

34P

38T

34B

Fig. 181
Weft G

17P

23T

25B

Fig. 179
Weft E

21P

24T

23B

Fig. 182
Weft H

14P

22T

24B

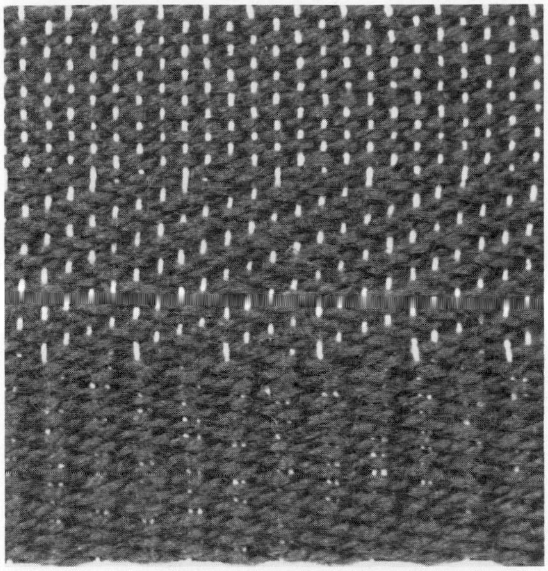

Fig. 183
Weft I

14P

20T

23B

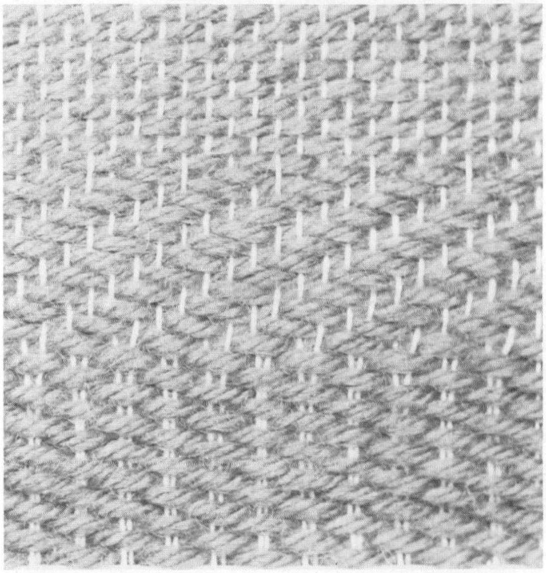

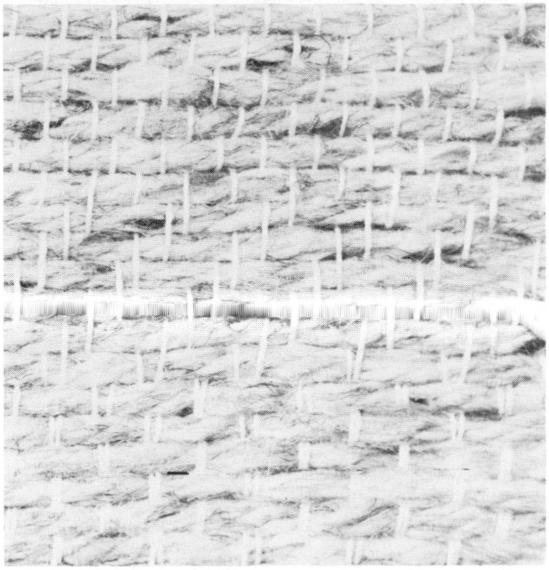

Fig.186
Weft L

6P

6T

6B

Fig. 184
Weft J

9P

12T

13B

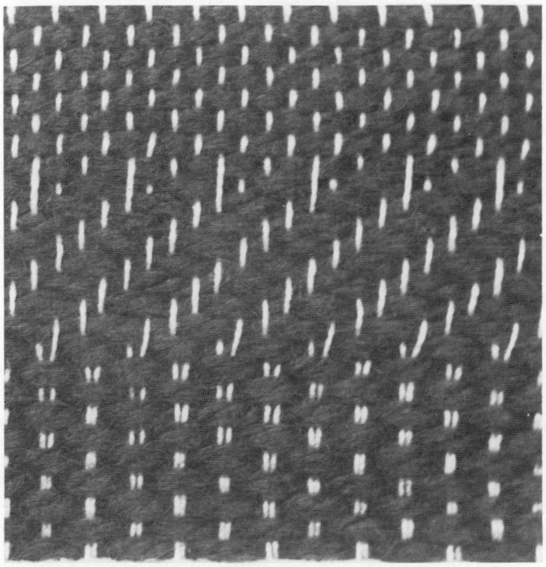

Fig. 185
Weft K

8P

9T

9B

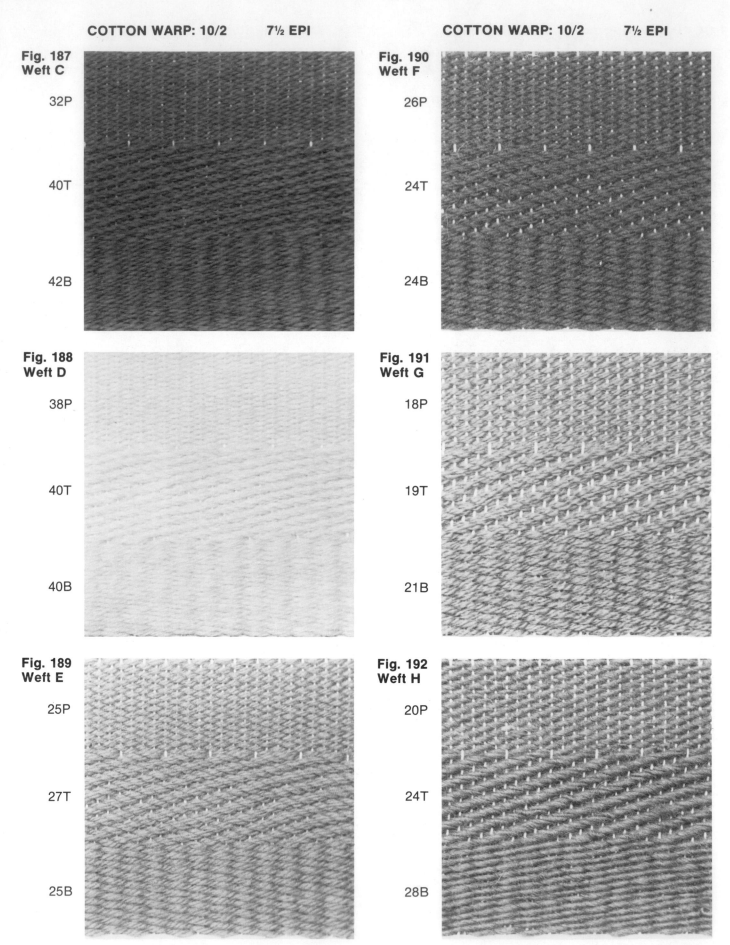

Fig. 187
Weft C

32P

40T

42B

Fig. 190
Weft F

26P

24T

24B

Fig. 188
Weft D

38P

40T

40B

Fig. 191
Weft G

18P

19T

21B

Fig. 189
Weft E

25P

27T

25B

Fig. 192
Weft H

20P

24T

28B

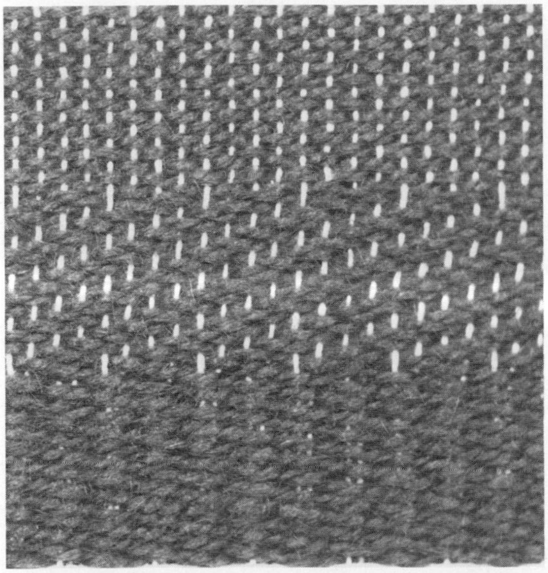

**Fig. 193
Weft I**

16P

18T

24B

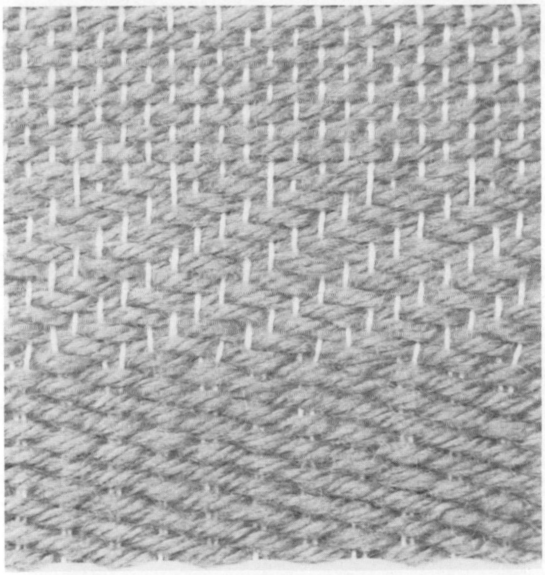

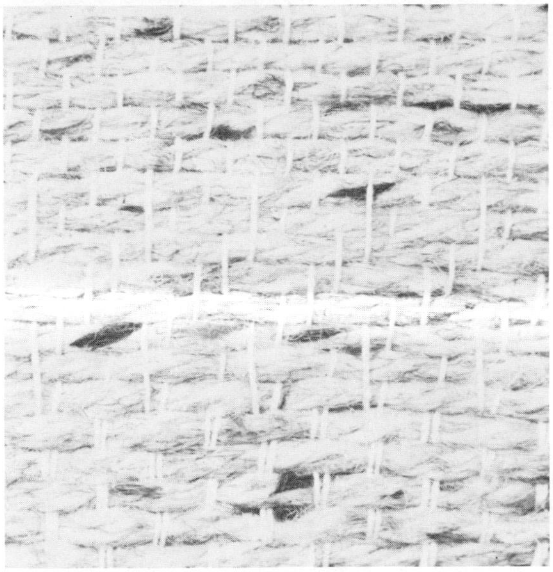

**Fig. 196
Weft L**

6P

6T

6B

**Fig. 194
Weft J**

9P

11T

16B

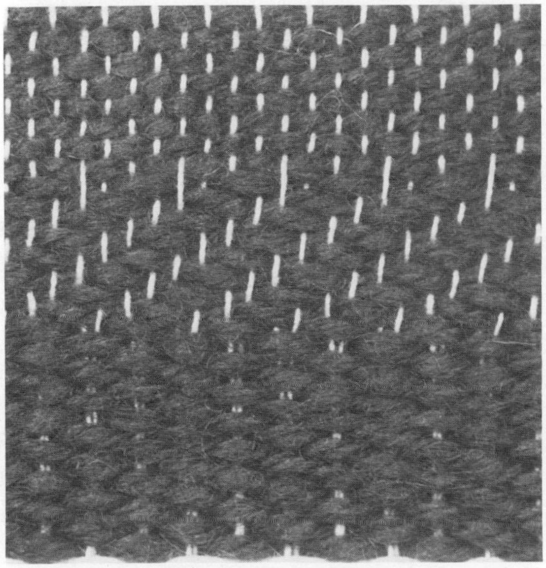

**Fig. 195
Weft K**

8P

9T

14B

45

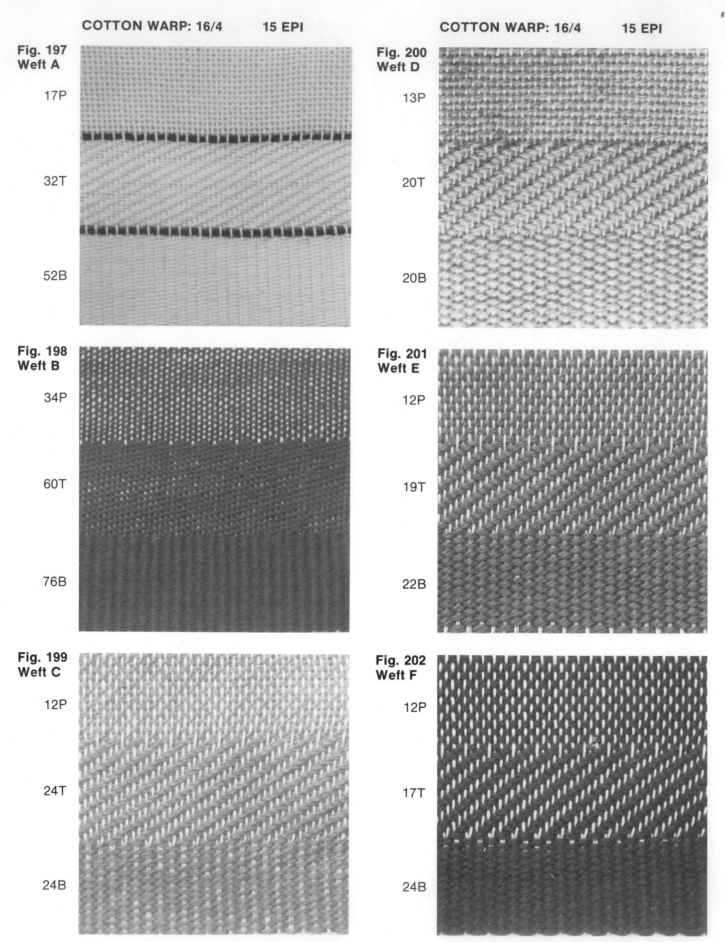

Fig. 197
Weft A

17P

32T

52B

Fig. 200
Weft D

13P

20T

20B

Fig. 198
Weft B

34P

60T

76B

Fig. 201
Weft E

12P

19T

22B

Fig. 199
Weft C

12P

24T

24B

Fig. 202
Weft F

12P

17T

24B

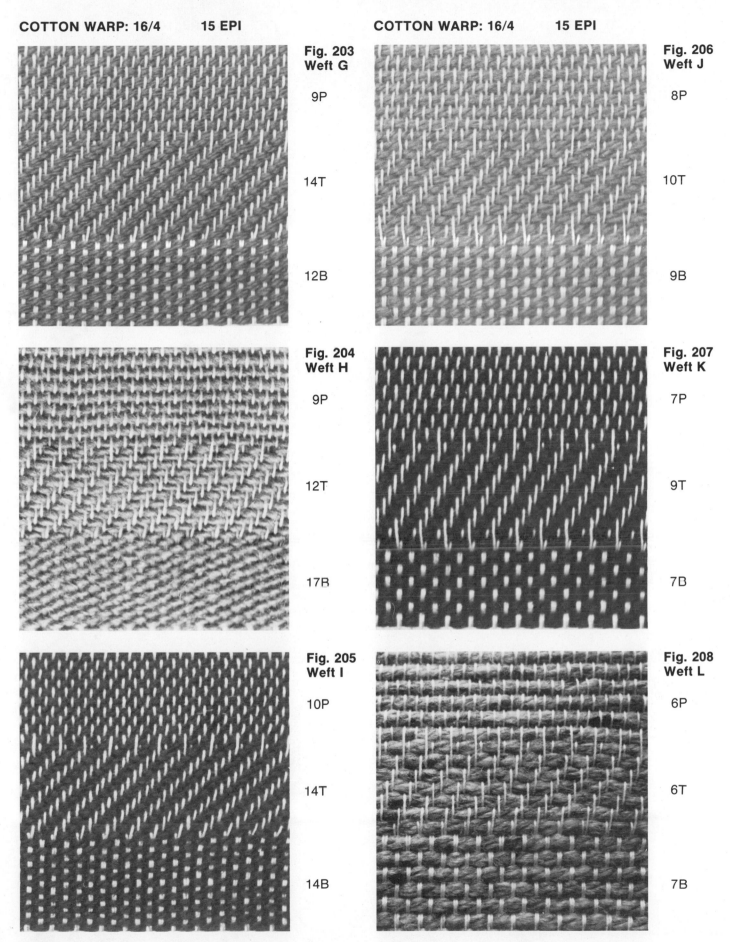

Fig. 203
Weft G

9P

14T

12B

Fig. 206
Weft J

8P

10T

9B

Fig. 204
Weft H

9P

12T

17B

Fig. 207
Weft K

7P

9T

7B

Fig. 205
Weft I

10P

14T

14B

Fig. 208
Weft L

6P

6T

7B

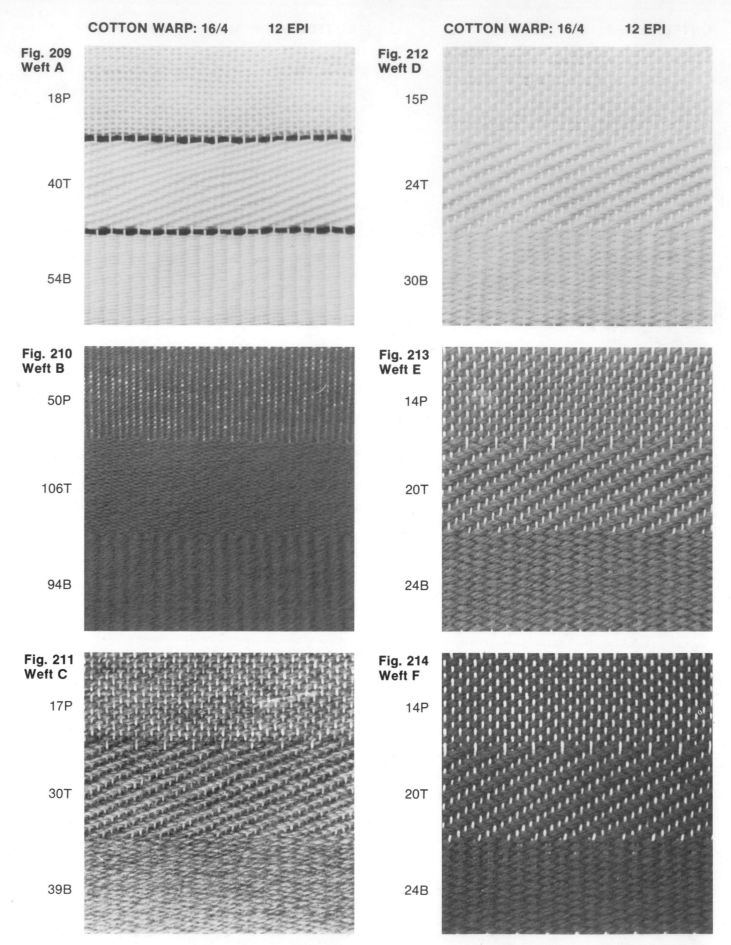

**Fig. 209
Weft A**

18P

40T

54B

**Fig. 212
Weft D**

15P

24T

30B

**Fig. 210
Weft B**

50P

106T

94B

**Fig. 213
Weft E**

14P

20T

24B

**Fig. 211
Weft C**

17P

30T

39B

**Fig. 214
Weft F**

14P

20T

24B

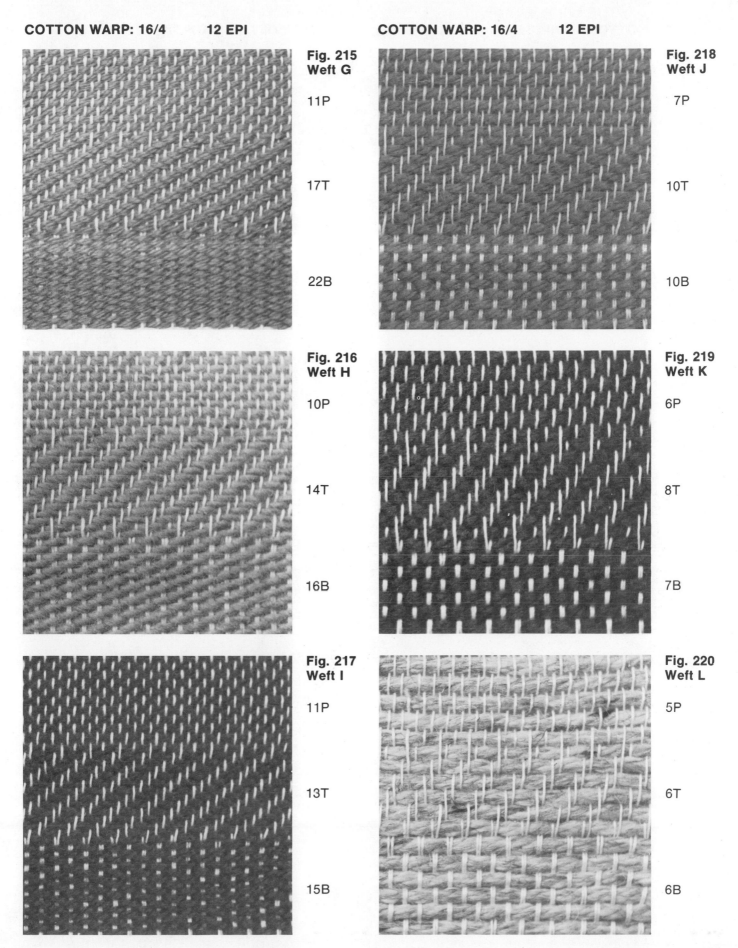

Fig. 215
Weft G

11P

17T

22B

Fig. 218
Weft J

7P

10T

10B

Fig. 216
Weft H

10P

14T

16B

Fig. 219
Weft K

6P

8T

7B

Fig. 217
Weft I

11P

13T

15B

Fig. 220
Weft L

5P

6T

6B

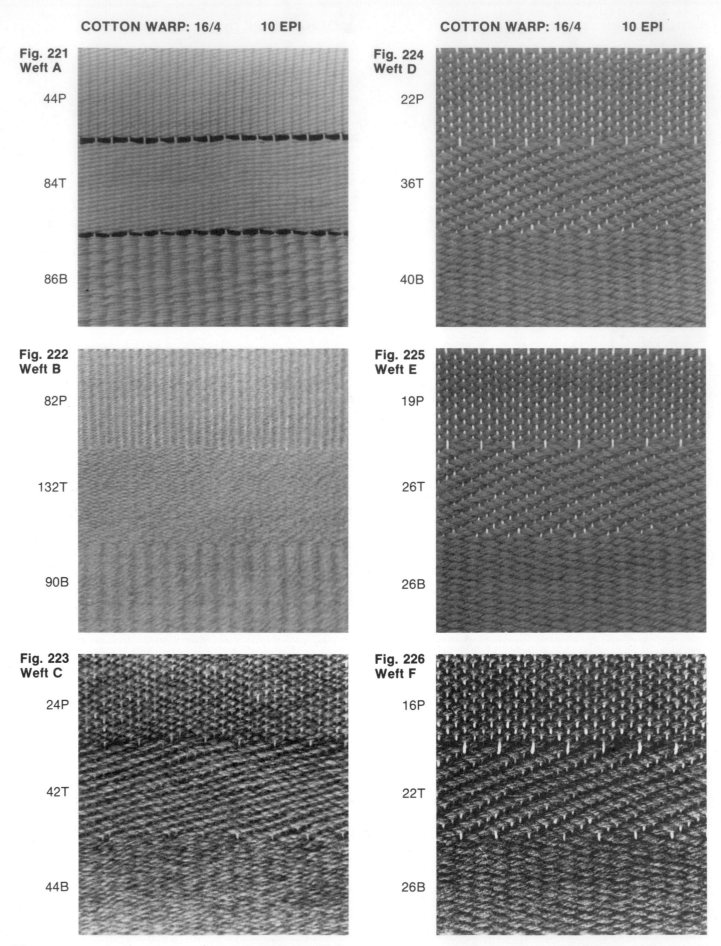

COTTON WARP: 16/4   10 EPI

Fig. 221
Weft A

44P

84T

86B

Fig. 224
Weft D

22P

36T

40B

Fig. 222
Weft B

82P

132T

90B

Fig. 225
Weft E

19P

26T

26B

Fig. 223
Weft C

24P

42T

44B

Fig. 226
Weft F

16P

22T

26B

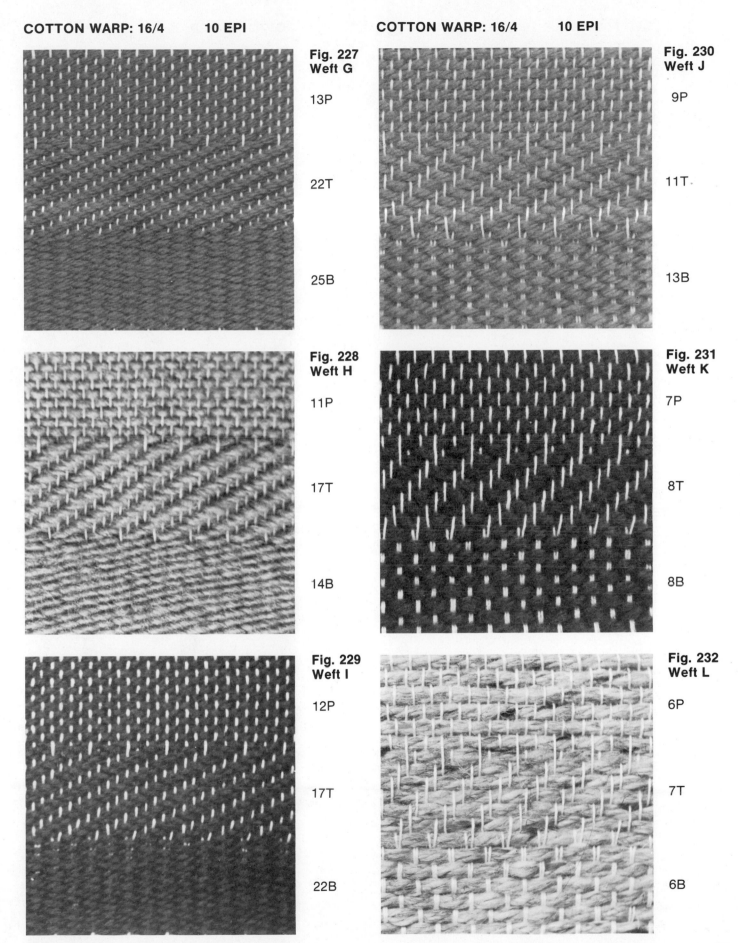

Fig. 227
Weft G

13P

22T

25B

Fig. 228
Weft H

11P

17T

14B

Fig. 229
Weft I

12P

17T

22B

Fig. 230
Weft J

9P

11T

13B

Fig. 231
Weft K

7P

8T

8B

Fig. 232
Weft L

6P

7T

6B

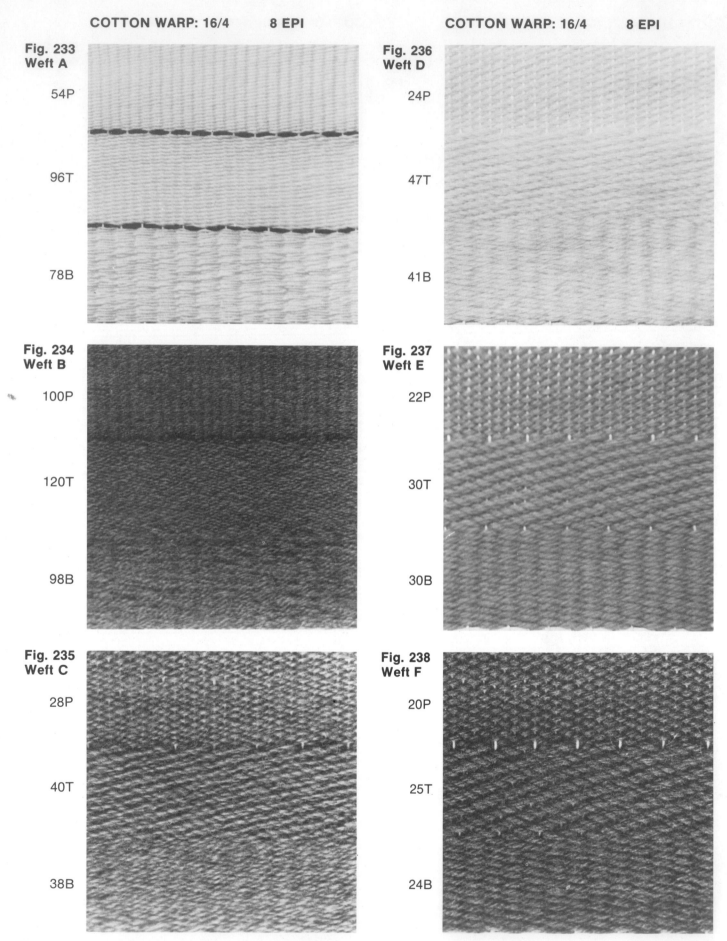

**Fig. 233
Weft A**

54P

96T

78B

**Fig. 236
Weft D**

24P

47T

41B

**Fig. 234
Weft B**

100P

120T

98B

**Fig. 237
Weft E**

22P

30T

30B

**Fig. 235
Weft C**

28P

40T

38B

**Fig. 238
Weft F**

20P

25T

24B

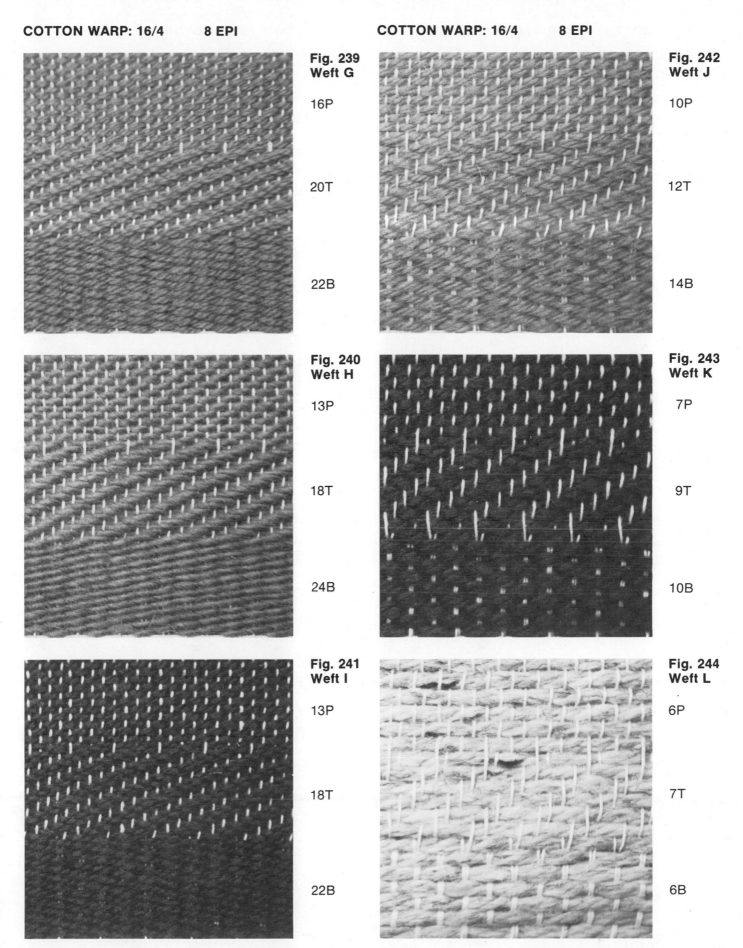

COTTON WARP: 16/4   8 EPI

COTTON WARP: 16/4   8 EPI

Fig. 239
Weft G

16P

20T

22B

Fig. 240
Weft H

13P

18T

24B

Fig. 241
Weft I

13P

18T

22B

Fig. 242
Weft J

10P

12T

14B

Fig. 243
Weft K

7P

9T

10B

Fig. 244
Weft L

6P

7T

6B

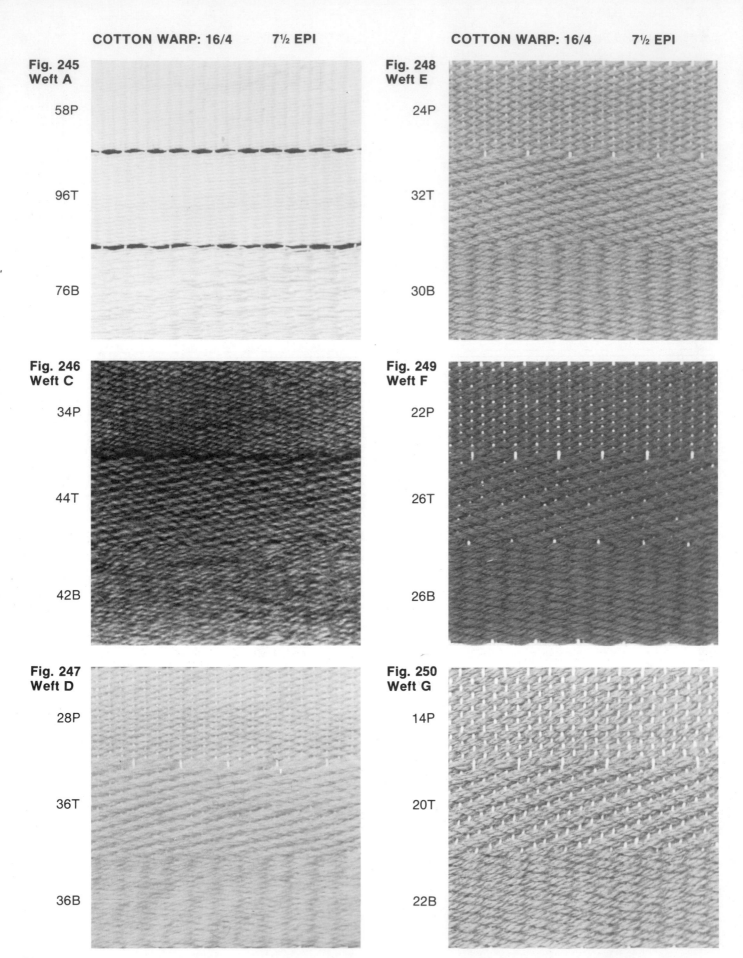

Fig. 245
Weft A

58P

96T

76B

Fig. 248
Weft E

24P

32T

30B

Fig. 246
Weft C

34P

44T

42B

Fig. 249
Weft F

22P

26T

26B

Fig. 247
Weft D

28P

36T

36B

Fig. 250
Weft G

14P

20T

22B

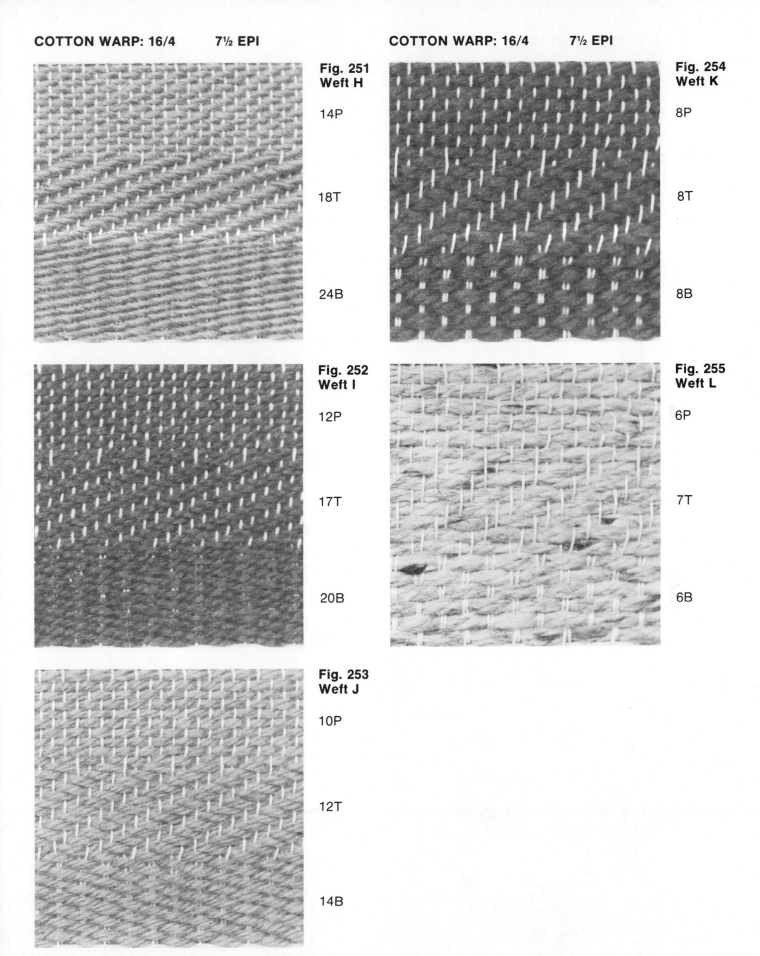

Fig. 251
Weft H

14P

18T

24B

Fig. 254
Weft K

8P

8T

8B

Fig. 252
Weft I

12P

17T

20B

Fig. 255
Weft L

6P

7T

6B

Fig. 253
Weft J

10P

12T

14B

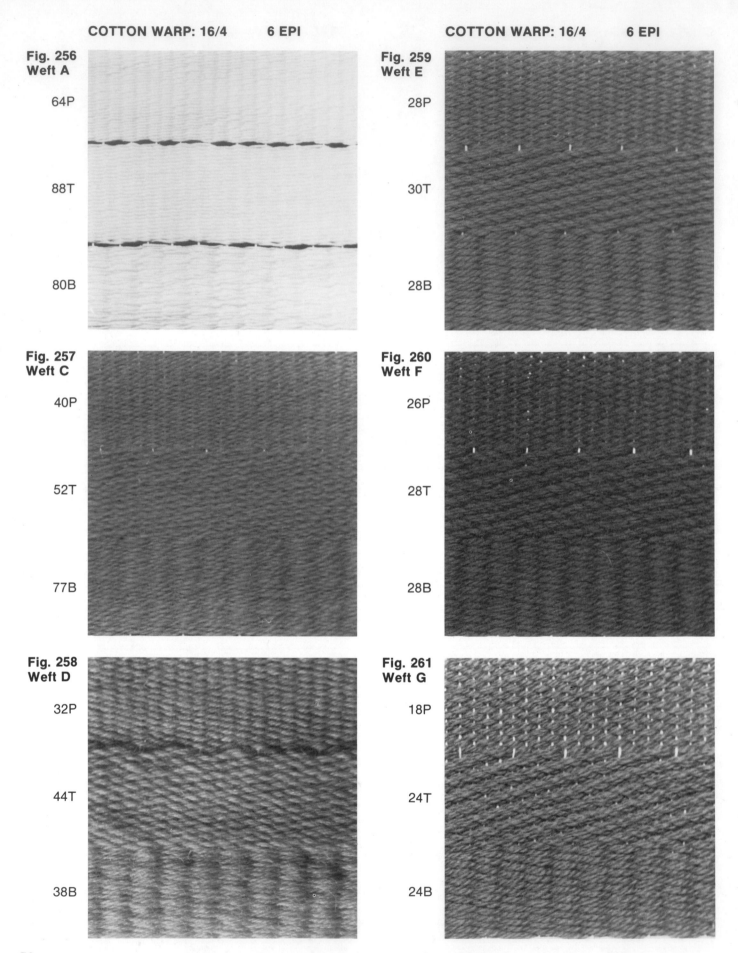

Fig. 256
Weft A

64P

88T

80B

Fig. 259
Weft E

28P

30T

28B

Fig. 257
Weft C

40P

52T

77B

Fig. 260
Weft F

26P

28T

28B

Fig. 258
Weft D

32P

44T

38B

Fig. 261
Weft G

18P

24T

24B

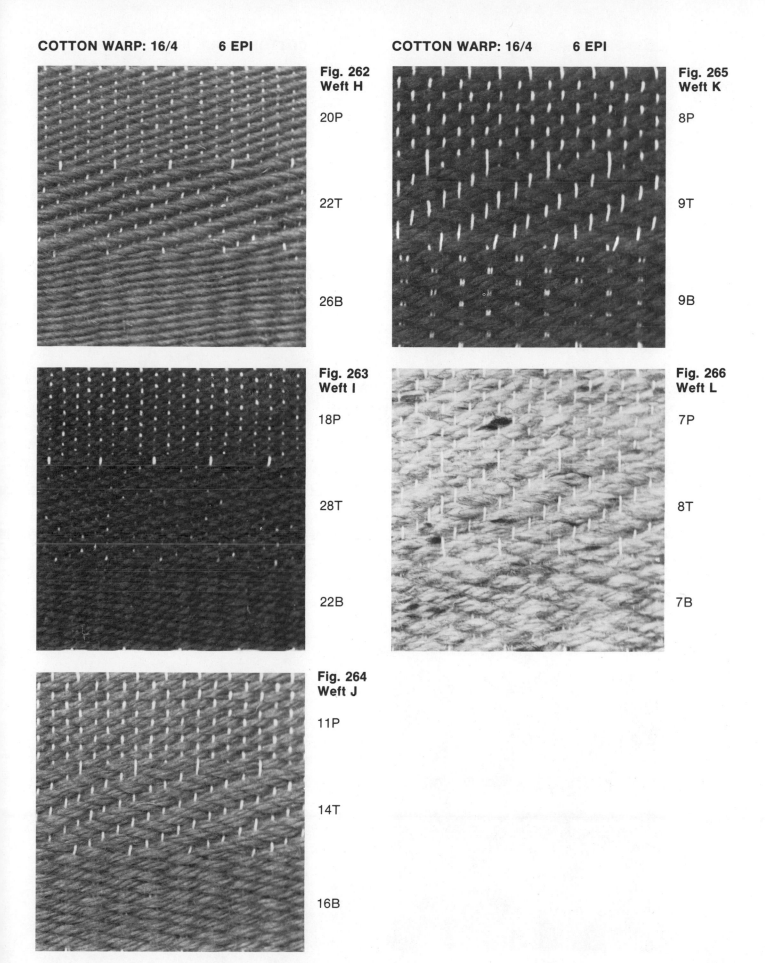

Fig. 262
Weft H

20P

22T

26B

Fig. 265
Weft K

8P

9T

9B

Fig. 263
Weft I

18P

28T

22B

Fig. 266
Weft L

7P

8T

7B

Fig. 264
Weft J

11P

14T

16B

57

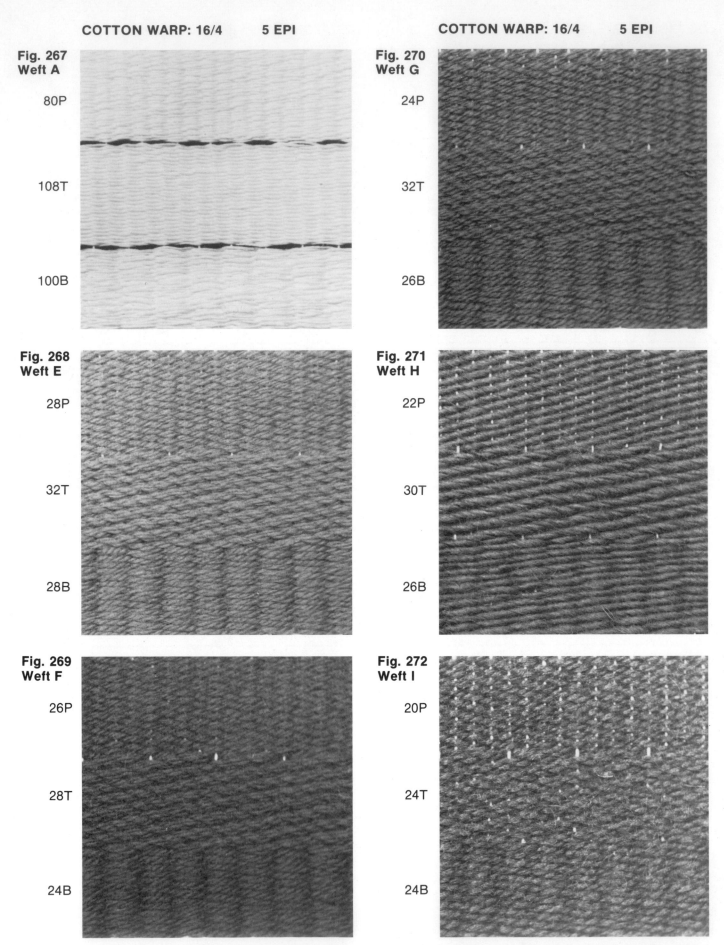

Fig. 267
Weft A

80P

108T

100B

Fig. 270
Weft G

24P

32T

26B

Fig. 268
Weft E

28P

32T

28B

Fig. 271
Weft H

22P

30T

26B

Fig. 269
Weft F

26P

28T

24B

Fig. 272
Weft I

20P

24T

24B

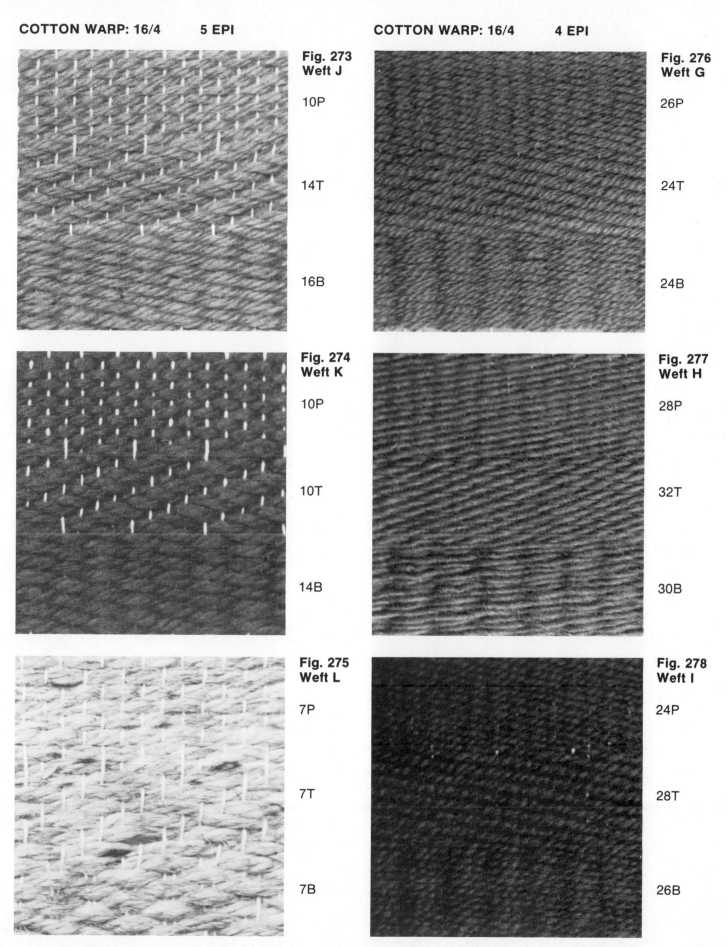

**Fig. 273
Weft J**

10P

14T

16B

**Fig. 274
Weft K**

10P

10T

14B

**Fig. 275
Weft L**

7P

7T

7B

**Fig. 276
Weft G**

26P

24T

24B

**Fig. 277
Weft H**

28P

32T

30B

**Fig. 278
Weft I**

24P

28T

26B

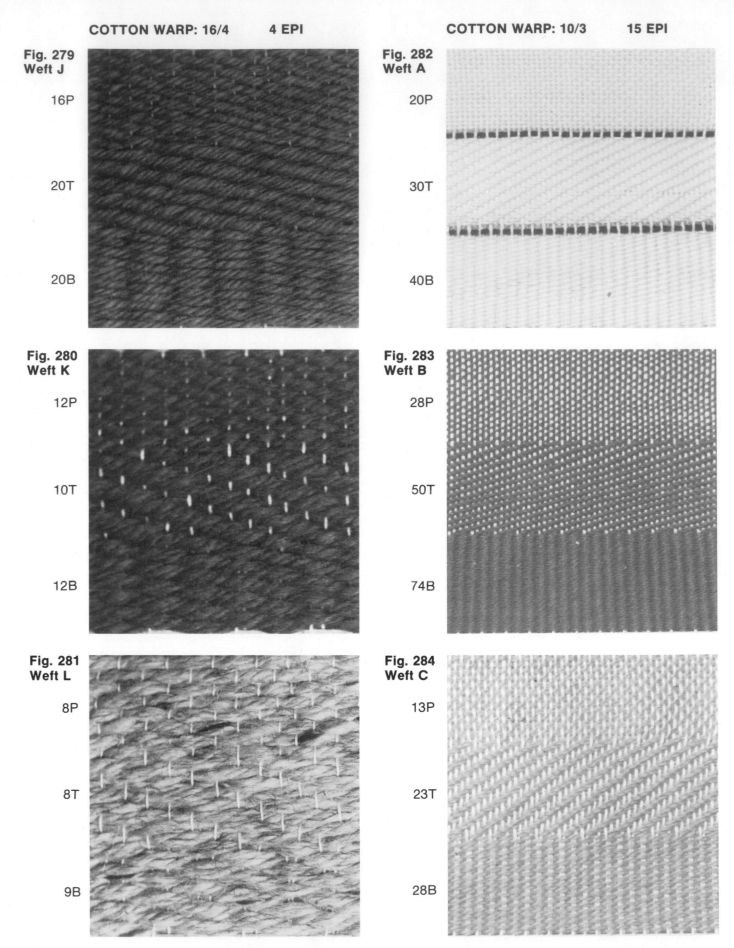

COTTON WARP: 16/4   4 EPI

Fig. 279
Weft J

16P

20T

20B

Fig. 280
Weft K

12P

10T

12B

Fig. 281
Weft L

8P

8T

9B

COTTON WARP: 10/3   15 EPI

Fig. 282
Weft A

20P

30T

40B

Fig. 283
Weft B

28P

50T

74B

Fig. 284
Weft C

13P

23T

28B

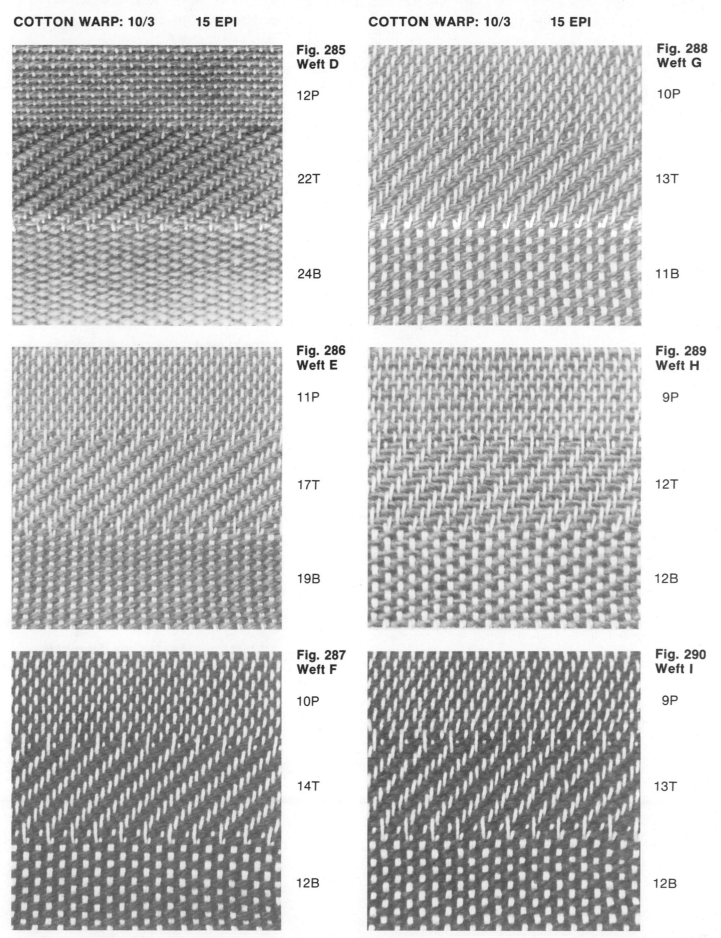

Fig. 285
Weft D

12P

22T

24B

COTTON WARP: 10/3   15 EPI

Fig. 288
Weft G

10P

13T

11B

Fig. 286
Weft E

11P

17T

19B

Fig. 289
Weft H

9P

12T

12B

Fig. 287
Weft F

10P

14T

12B

Fig. 290
Weft I

9P

13T

12B

**Fig. 291
Weft J**

8P

10T

9B

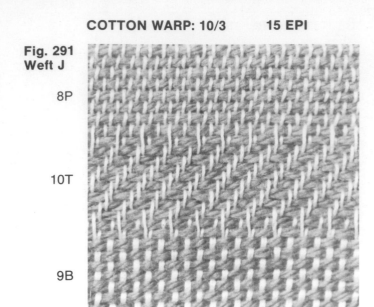

**Fig. 292
Weft A**

24P

50T

60B

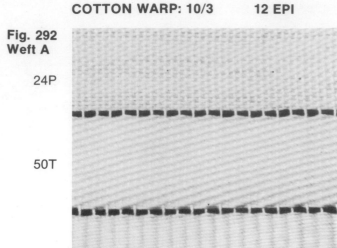

**Fig. 293
Weft B**

50P

108T

84B

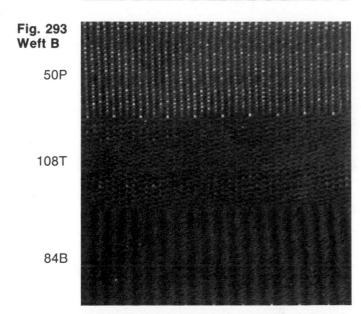

**Fig. 294
Weft C**

18P

30T

34B

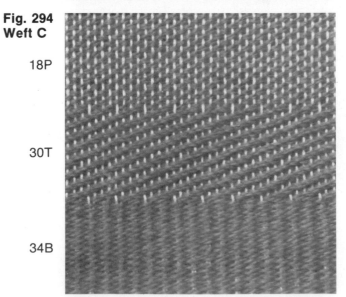

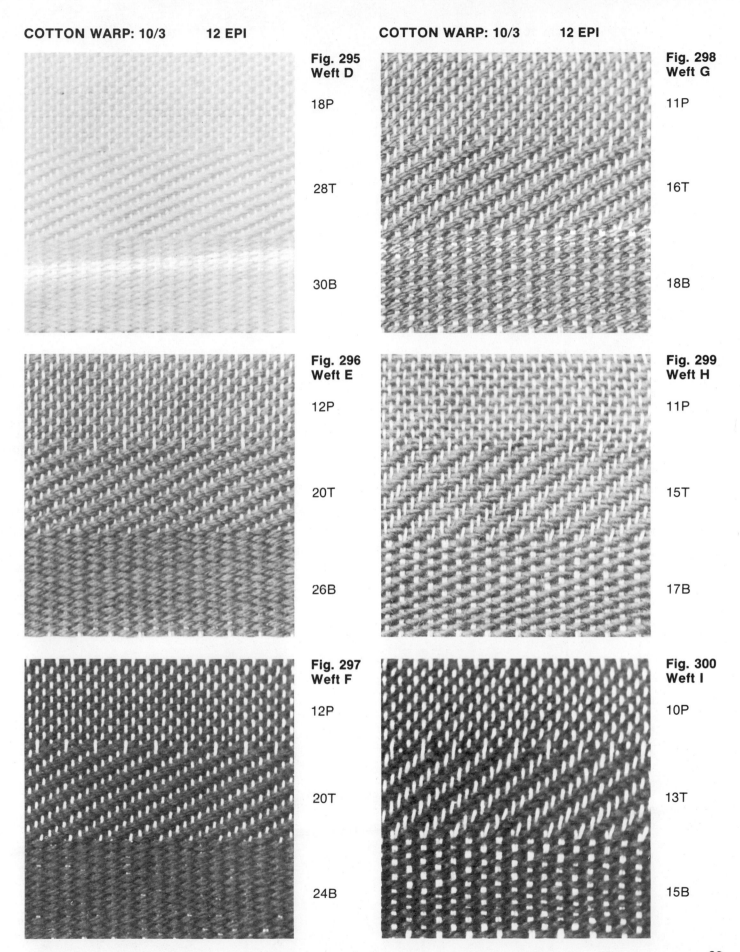

Fig. 295
Weft D

18P

28T

30B

Fig. 298
Weft G

11P

16T

18B

Fig. 296
Weft E

12P

20T

26B

Fig. 299
Weft H

11P

15T

17B

Fig. 297
Weft F

12P

20T

24B

Fig. 300
Weft I

10P

13T

15B

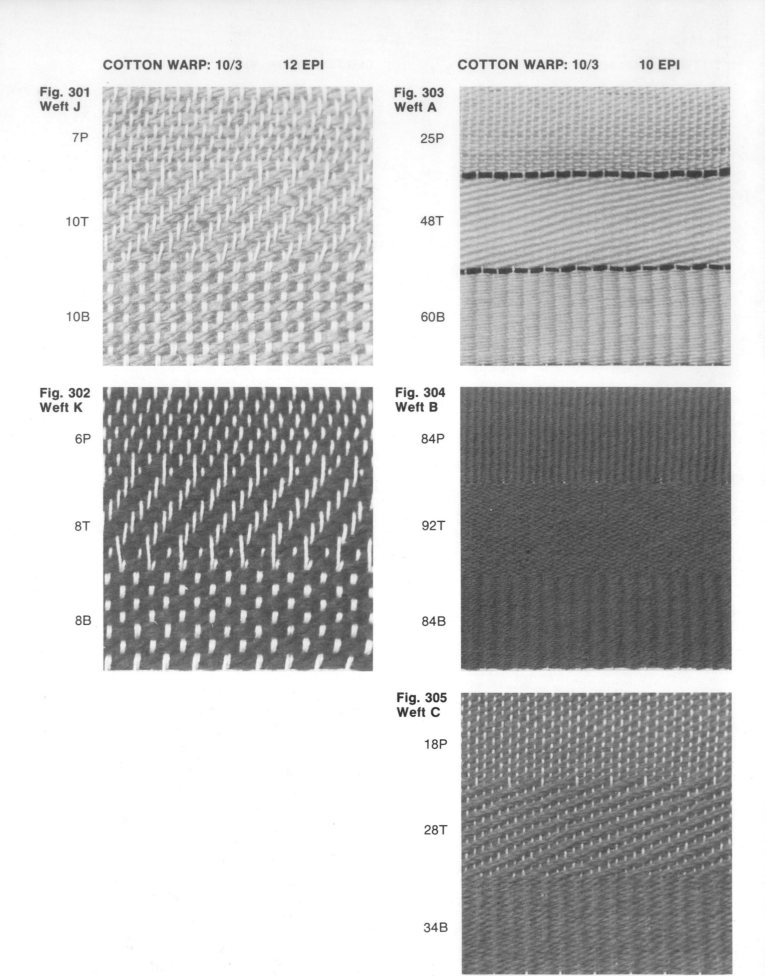

COTTON WARP: 10/3   12 EPI

COTTON WARP: 10/3   10 EPI

**Fig. 301
Weft J**

7P

10T

10B

**Fig. 302
Weft K**

6P

8T

8B

**Fig. 303
Weft A**

25P

48T

60B

**Fig. 304
Weft B**

84P

92T

84B

**Fig. 305
Weft C**

18P

28T

34B

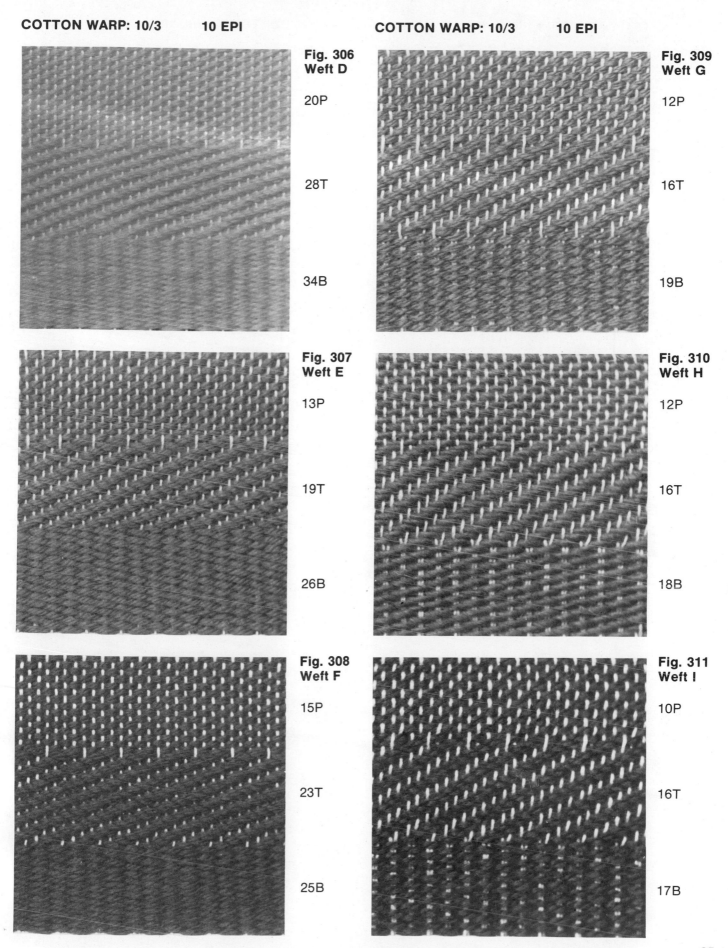

Fig. 306
Weft D

20P

28T

34B

Fig. 309
Weft G

12P

16T

19B

Fig. 307
Weft E

13P

19T

26B

Fig. 310
Weft H

12P

16T

18B

Fig. 308
Weft F

15P

23T

25B

Fig. 311
Weft I

10P

16T

17B

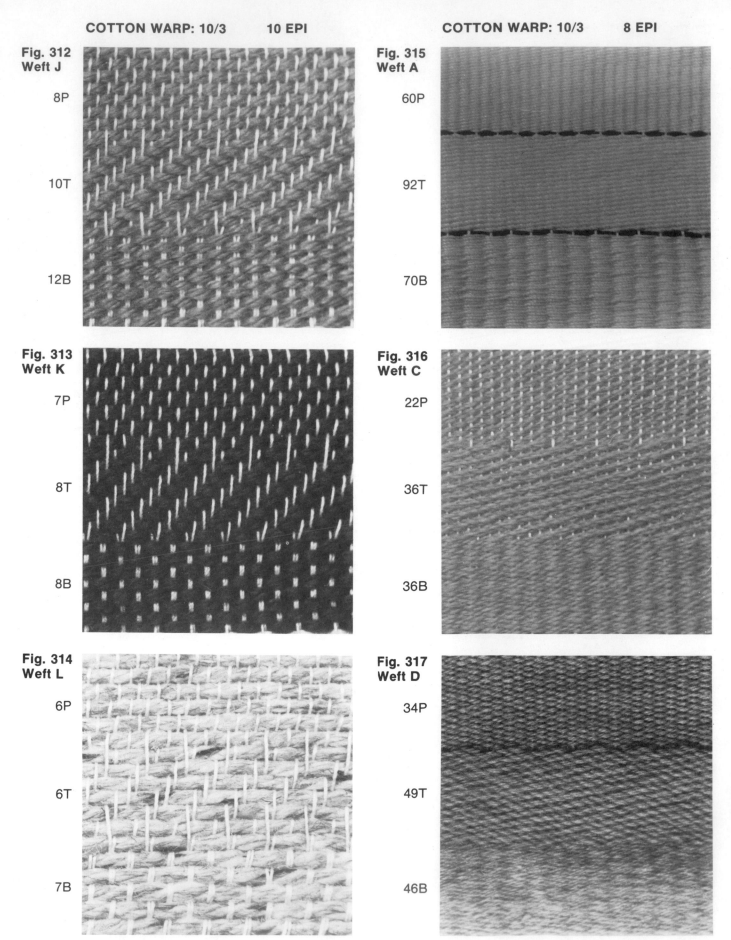

Fig. 312
Weft J

8P

10T

12B

Fig. 313
Weft K

7P

8T

8B

Fig. 314
Weft L

6P

6T

7B

Fig. 315
Weft A

60P

92T

70B

Fig. 316
Weft C

22P

36T

36B

Fig. 317
Weft D

34P

49T

46B

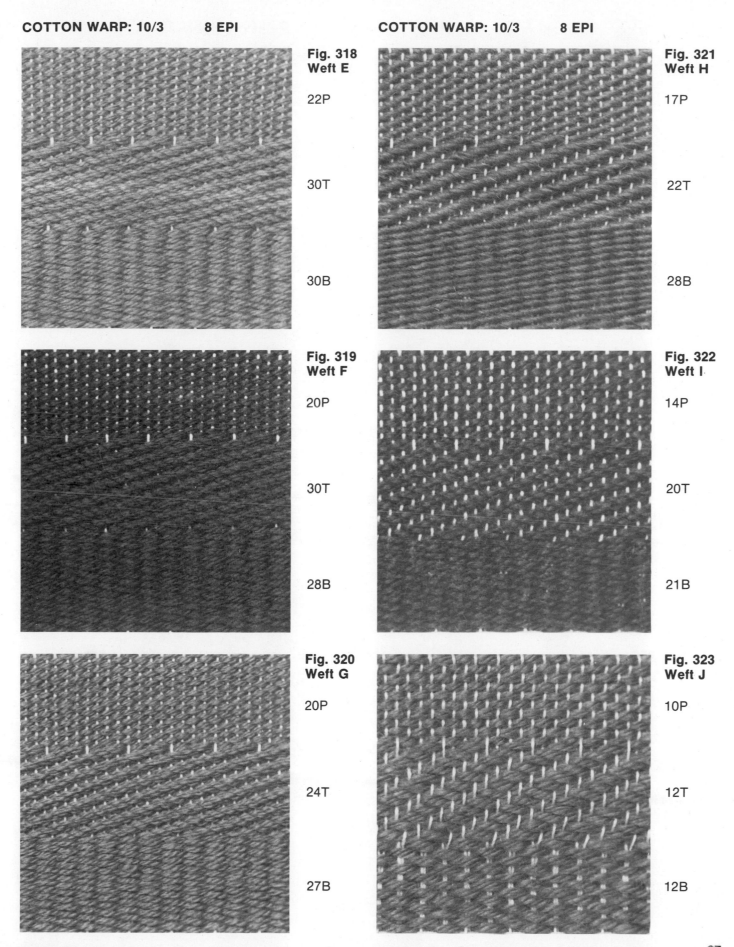

Fig. 318
Weft E

22P

30T

30B

Fig. 321
Weft H

17P

22T

28B

Fig. 319
Weft F

20P

30T

28B

Fig. 322
Weft I

14P

20T

21B

Fig. 320
Weft G

20P

24T

27B

Fig. 323
Weft J

10P

12T

12B

COTTON WARP: 10/3 8 EPI

Fig. 324
Weft K

8P

9T

12B

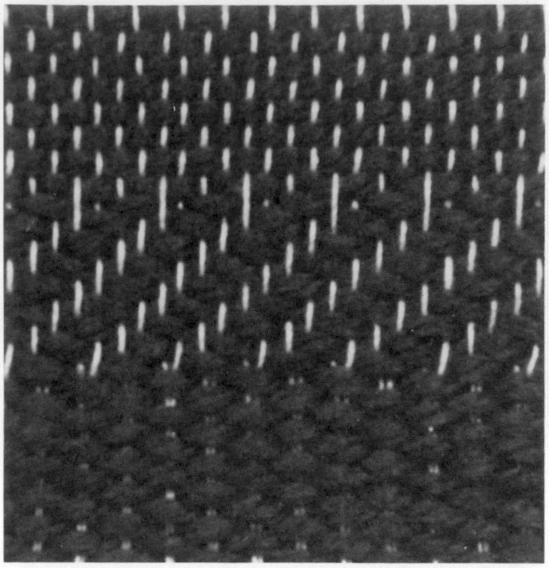

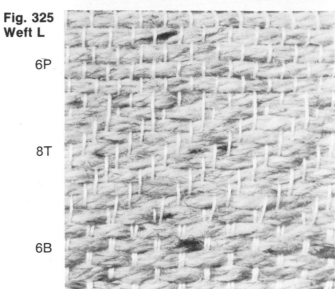

Fig. 325
Weft L

6P

8T

6B

COTTON WARP: 10/3 7½ EPI

Fig. 326
Weft A

71P

Fig. 327
Weft C

44P

Fig. 328
Weft E

32P

39T

34B

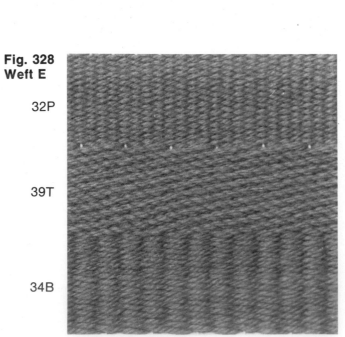

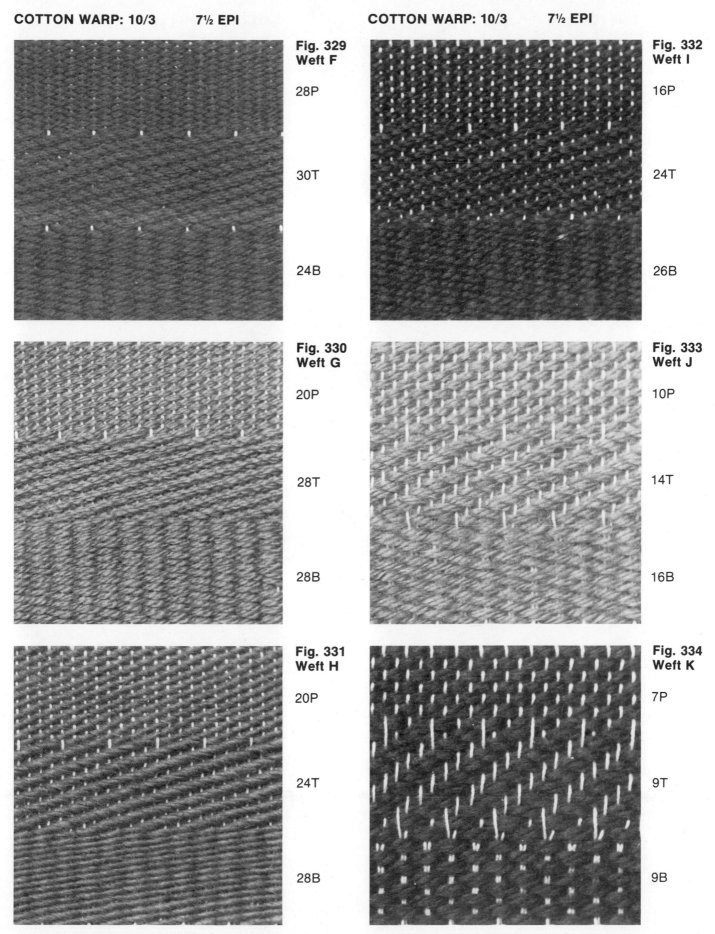

Fig. 329
Weft F

28P

30T

24B

Fig. 332
Weft I

16P

24T

26B

Fig. 330
Weft G

20P

28T

28B

Fig. 333
Weft J

10P

14T

16B

Fig. 331
Weft H

20P

24T

28B

Fig. 334
Weft K

7P

9T

9B

**Fig. 335
Weft L**

6P

7T

7B

**Fig. 336
Weft G**

28P

32T

24B

**Fig. 337
Weft H**

21P

36T

28B

**Fig. 338
Weft I**

26P

34T

26B

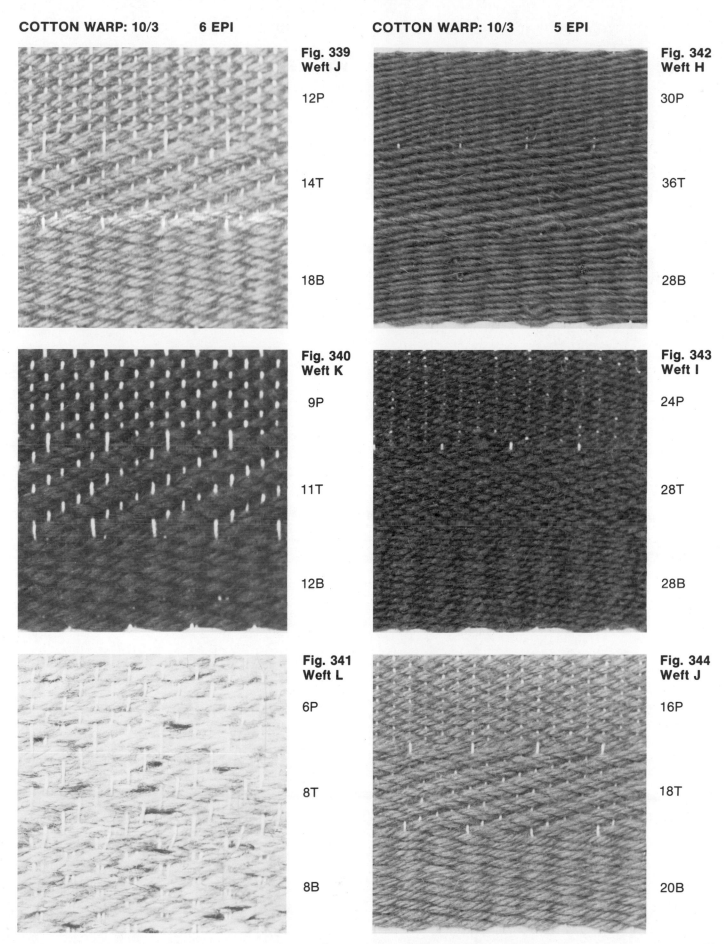

Fig. 339
Weft J

12P

14T

18B

Fig. 342
Weft H

30P

36T

28B

Fig. 340
Weft K

9P

11T

12B

Fig. 343
Weft I

24P

28T

28B

Fig. 341
Weft L

6P

8T

8B

Fig. 344
Weft J

16P

18T

20B

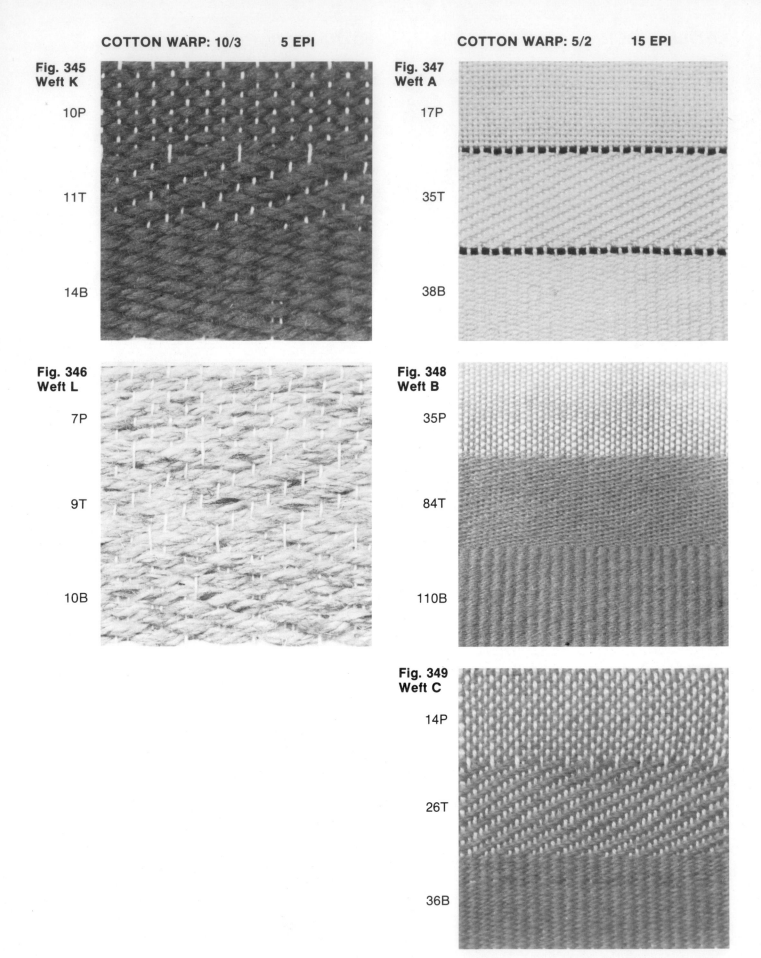

COTTON WARP: 10/3   5 EPI

COTTON WARP: 5/2   15 EPI

Fig. 345
Weft K

10P

11T

14B

Fig. 346
Weft L

7P

9T

10B

Fig. 347
Weft A

17P

35T

38B

Fig. 348
Weft B

35P

84T

110B

Fig. 349
Weft C

14P

26T

36B

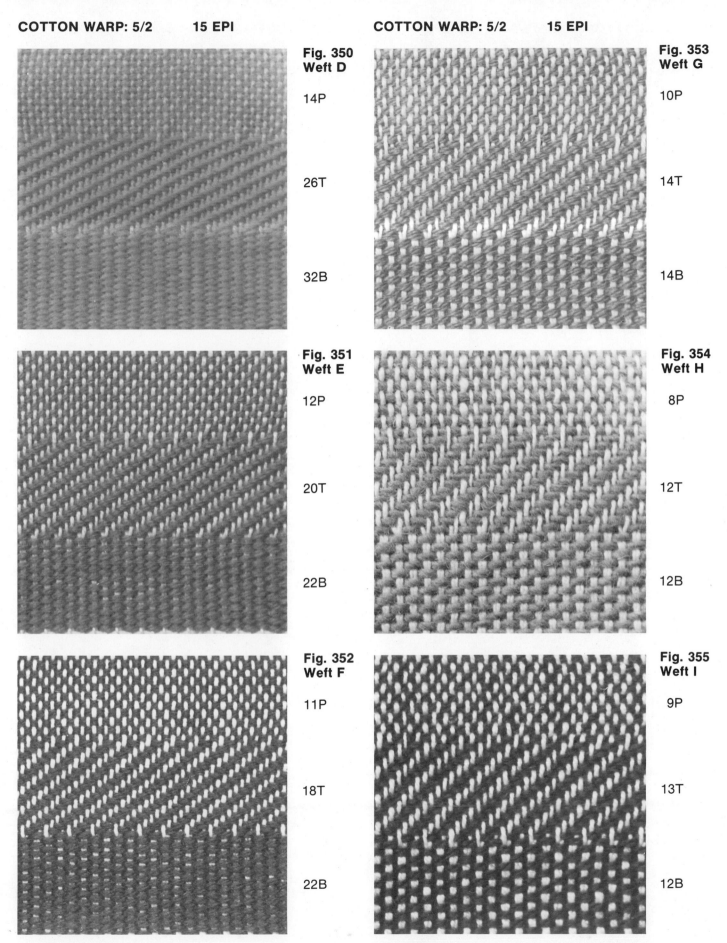

Fig. 350
Weft D

14P

26T

32B

Fig. 353
Weft G

10P

14T

14B

Fig. 351
Weft E

12P

20T

22B

Fig. 354
Weft H

8P

12T

12B

Fig. 352
Weft F

11P

18T

22B

Fig. 355
Weft I

9P

13T

12B

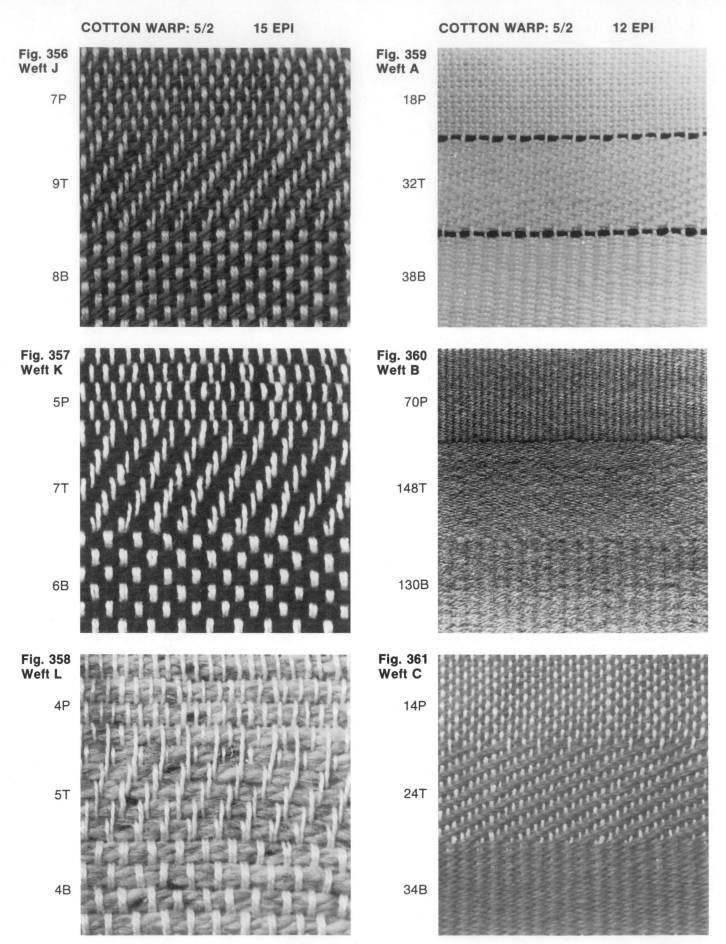

Fig. 356
Weft J

7P

9T

8B

Fig. 359
Weft A

18P

32T

38B

Fig. 357
Weft K

5P

7T

6B

Fig. 360
Weft B

70P

148T

130B

Fig. 358
Weft L

4P

5T

4B

Fig. 361
Weft C

14P

24T

34B

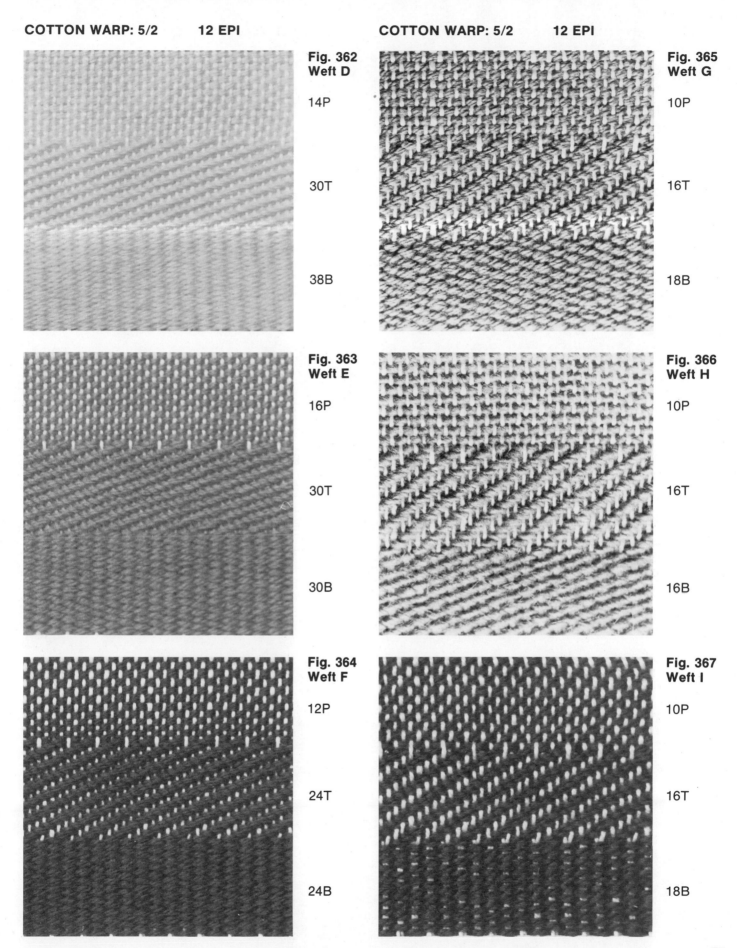

Fig. 362
Weft D

14P

30T

38B

Fig. 365
Weft G

10P

16T

18B

Fig. 363
Weft E

16P

30T

30B

Fig. 366
Weft H

10P

16T

16B

Fig. 364
Weft F

12P

24T

24B

Fig. 367
Weft I

10P

16T

18B

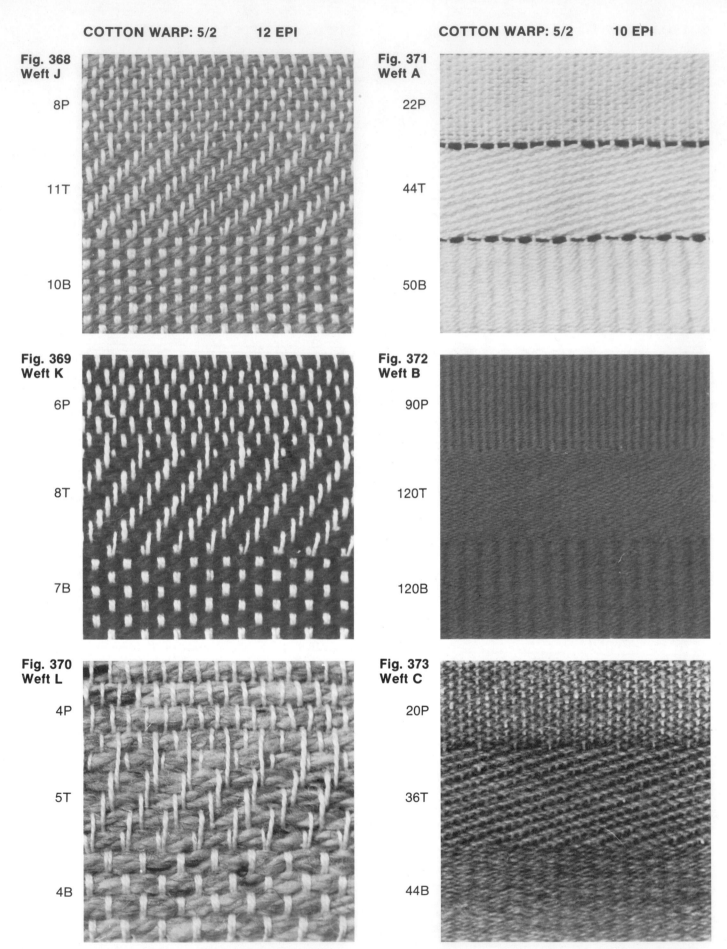

Fig. 368
Weft J

8P

11T

10B

Fig. 371
Weft A

22P

44T

50B

Fig. 369
Weft K

6P

8T

7B

Fig. 372
Weft B

90P

120T

120B

Fig. 370
Weft L

4P

5T

4B

Fig. 373
Weft C

20P

36T

44B

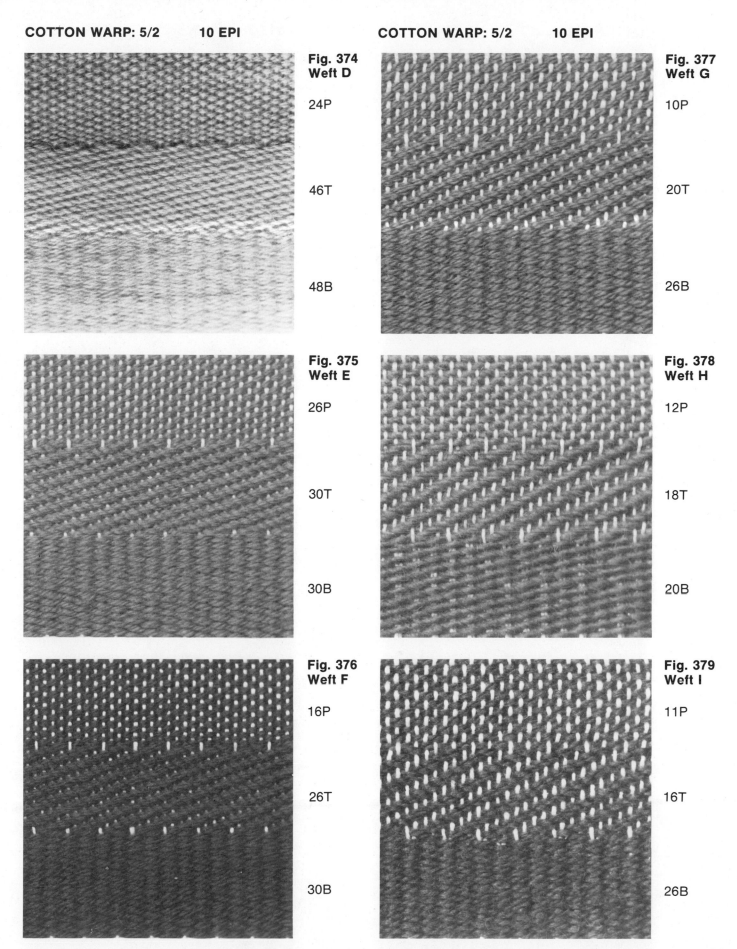

COTTON WARP: 5/2   10 EPI

Fig. 374
Weft D

24P

46T

48B

COTTON WARP: 5/2   10 EPI

Fig. 377
Weft G

10P

20T

26B

Fig. 375
Weft E

26P

30T

30B

Fig. 378
Weft H

12P

18T

20B

Fig. 376
Weft F

16P

26T

30B

Fig. 379
Weft I

11P

16T

26B

77

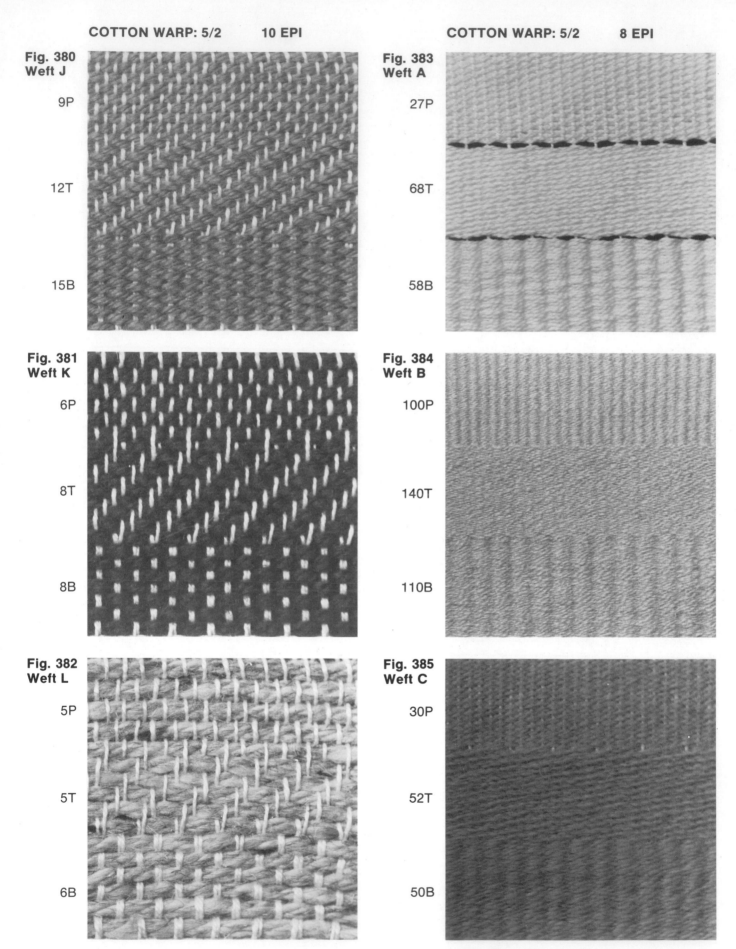

COTTON WARP: 5/2   10 EPI

**Fig. 380
Weft J**

9P

12T

15B

**Fig. 381
Weft K**

6P

8T

8B

**Fig. 382
Weft L**

5P

5T

6B

COTTON WARP: 5/2   8 EPI

**Fig. 383
Weft A**

27P

68T

58B

**Fig. 384
Weft B**

100P

140T

110B

**Fig. 385
Weft C**

30P

52T

50B

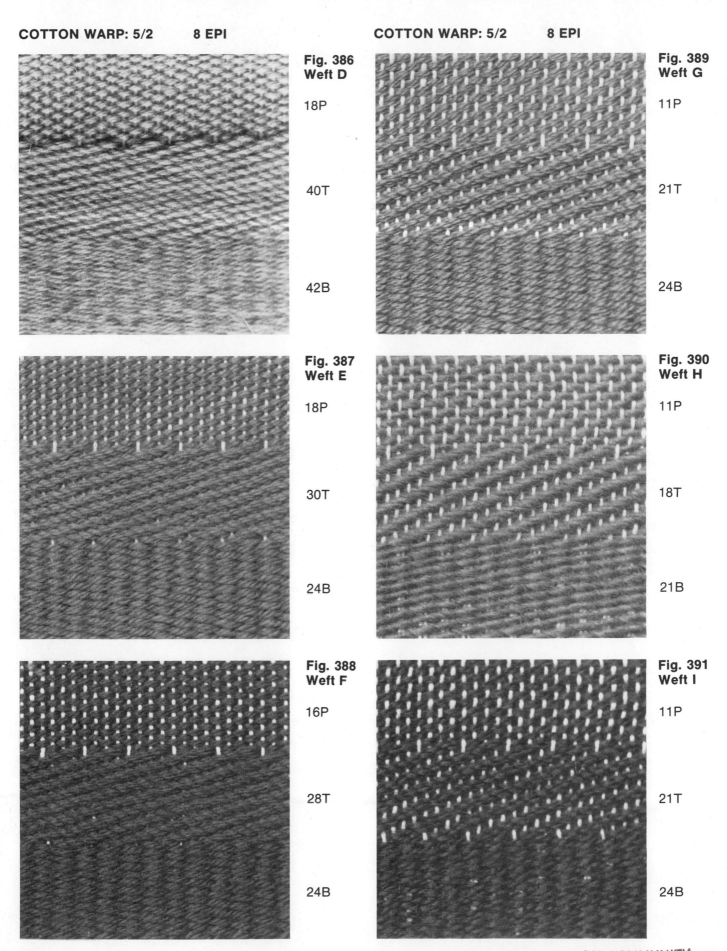

COTTON WARP: 5/2   8 EPI

Fig. 386
Weft D

18P

40T

42B

COTTON WARP: 5/2   8 EPI

Fig. 389
Weft G

11P

21T

24B

Fig. 387
Weft E

18P

30T

24B

Fig. 390
Weft H

11P

18T

21B

Fig. 388
Weft F

16P

28T

24B

Fig. 391
Weft I

11P

21T

24B

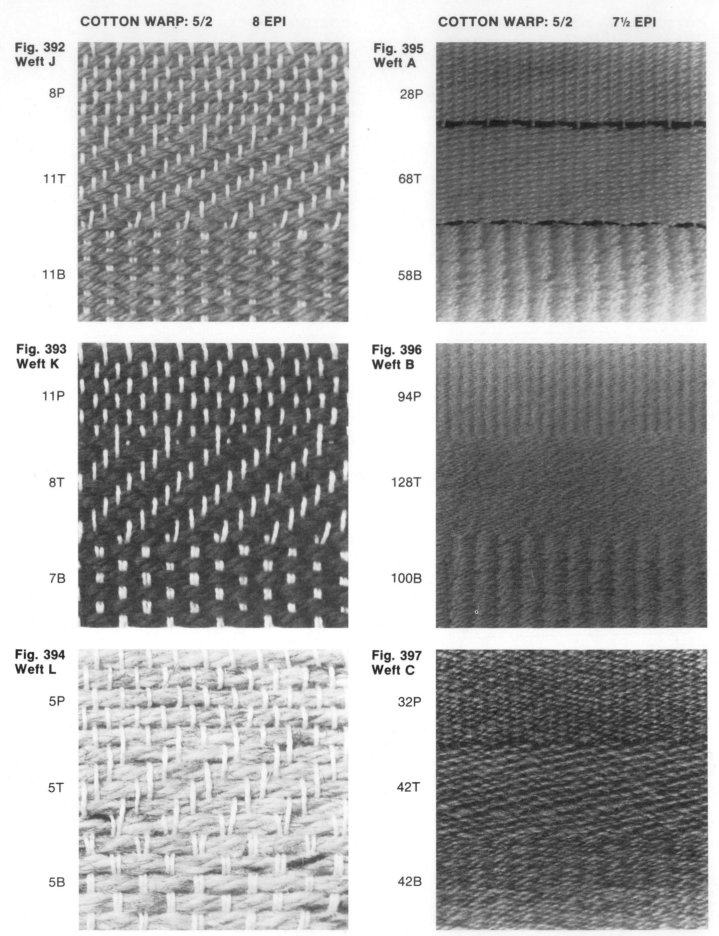

Fig. 392
Weft J

8P

11T

11B

Fig. 395
Weft A

28P

68T

58B

Fig. 393
Weft K

11P

8T

7B

Fig. 396
Weft B

94P

128T

100B

Fig. 394
Weft L

5P

5T

5B

Fig. 397
Weft C

32P

42T

42B

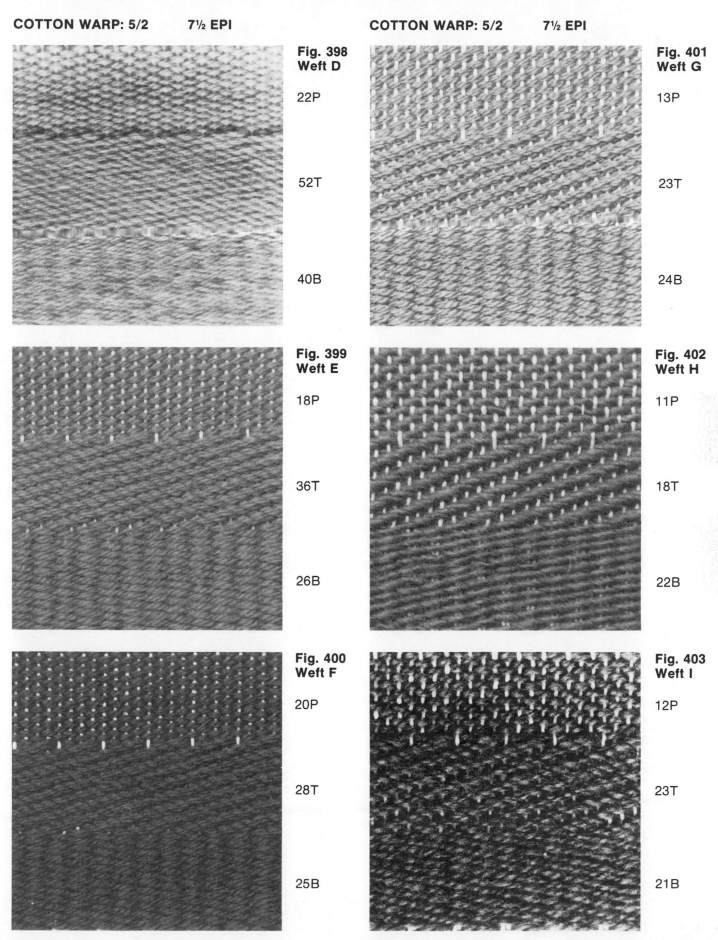

Fig. 398
Weft D

22P

52T

40B

Fig. 401
Weft G

13P

23T

24B

Fig. 399
Weft E

18P

36T

26B

Fig. 402
Weft H

11P

18T

22B

Fig. 400
Weft F

20P

28T

25B

Fig. 403
Weft I

12P

23T

21B

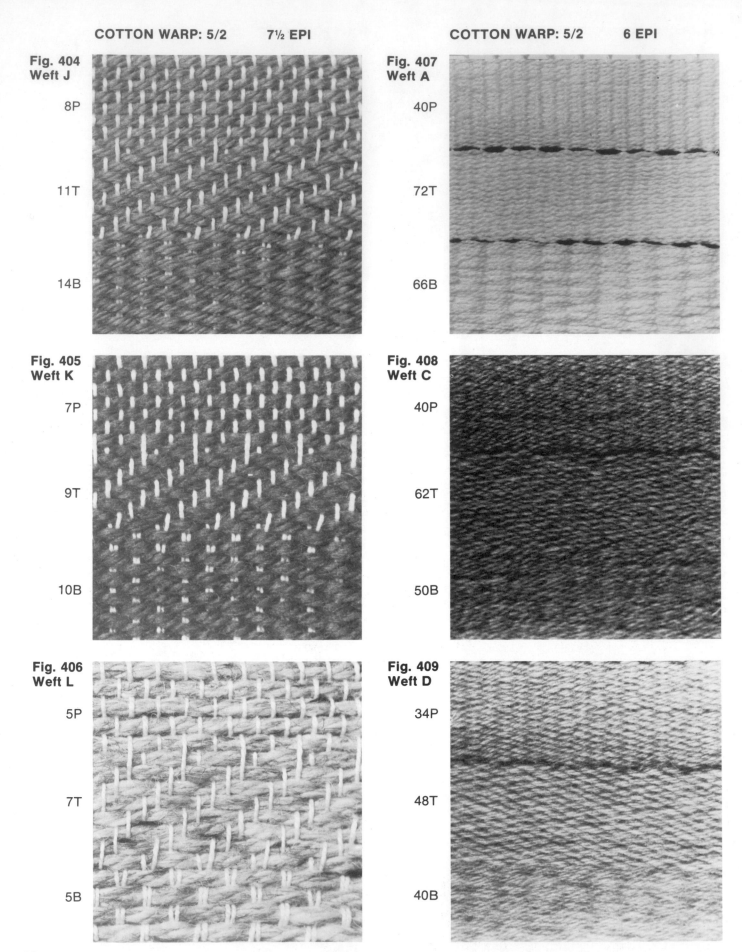

Fig. 404
Weft J

8P

11T

14B

Fig. 407
Weft A

40P

72T

66B

Fig. 405
Weft K

7P

9T

10B

Fig. 408
Weft C

40P

62T

50B

Fig. 406
Weft L

5P

7T

5B

Fig. 409
Weft D

34P

48T

40B

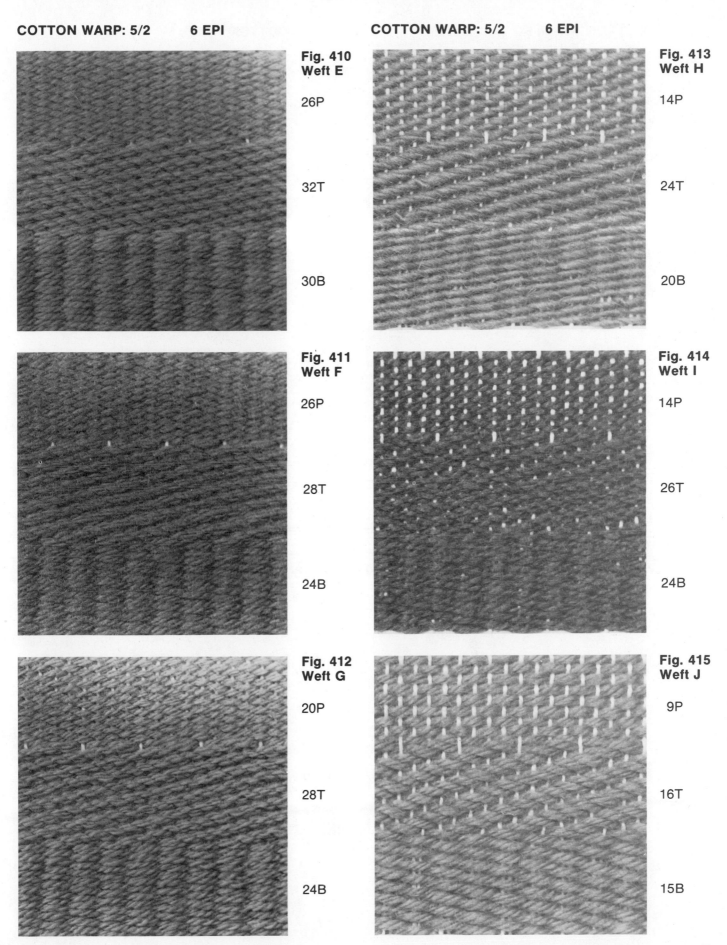

Fig. 410
Weft E

26P

32T

30B

Fig. 411
Weft F

26P

28T

24B

Fig. 412
Weft G

20P

28T

24B

Fig. 413
Weft H

14P

24T

20B

Fig. 414
Weft I

14P

26T

24B

Fig. 415
Weft J

9P

16T

15B

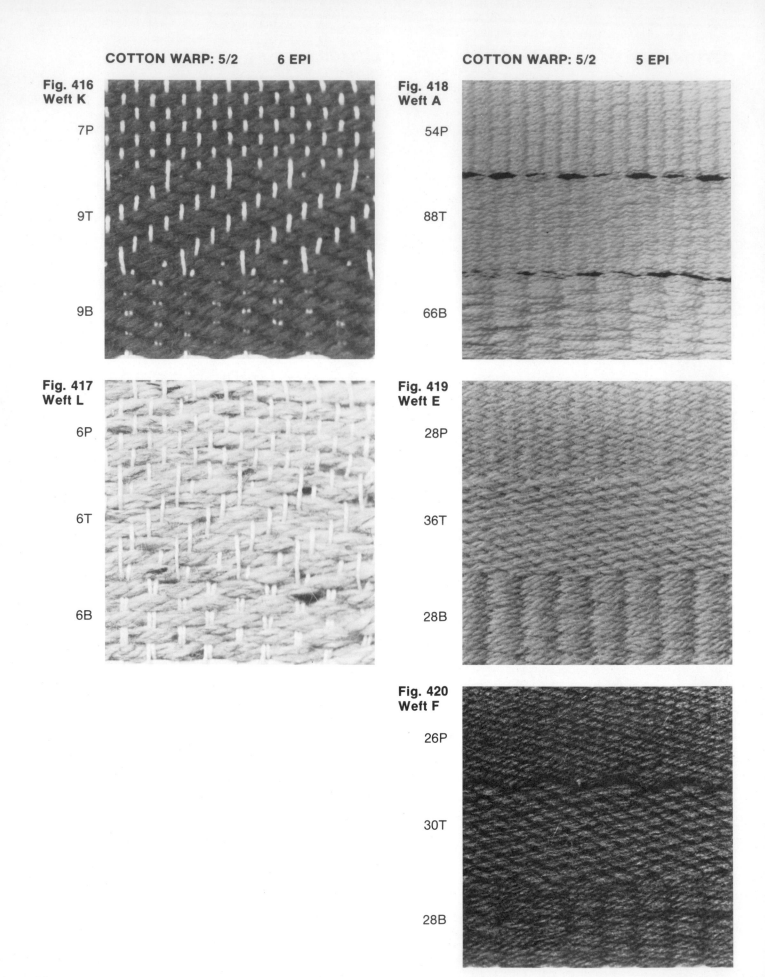

Fig. 416
Weft K

7P

9T

9B

Fig. 418
Weft A

54P

88T

66B

Fig. 417
Weft L

6P

6T

6B

Fig. 419
Weft E

28P

36T

28B

Fig. 420
Weft F

26P

30T

28B

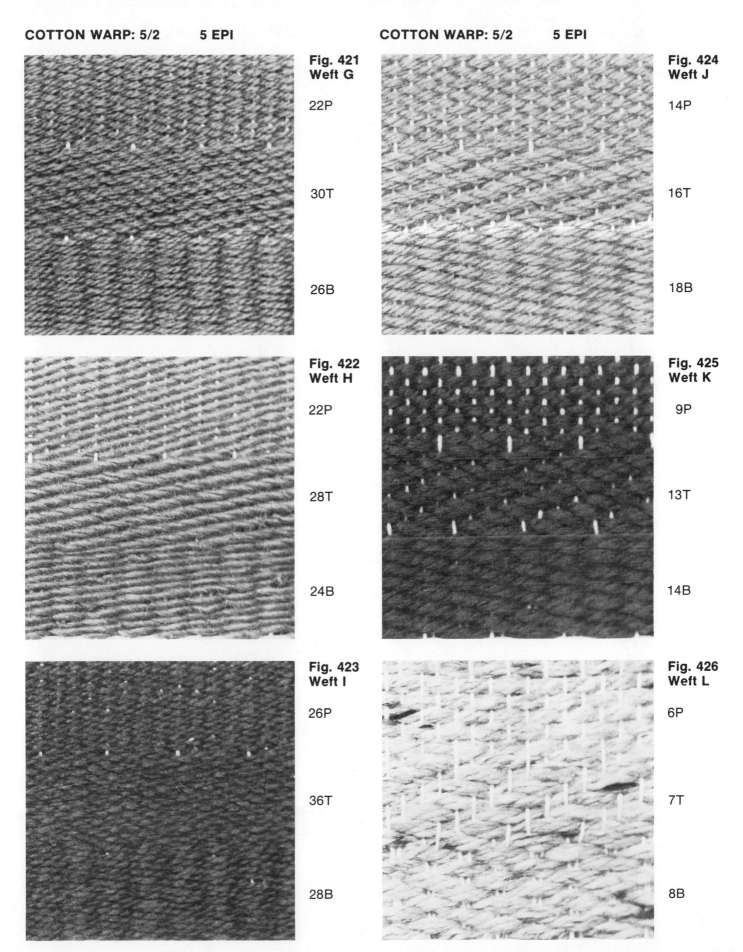

COTTON WARP: 5/2   5 EPI

Fig. 421
Weft G

22P

30T

26B

Fig. 422
Weft H

22P

28T

24B

Fig. 423
Weft I

26P

36T

28B

Fig. 424
Weft J

14P

16T

18B

Fig. 425
Weft K

9P

13T

14B

Fig. 426
Weft L

6P

7T

8B

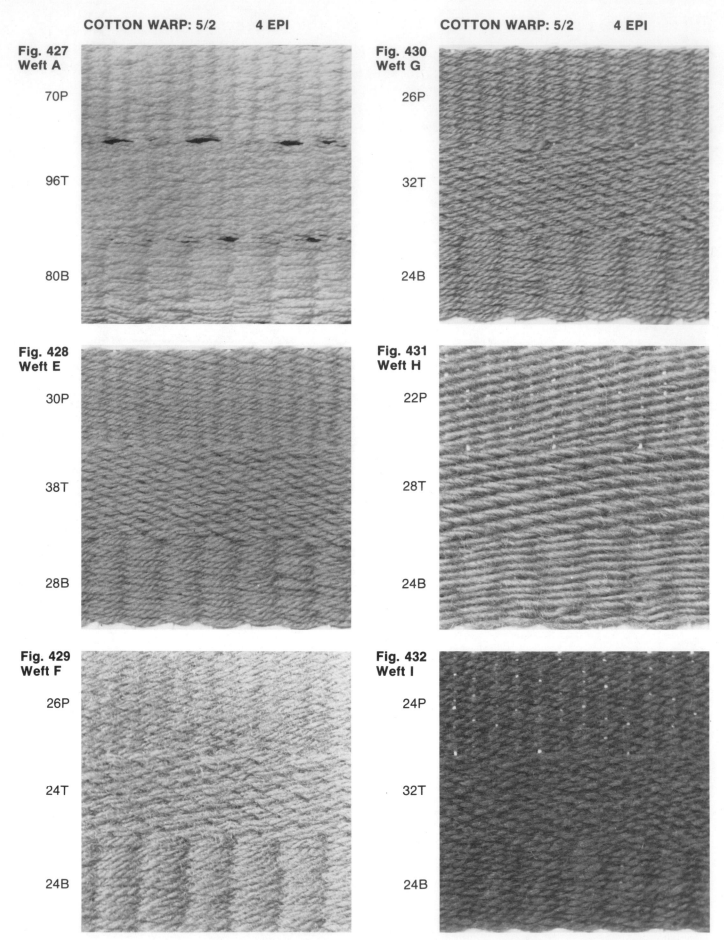

COTTON WARP: 5/2   4 EPI

COTTON WARP: 5/2   4 EPI

COTTON WARP: 5/2   4 EPI

Fig. 427
Weft A

70P

96T

80B

Fig. 430
Weft G

26P

32T

24B

Fig. 428
Weft E

30P

38T

28B

Fig. 431
Weft H

22P

28T

24B

Fig. 429
Weft F

26P

24T

24B

Fig. 432
Weft I

24P

32T

24B

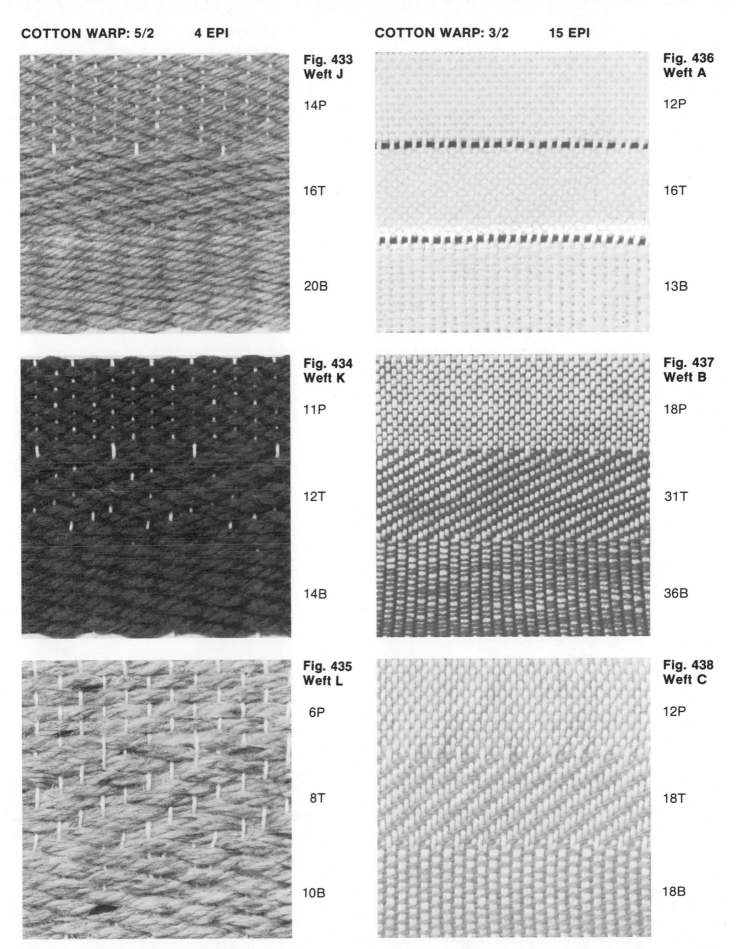

Fig. 433
Weft J

14P

16T

20B

Fig. 436
Weft A

12P

16T

13B

Fig. 434
Weft K

11P

12T

14B

Fig. 437
Weft B

18P

31T

36B

Fig. 435
Weft L

6P

8T

10B

Fig. 438
Weft C

12P

18T

18B

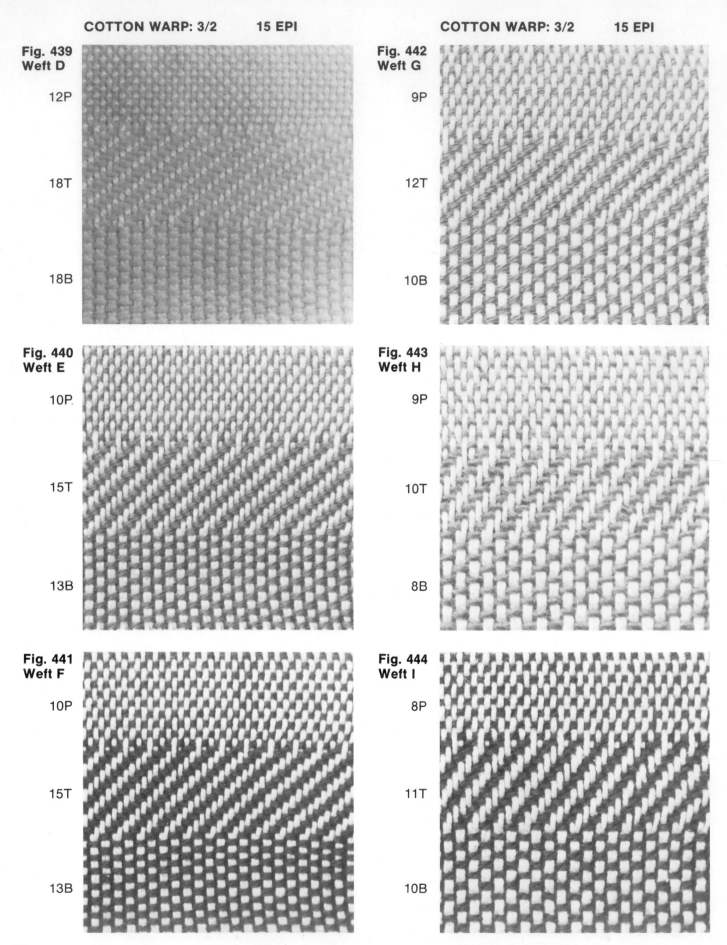

Fig. 439
Weft D

12P

18T

18B

Fig. 442
Weft G

9P

12T

10B

Fig. 440
Weft E

10P

15T

13B

Fig. 443
Weft H

9P

10T

8B

Fig. 441
Weft F

10P

15T

13B

Fig. 444
Weft I

8P

11T

10B

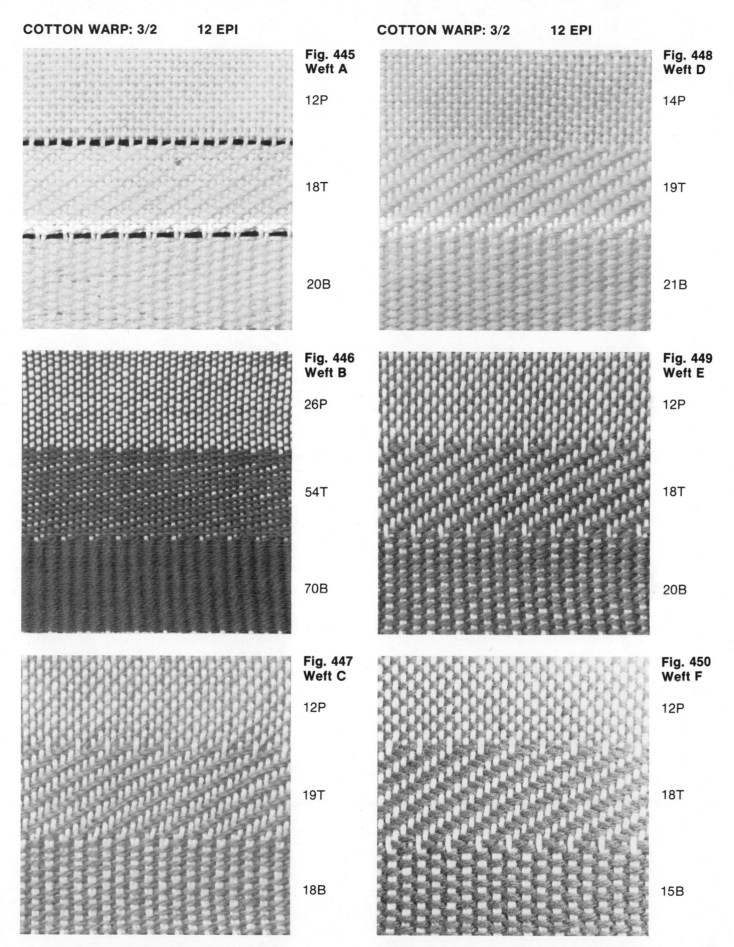

COTTON WARP: 3/2   12 EPI

**Fig. 445
Weft A**

12P

18T

20B

COTTON WARP: 3/2   12 EPI

**Fig. 448
Weft D**

14P

19T

21B

**Fig. 446
Weft B**

26P

54T

70B

**Fig. 449
Weft E**

12P

18T

20B

**Fig. 447
Weft C**

12P

19T

18B

**Fig. 450
Weft F**

12P

18T

15B

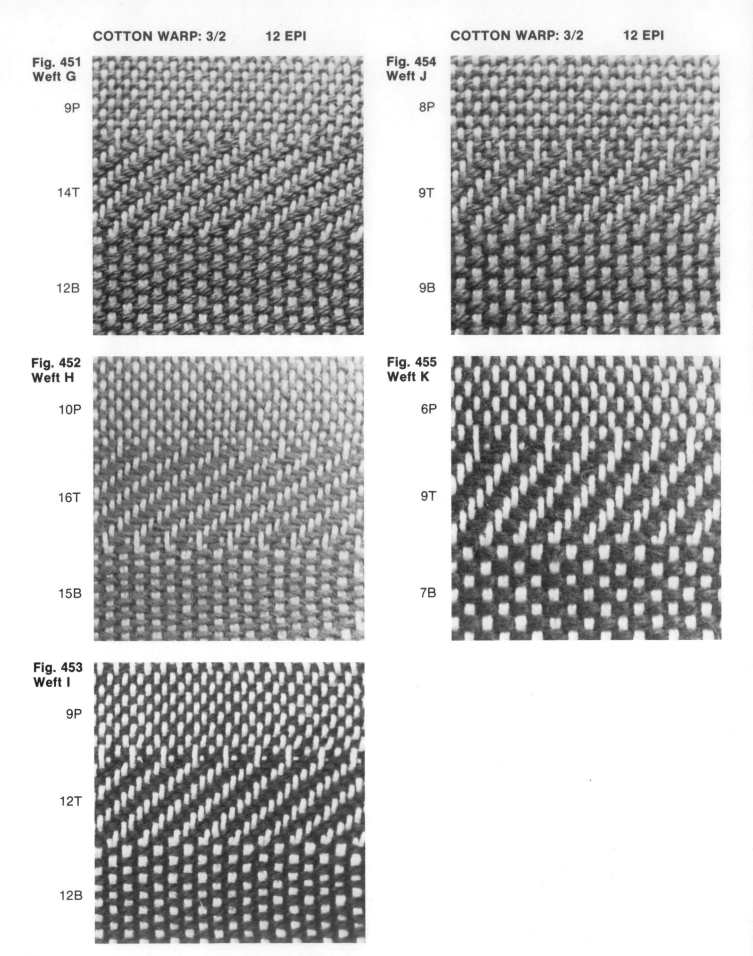

COTTON WARP: 3/2   12 EPI

Fig. 451
Weft G

9P

14T

12B

COTTON WARP: 3/2   12 EPI

Fig. 454
Weft J

8P

9T

9B

Fig. 452
Weft H

10P

16T

15B

Fig. 455
Weft K

6P

9T

7B

Fig. 453
Weft I

9P

12T

12B

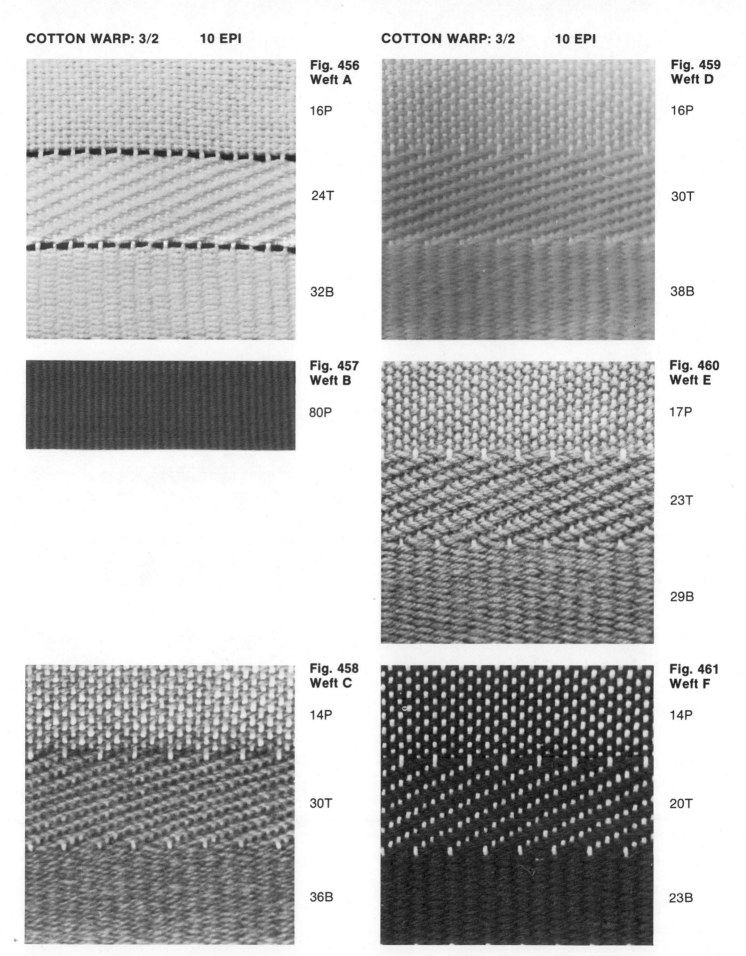

Fig. 456
Weft A

16P

24T

32B

Fig. 459
Weft D

16P

30T

38B

Fig. 457
Weft B

80P

Fig. 460
Weft E

17P

23T

29B

Fig. 458
Weft C

14P

30T

36B

Fig. 461
Weft F

14P

20T

23B

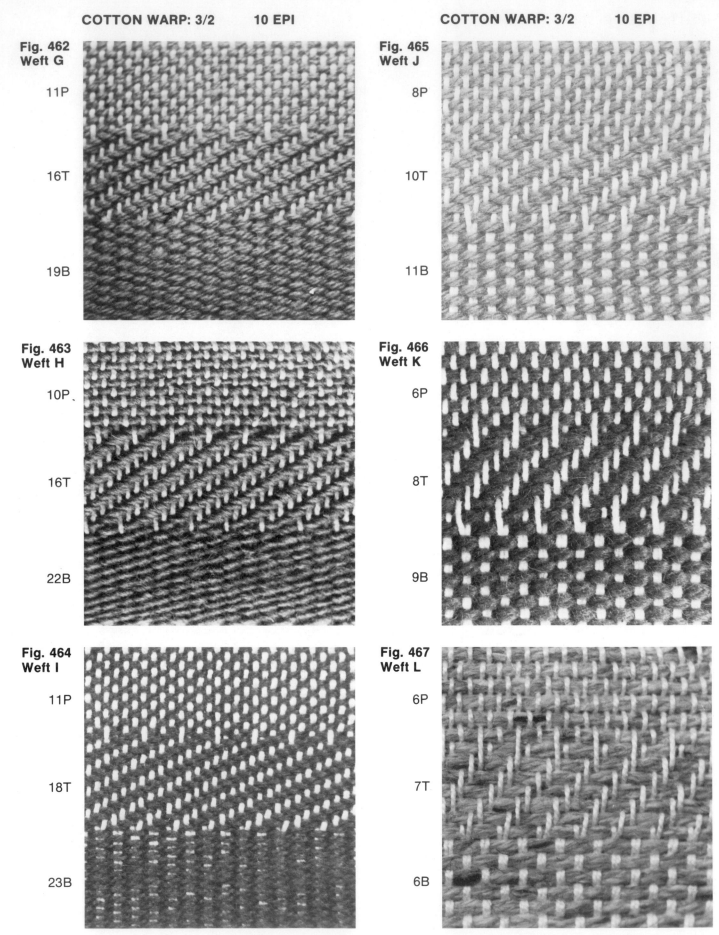

Fig. 462
Weft G

11P

16T

19B

Fig. 463
Weft H

10P

16T

22B

Fig. 464
Weft I

11P

18T

23B

Fig. 465
Weft J

8P

10T

11B

Fig. 466
Weft K

6P

8T

9B

Fig. 467
Weft L

6P

7T

6B

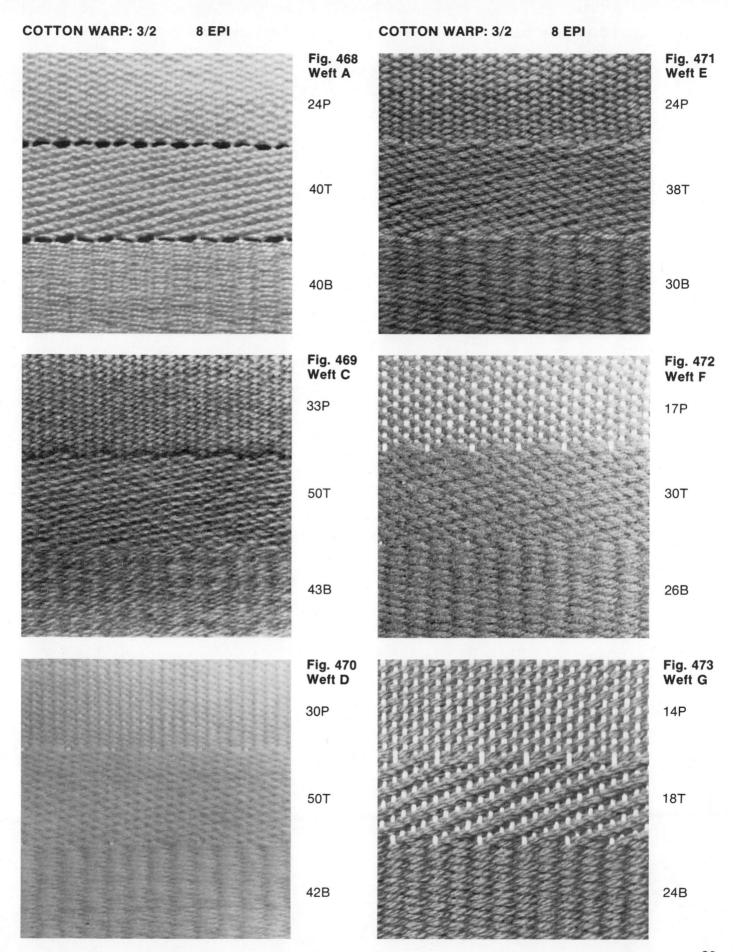

Fig. 468
Weft A

24P

40T

40B

Fig. 471
Weft E

24P

38T

30B

Fig. 469
Weft C

33P

50T

43B

Fig. 472
Weft F

17P

30T

26B

Fig. 470
Weft D

30P

50T

42B

Fig. 473
Weft G

14P

18T

24B

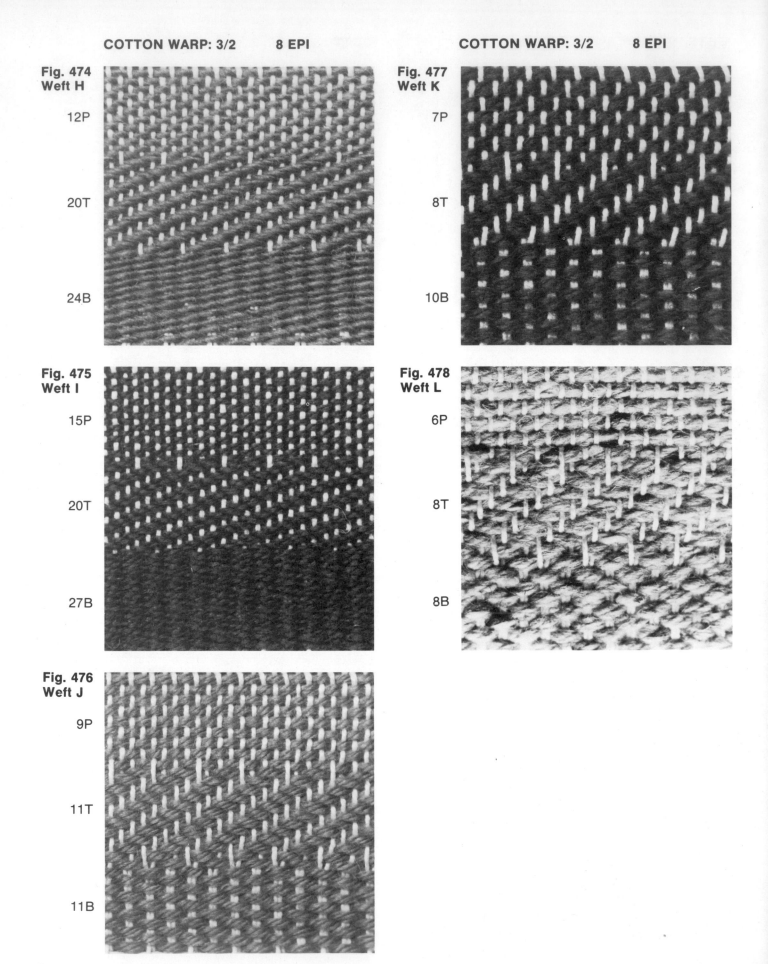

Fig. 474
Weft H

12P

20T

24B

Fig. 475
Weft I

15P

20T

27B

Fig. 476
Weft J

9P

11T

11B

Fig. 477
Weft K

7P

8T

10B

Fig. 478
Weft L

6P

8T

8B

COTTON WARP: 3/2   7½ EPI

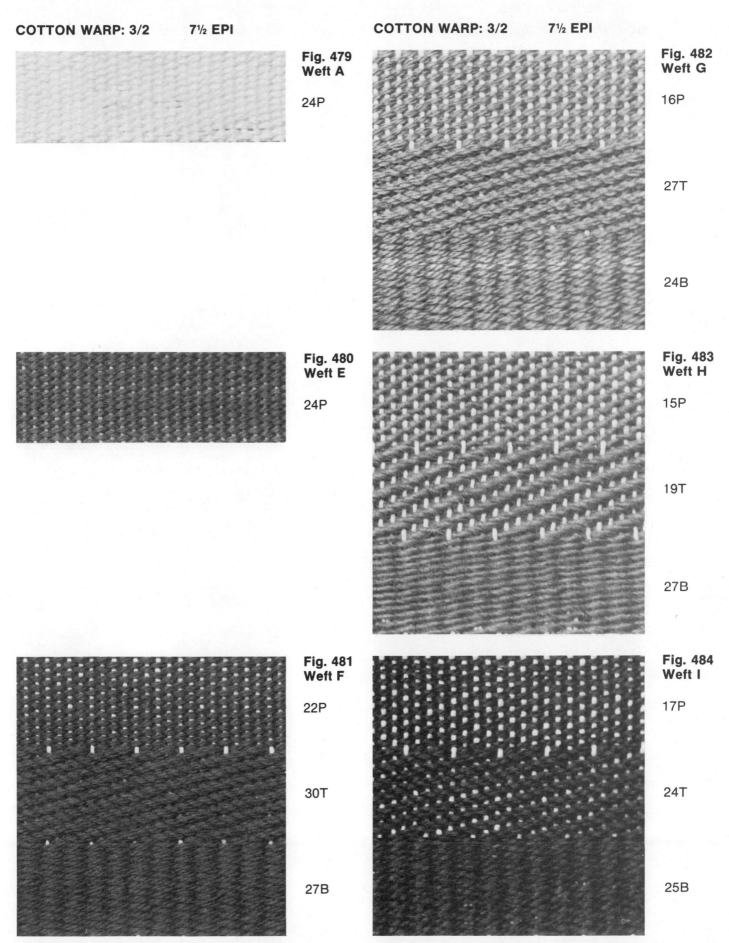

Fig. 479
Weft A

24P

Fig. 480
Weft E

24P

Fig. 481
Weft F

22P

30T

27B

Fig. 482
Weft G

16P

27T

24B

Fig. 483
Weft H

15P

19T

27B

Fig. 484
Weft I

17P

24T

25B

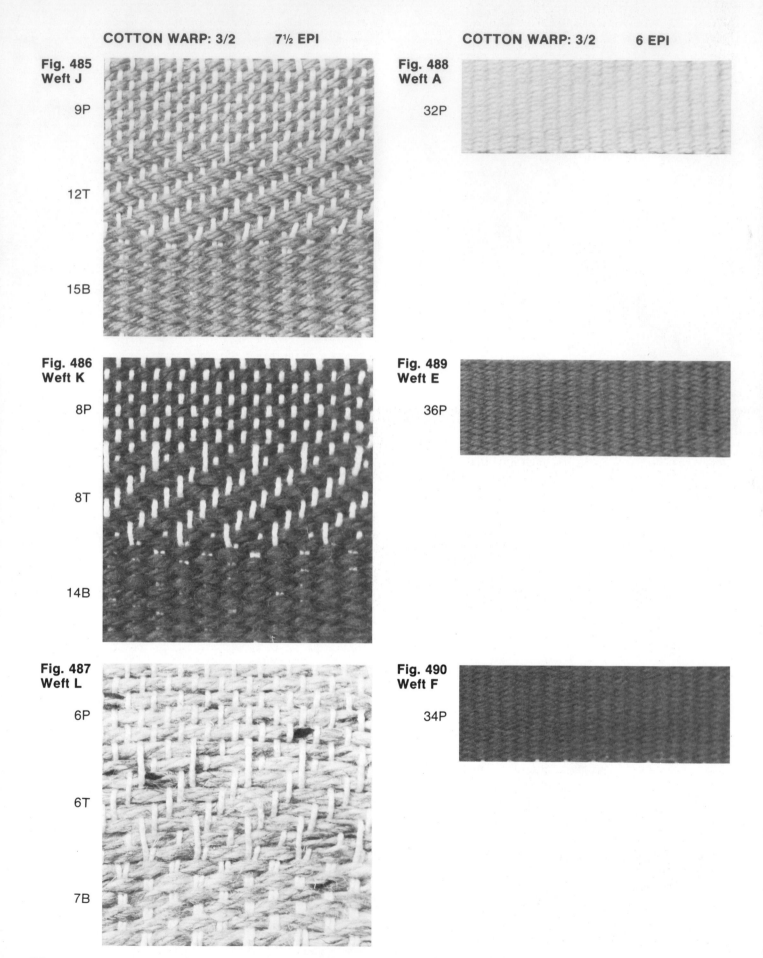

COTTON WARP: 3/2   7½ EPI

COTTON WARP: 3/2   6 EPI

Fig. 485
Weft J

9P

12T

15B

Fig. 486
Weft K

8P

8T

14B

Fig. 487
Weft L

6P

6T

7B

Fig. 488
Weft A

32P

Fig. 489
Weft E

36P

Fig. 490
Weft F

34P

**Fig. 491
Weft G**

24P

**Fig. 494
Weft J**

11P

16T

19B

**Fig. 492
Weft H**

13P

40T

32B

**Fig. 495
Weft K**

9P

9T

12B

**Fig. 493
Weft I**

20P

30T

28B

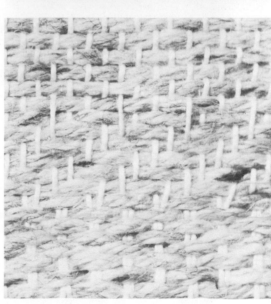

**Fig. 496
Weft L**

6P

7T

7B

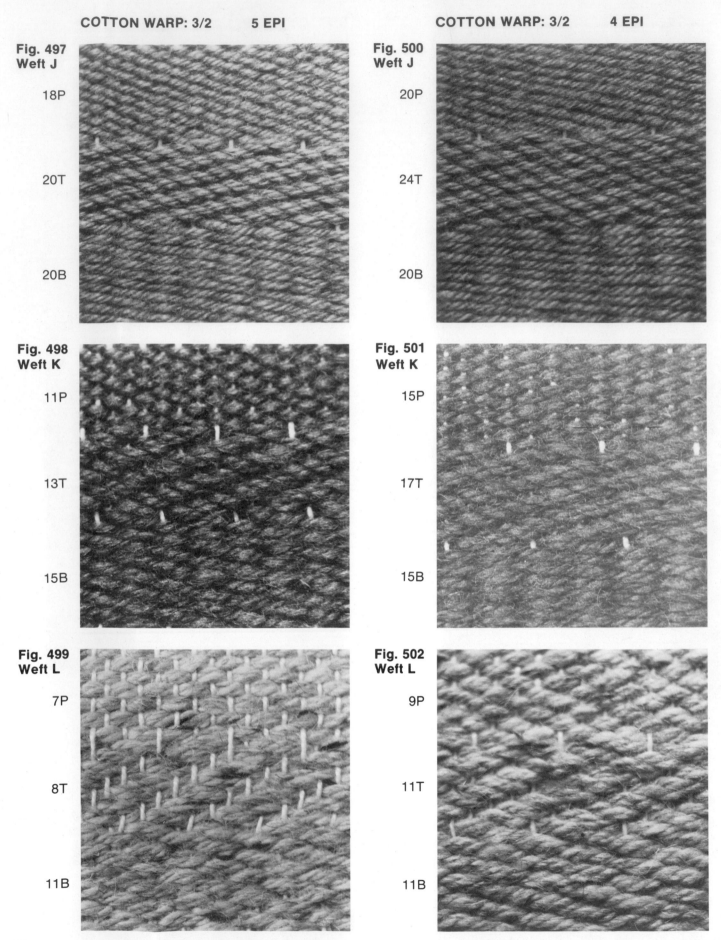

Fig. 497
Weft J

18P

20T

20B

Fig. 500
Weft J

20P

24T

20B

Fig. 498
Weft K

11P

13T

15B

Fig. 501
Weft K

15P

17T

15B

Fig. 499
Weft L

7P

8T

11B

Fig. 502
Weft L

9P

11T

11B

98

Linen Warps

Figures 503-795

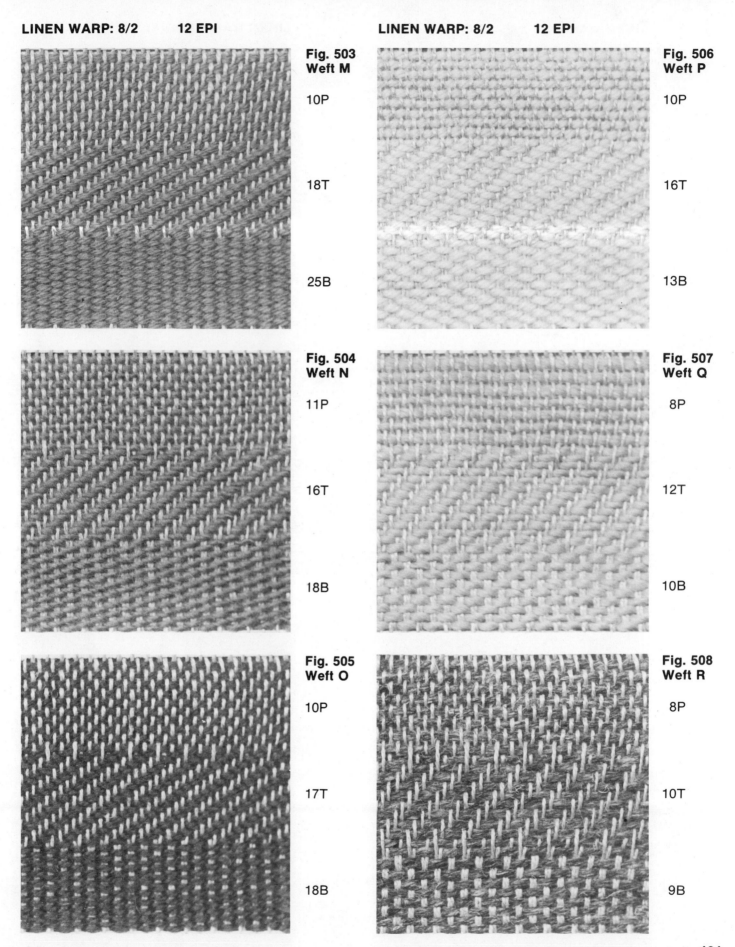

Fig. 503 Weft M
10P
18T
25B

Fig. 506 Weft P
10P
16T
13B

Fig. 504 Weft N
11P
16T
18B

Fig. 507 Weft Q
8P
12T
10B

Fig. 505 Weft O
10P
17T
18B

Fig. 508 Weft R
8P
10T
9B

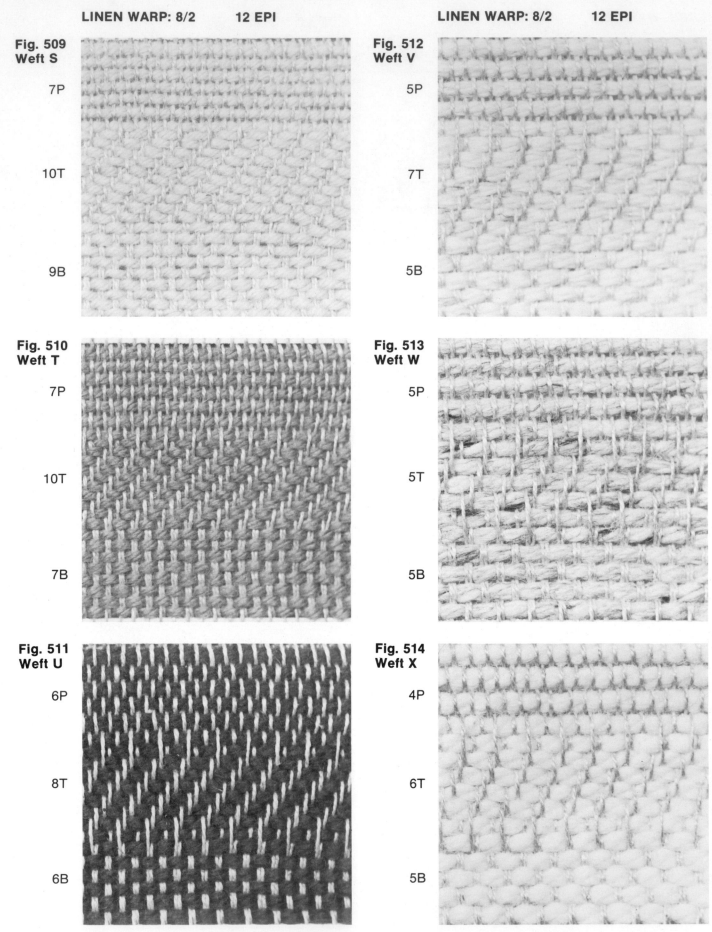

Fig. 509
Weft S

7P

10T

9B

Fig. 512
Weft V

5P

7T

5B

Fig. 510
Weft T

7P

10T

7B

Fig. 513
Weft W

5P

5T

5B

Fig. 511
Weft U

6P

8T

6B

Fig. 514
Weft X

4P

6T

5B

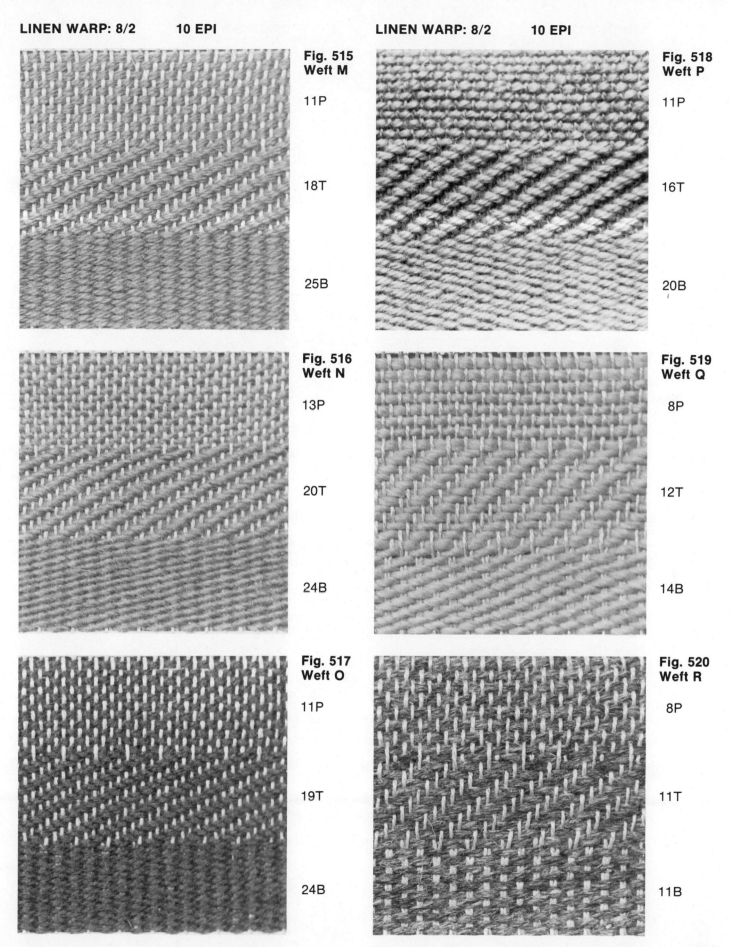

**Fig. 515
Weft M**

11P

18T

25B

**Fig. 518
Weft P**

11P

16T

20B

**Fig. 516
Weft N**

13P

20T

24B

**Fig. 519
Weft Q**

8P

12T

14B

**Fig. 517
Weft O**

11P

19T

24B

**Fig. 520
Weft R**

8P

11T

11B

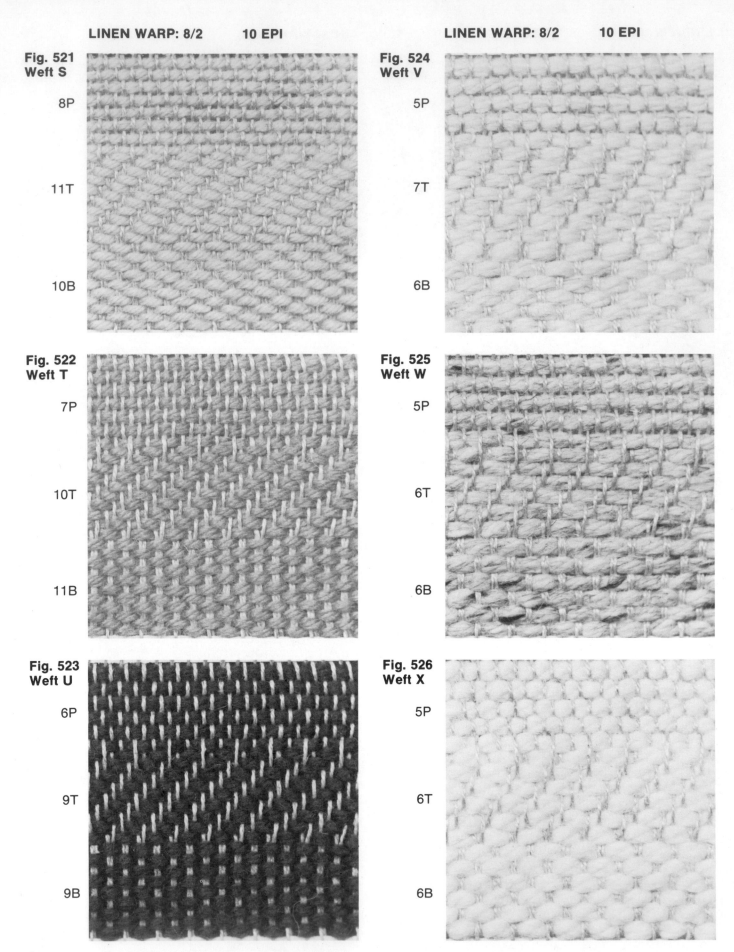

Fig. 521
Weft S

8P

11T

10B

Fig. 524
Weft V

5P

7T

6B

Fig. 522
Weft T

7P

10T

11B

Fig. 525
Weft W

5P

6T

6B

Fig. 523
Weft U

6P

9T

9B

Fig. 526
Weft X

5P

6T

6B

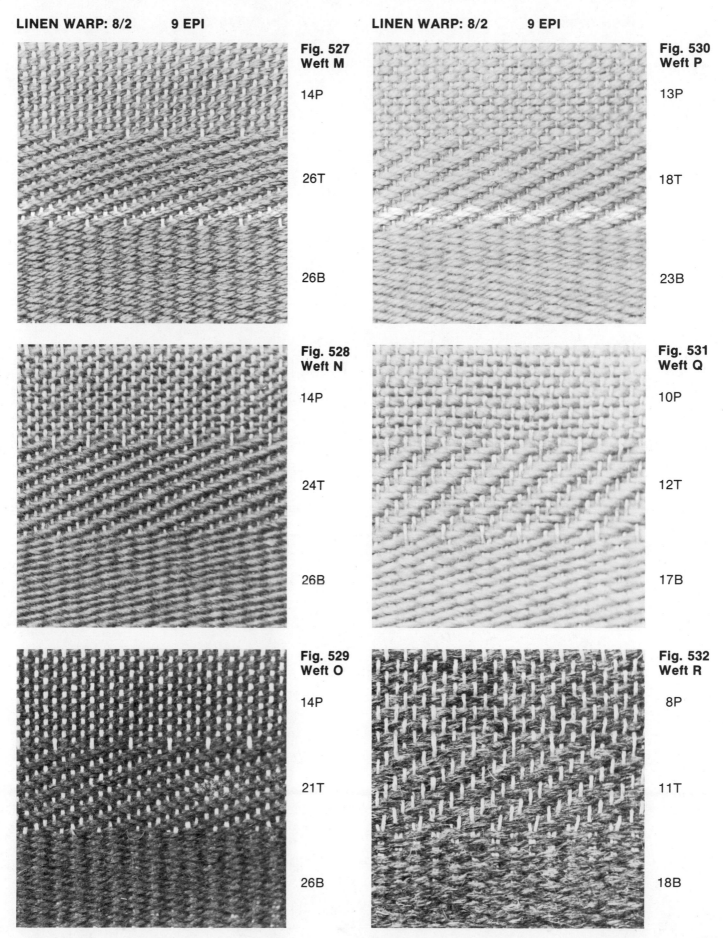

Fig. 527
Weft M

14P

26T

26B

Fig. 530
Weft P

13P

18T

23B

Fig. 528
Weft N

14P

24T

26B

Fig. 531
Weft Q

10P

12T

17B

Fig. 529
Weft O

14P

21T

26B

Fig. 532
Weft R

8P

11T

18B

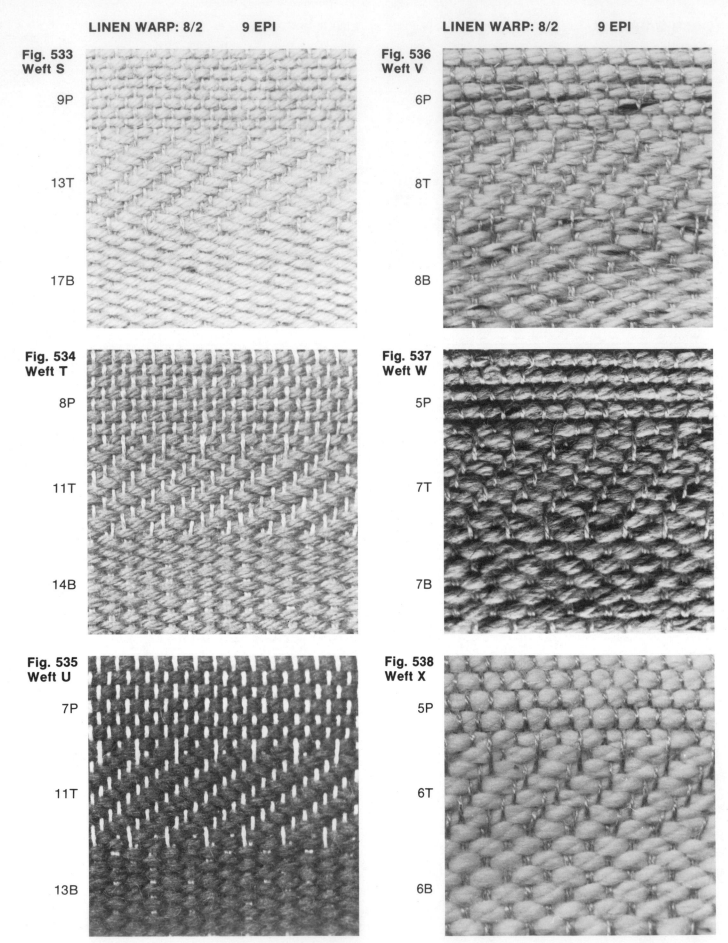

Fig. 533
Weft S

9P

13T

17B

Fig. 536
Weft V

6P

8T

8B

Fig. 534
Weft T

8P

11T

14B

Fig. 537
Weft W

5P

7T

7B

Fig. 535
Weft U

7P

11T

13B

Fig. 538
Weft X

5P

6T

6B

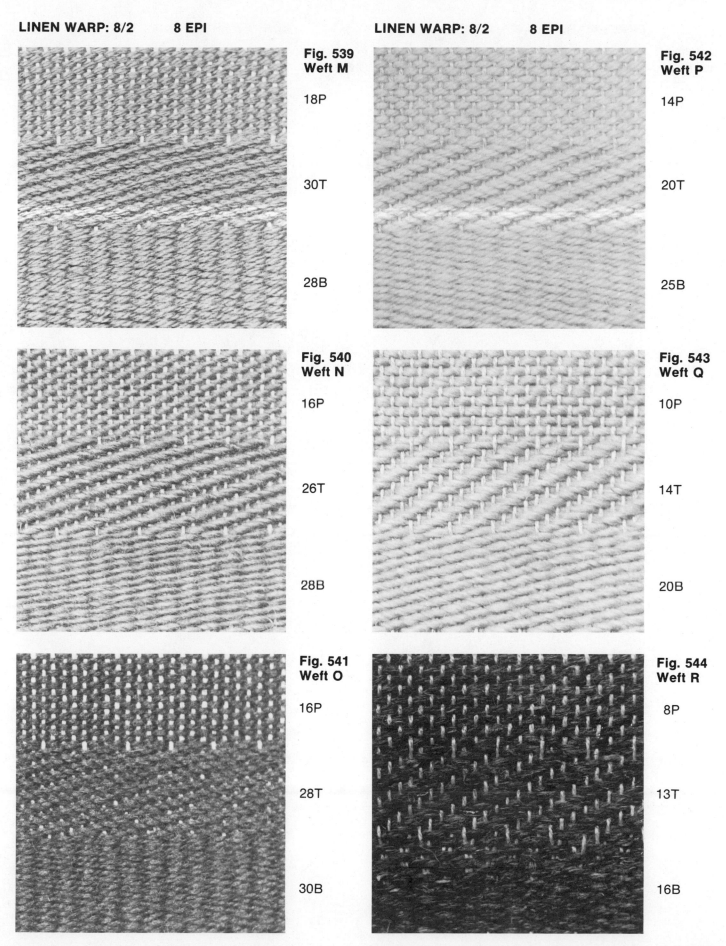

Fig. 539
Weft M

18P

30T

28B

Fig. 542
Weft P

14P

20T

25B

Fig. 540
Weft N

16P

26T

28B

Fig. 543
Weft Q

10P

14T

20B

Fig. 541
Weft O

16P

28T

30B

Fig. 544
Weft R

8P

13T

16B

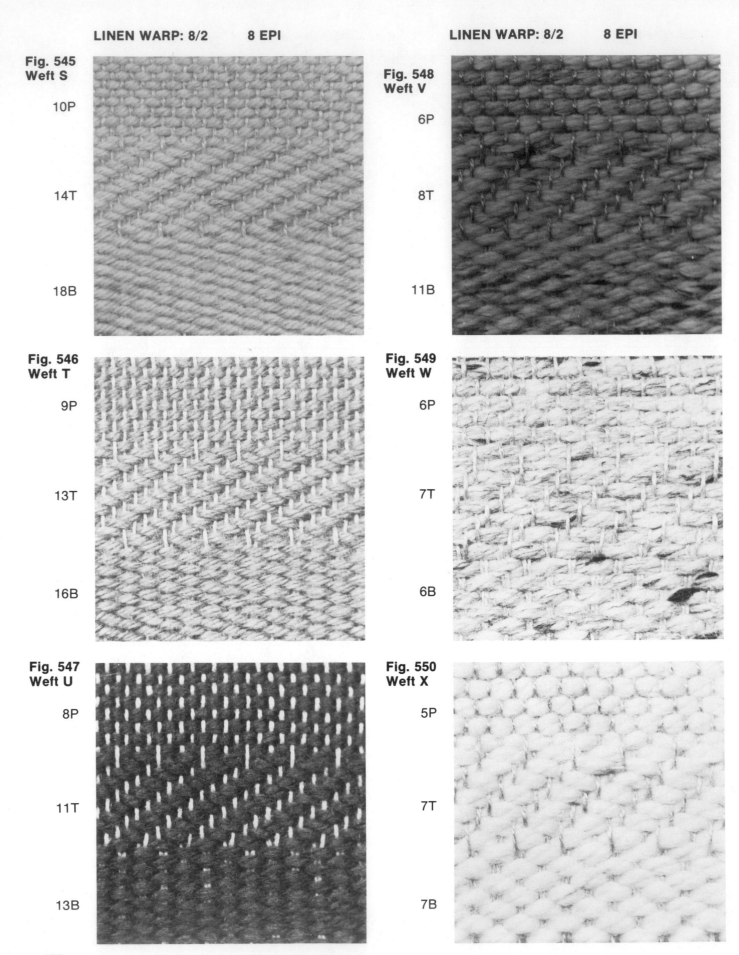

Fig. 545
Weft S

10P

14T

18B

Fig. 548
Weft V

6P

8T

11B

Fig. 546
Weft T

9P

13T

16B

Fig. 549
Weft W

6P

7T

6B

Fig. 547
Weft U

8P

11T

13B

Fig. 550
Weft X

5P

7T

7B

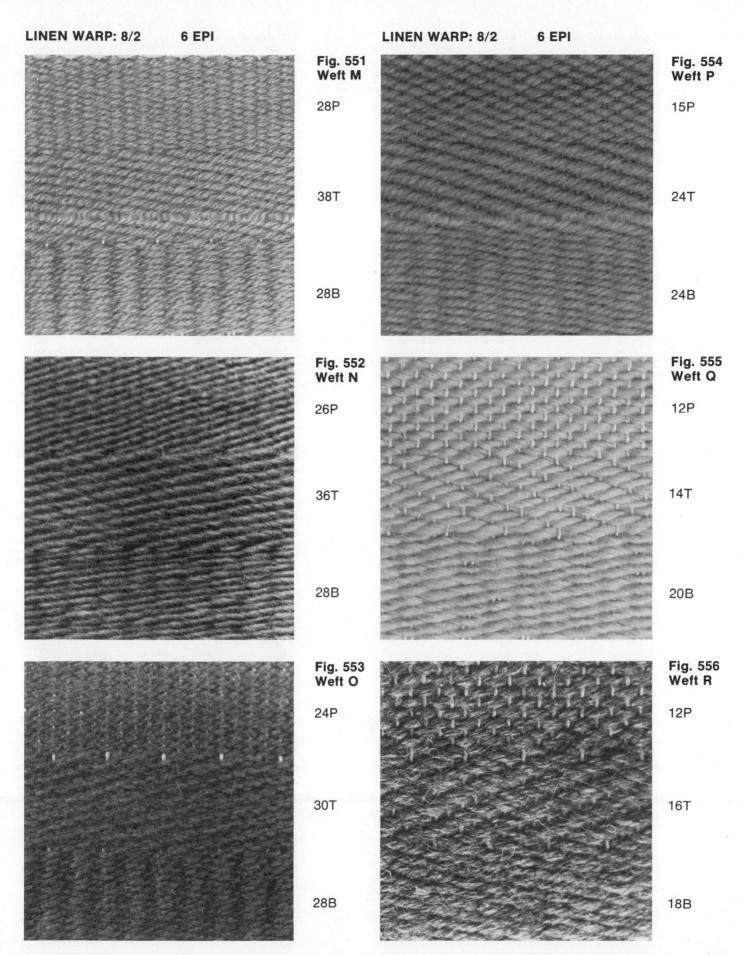

Fig. 551
Weft M

28P

38T

28B

Fig. 552
Weft N

26P

36T

28B

Fig. 553
Weft O

24P

30T

28B

Fig. 554
Weft P

15P

24T

24B

Fig. 555
Weft Q

12P

14T

20B

Fig. 556
Weft R

12P

16T

18B

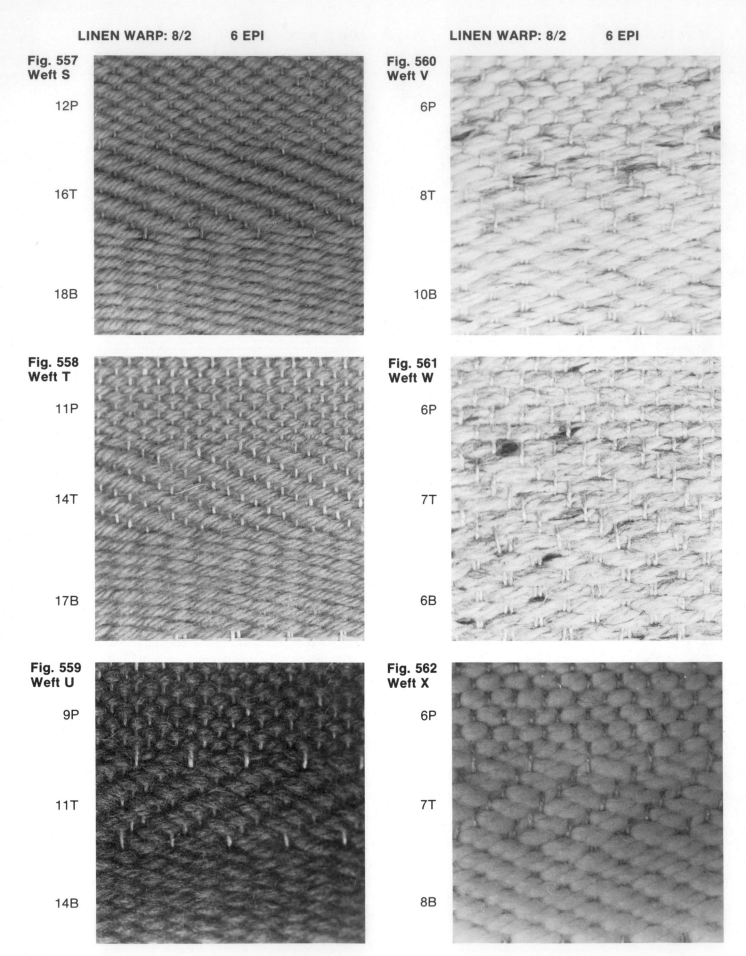

Fig. 557
Weft S

12P

16T

18B

Fig. 560
Weft V

6P

8T

10B

Fig. 558
Weft T

11P

14T

17B

Fig. 561
Weft W

6P

7T

6B

Fig. 559
Weft U

9P

11T

14B

Fig. 562
Weft X

6P

7T

8B

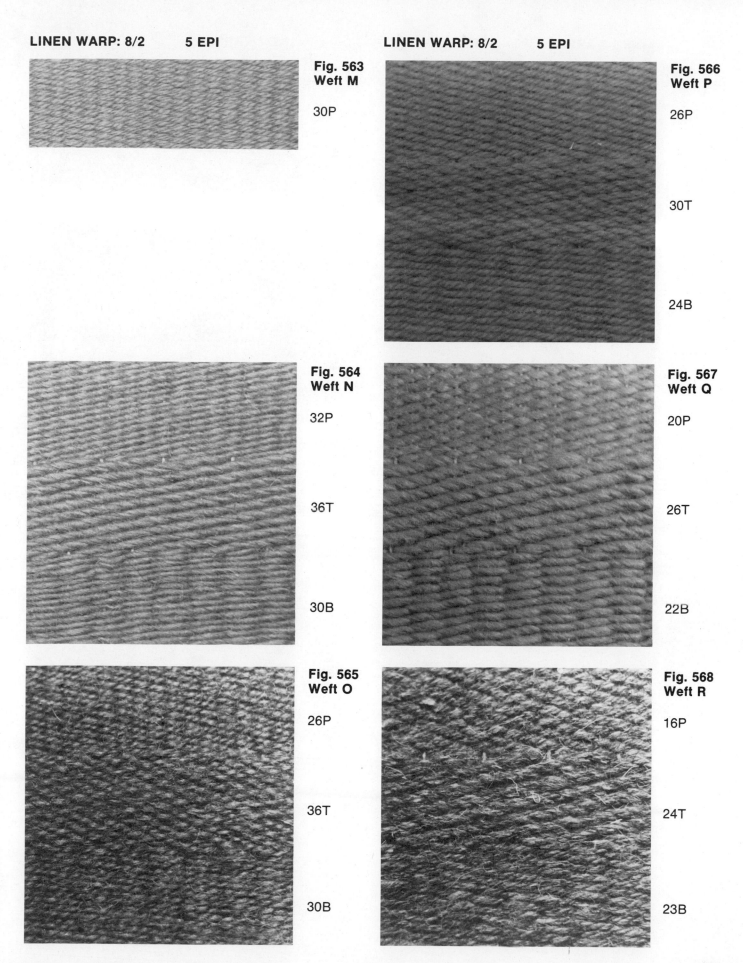

Fig. 563
Weft M

30P

Fig. 564
Weft N

32P

36T

30B

Fig. 565
Weft O

26P

36T

30B

Fig. 566
Weft P

26P

30T

24B

Fig. 567
Weft Q

20P

26T

22B

Fig. 568
Weft R

16P

24T

23B

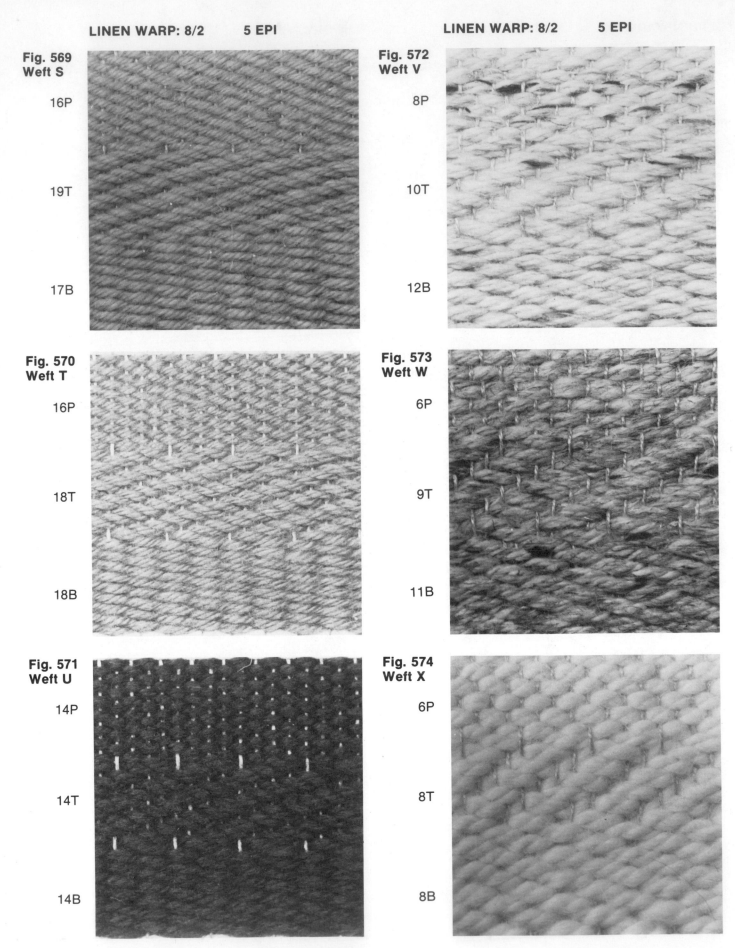

Fig. 569
Weft S

16P

19T

17B

Fig. 570
Weft T

16P

18T

18B

Fig. 571
Weft U

14P

14T

14B

Fig. 572
Weft V

8P

10T

12B

Fig. 573
Weft W

6P

9T

11B

Fig. 574
Weft X

6P

8T

8B

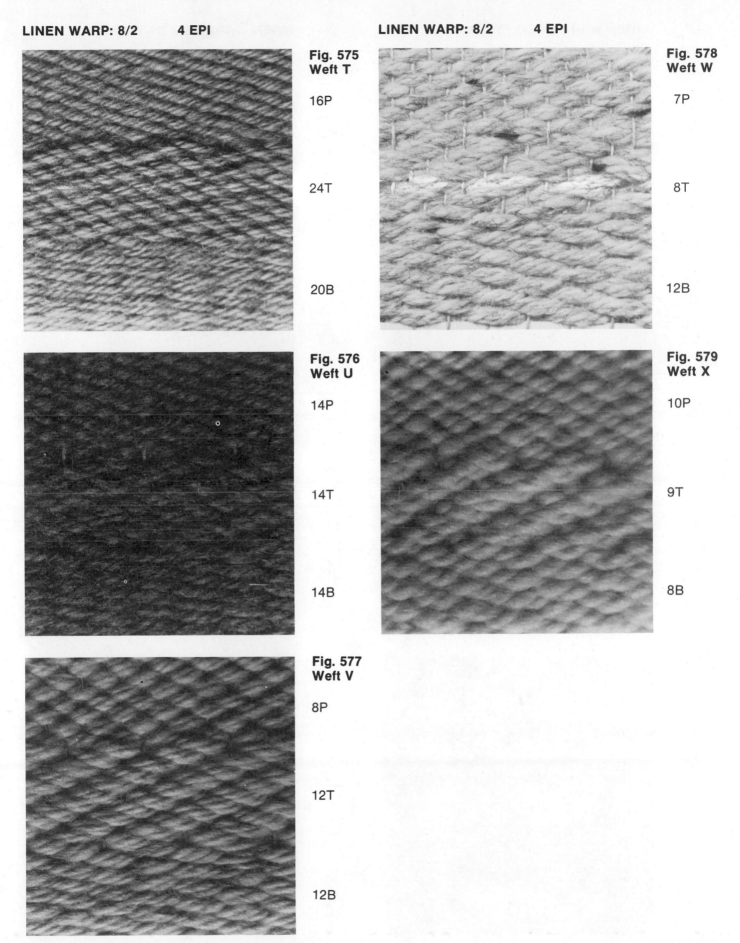

**Fig. 575
Weft T**

16P

24T

20B

**Fig. 576
Weft U**

14P

14T

14B

**Fig. 577
Weft V**

8P

12T

12B

**Fig. 578
Weft W**

7P

8T

12B

**Fig. 579
Weft X**

10P

9T

8B

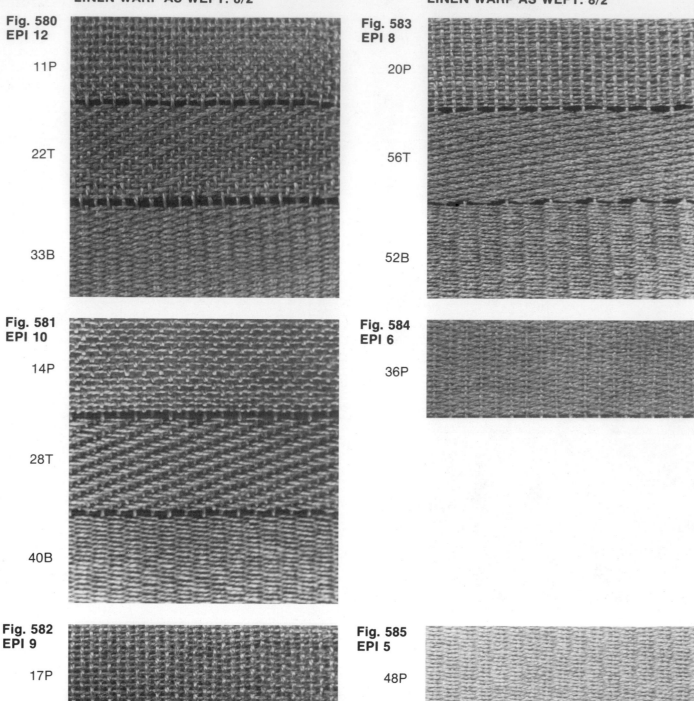

Fig. 580
EPI 12

11P

22T

33B

Fig. 581
EPI 10

14P

28T

40B

Fig. 582
EPI 9

17P

40T

48B

LINEN WARP AS WEFT: 8/2

Fig. 583
EPI 8

20P

56T

52B

Fig. 584
EPI 6

36P

Fig. 585
EPI 5

48P

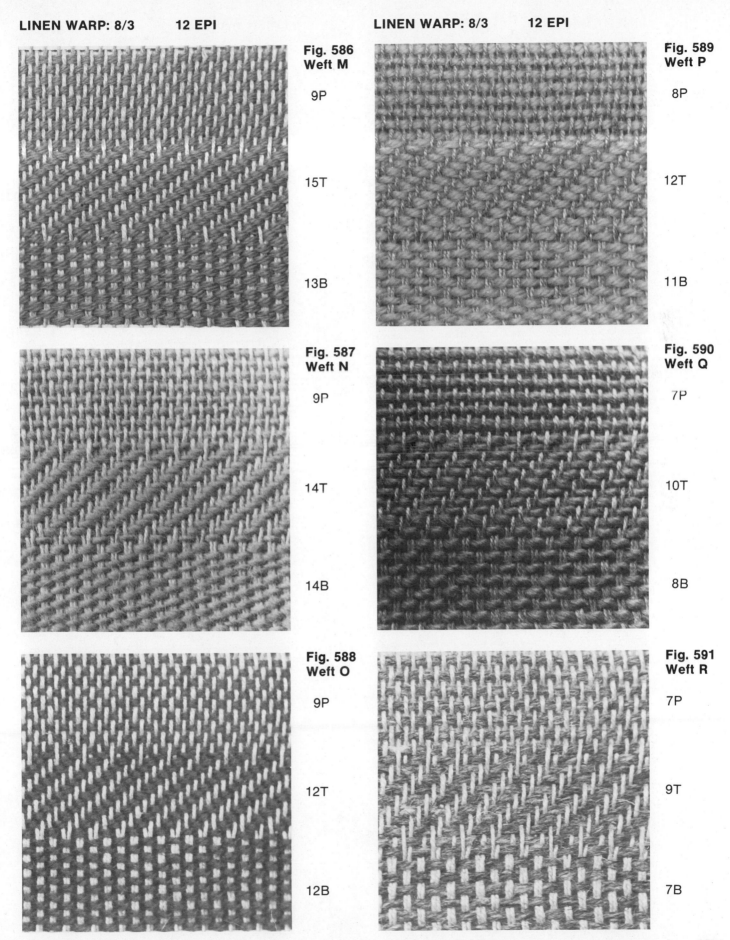

Fig. 586
Weft M

9P

15T

13B

Fig. 587
Weft N

9P

14T

14B

Fig. 588
Weft O

9P

12T

12B

Fig. 589
Weft P

8P

12T

11B

Fig. 590
Weft Q

7P

10T

8B

Fig. 591
Weft R

7P

9T

7B

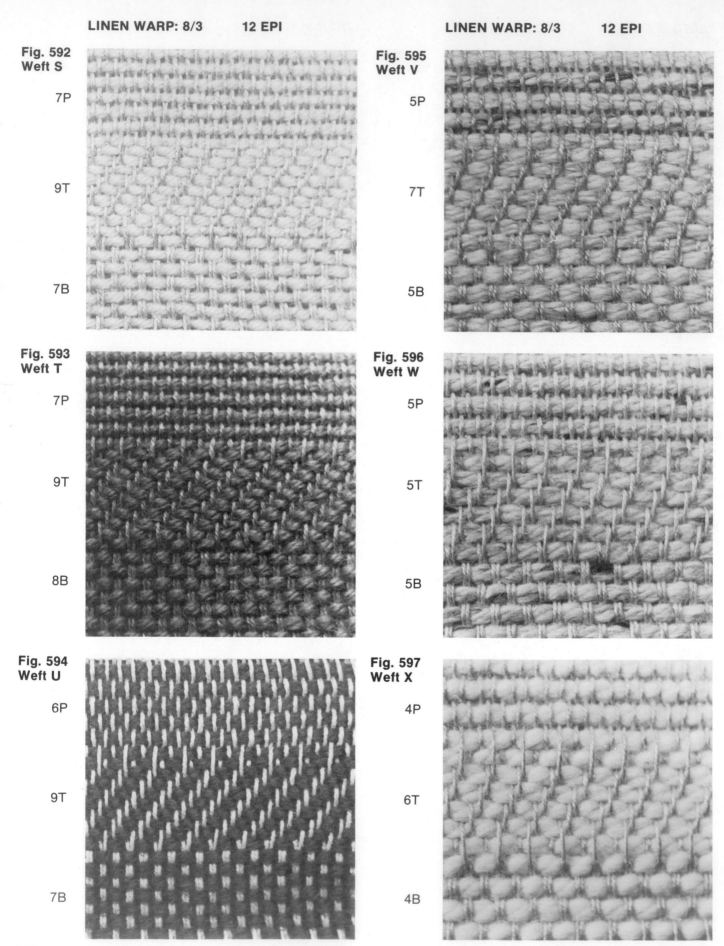

Fig. 592
Weft S

7P

9T

7B

Fig. 595
Weft V

5P

7T

5B

Fig. 593
Weft T

7P

9T

8B

Fig. 596
Weft W

5P

5T

5B

Fig. 594
Weft U

6P

9T

7B

Fig. 597
Weft X

4P

6T

4B

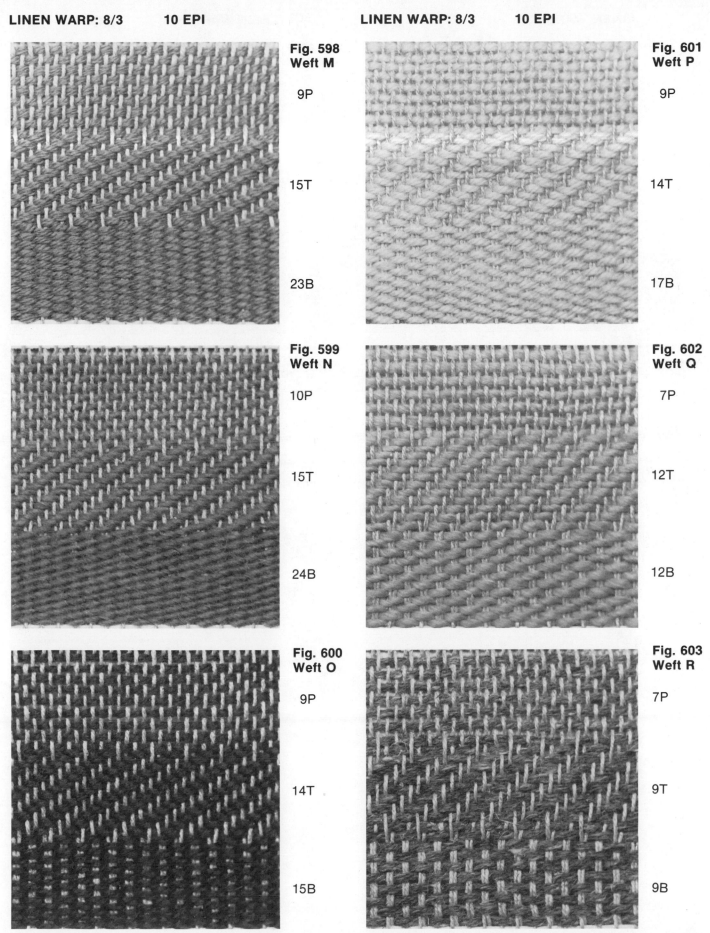

Fig. 598
Weft M

9P

15T

23B

Fig. 601
Weft P

9P

14T

17B

Fig. 599
Weft N

10P

15T

24B

Fig. 602
Weft Q

7P

12T

12B

Fig. 600
Weft O

9P

14T

15B

Fig. 603
Weft R

7P

9T

9B

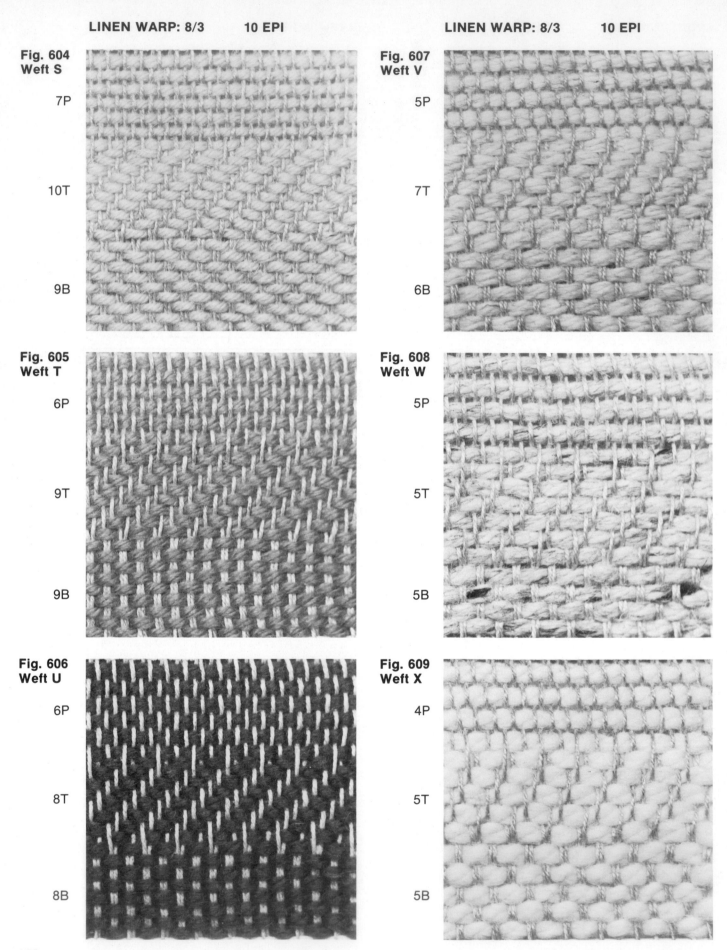

**Fig. 604
Weft S**

7P

10T

9B

**Fig. 605
Weft T**

6P

9T

9B

**Fig. 606
Weft U**

6P

8T

8B

**Fig. 607
Weft V**

5P

7T

6B

**Fig. 608
Weft W**

5P

5T

5B

**Fig. 609
Weft X**

4P

5T

5B

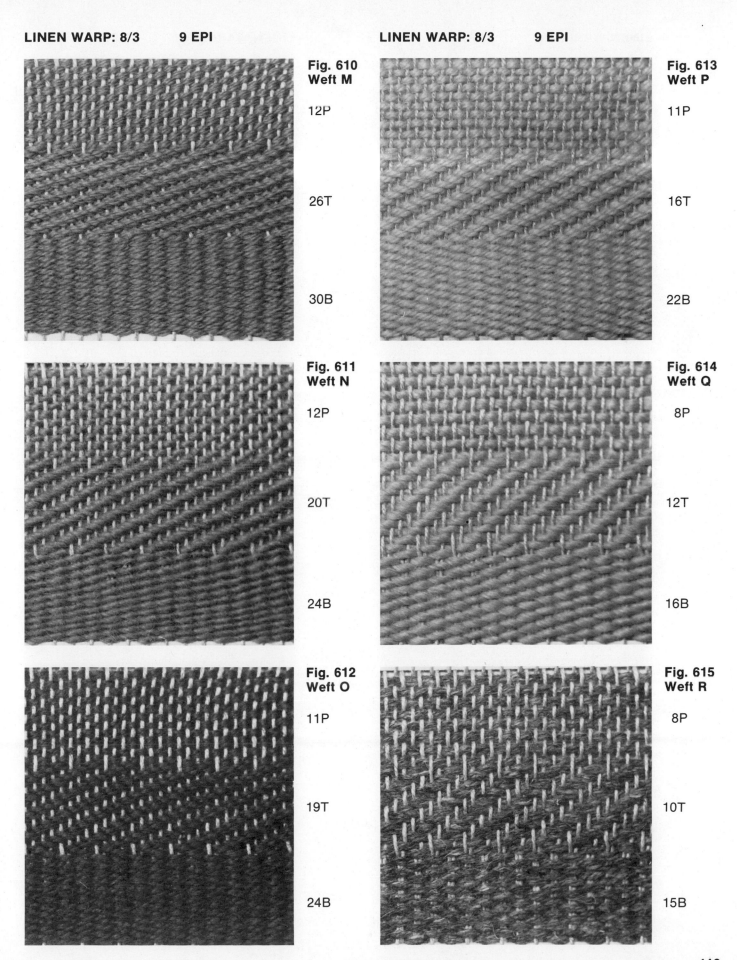

Fig. 610
Weft M

12P

26T

30B

Fig. 613
Weft P

11P

16T

22B

Fig. 611
Weft N

12P

20T

24B

Fig. 614
Weft Q

8P

12T

16B

Fig. 612
Weft O

11P

19T

24B

Fig. 615
Weft R

8P

10T

15B

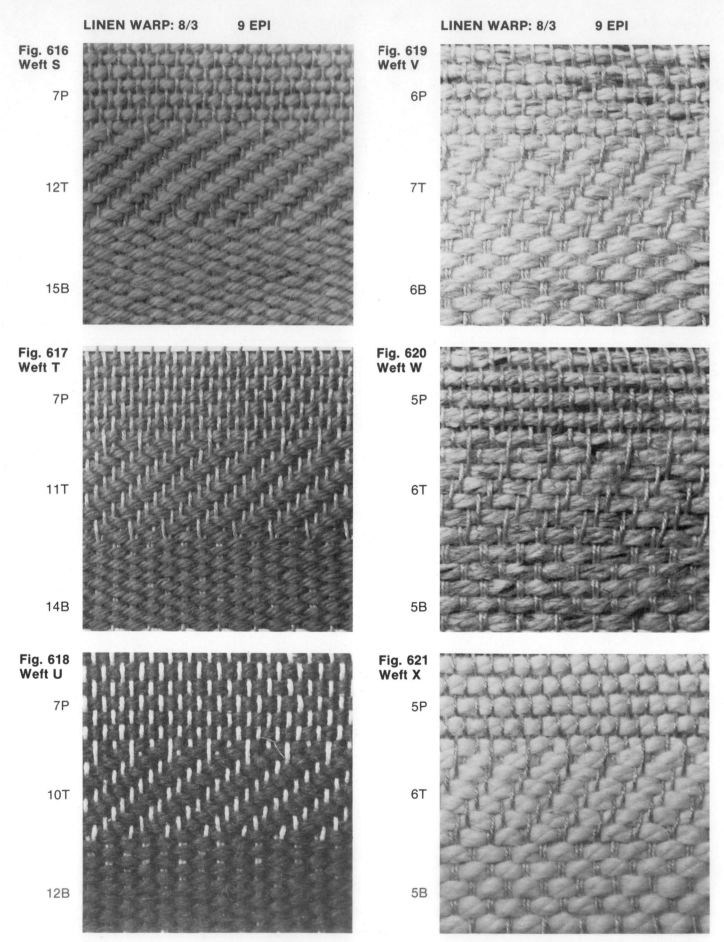

Fig. 616
Weft S

7P

12T

15B

LINEN WARP: 8/3   9 EPI

Fig. 619
Weft V

6P

7T

6B

Fig. 617
Weft T

7P

11T

14B

Fig. 620
Weft W

5P

6T

5B

Fig. 618
Weft U

7P

10T

12B

Fig. 621
Weft X

5P

6T

5B

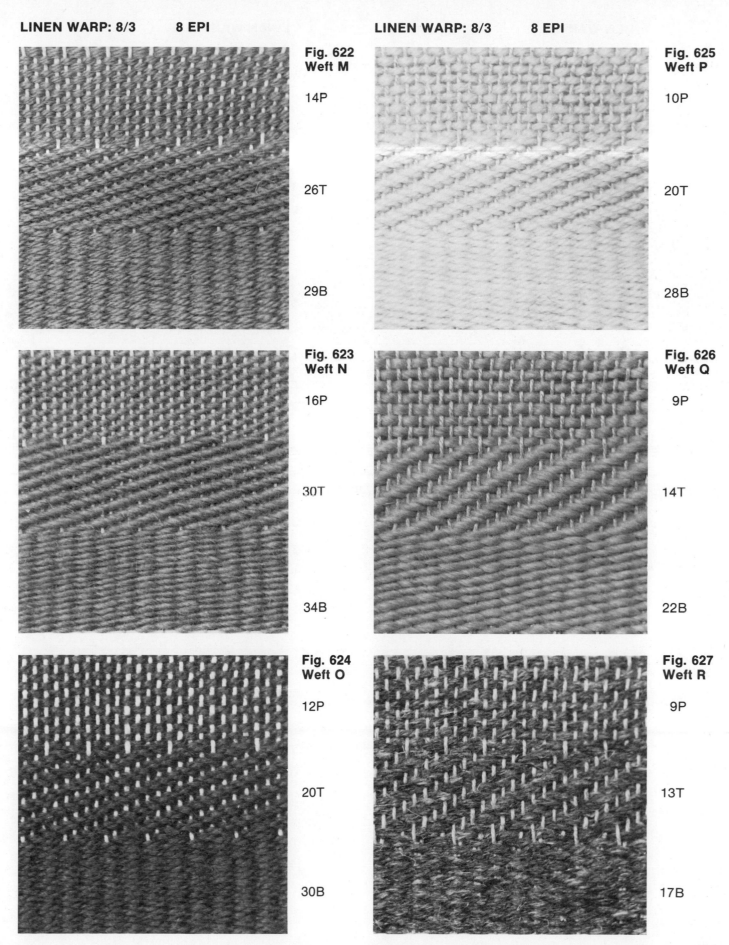

Fig. 622
Weft M

14P

26T

29B

Fig. 625
Weft P

10P

20T

28B

Fig. 623
Weft N

16P

30T

34B

Fig. 626
Weft Q

9P

14T

22B

Fig. 624
Weft O

12P

20T

30B

Fig. 627
Weft R

9P

13T

17B

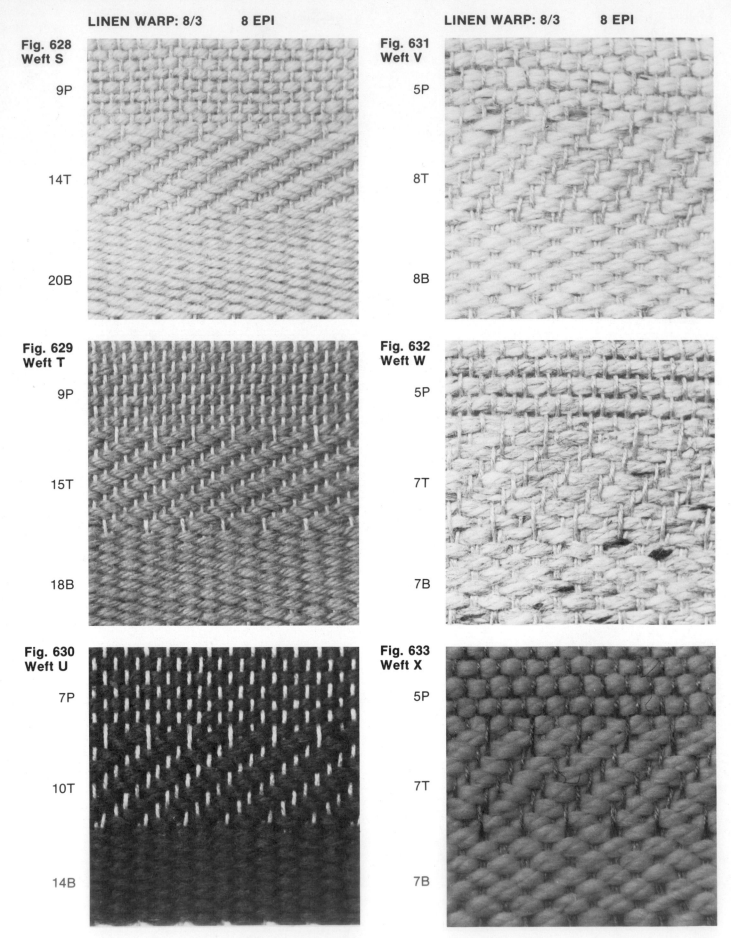

**Fig. 628
Weft S**

9P

14T

20B

**Fig. 629
Weft T**

9P

15T

18B

**Fig. 630
Weft U**

7P

10T

14B

**Fig. 631
Weft V**

5P

8T

8B

**Fig. 632
Weft W**

5P

7T

7B

**Fig. 633
Weft X**

5P

7T

7B

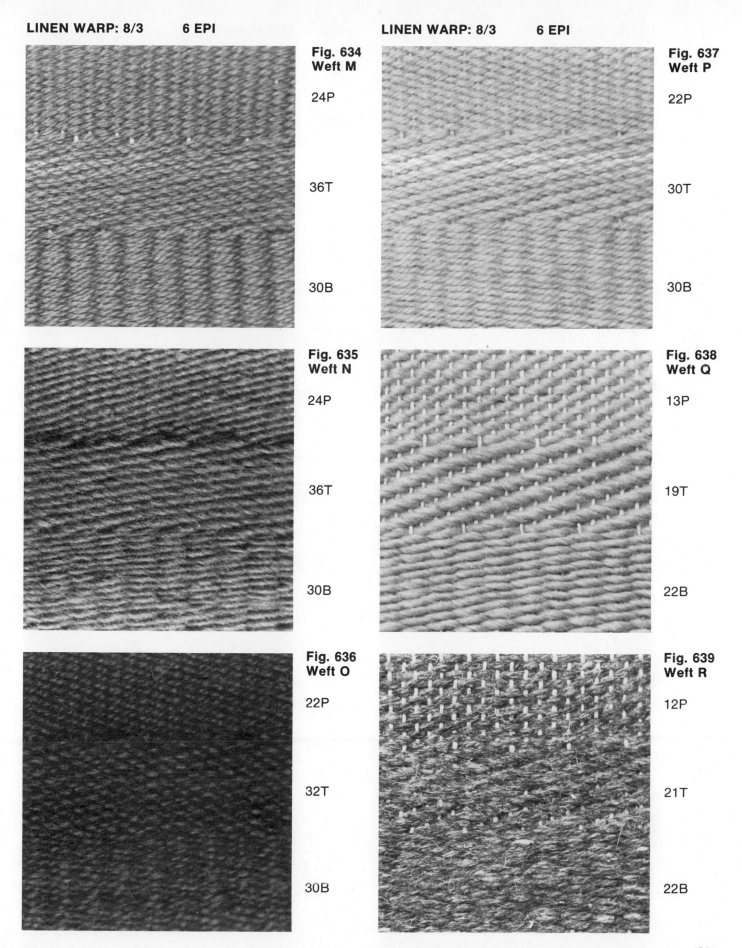

Fig. 634
Weft M

24P

36T

30B

Fig. 637
Weft P

22P

30T

30B

Fig. 635
Weft N

24P

36T

30B

Fig. 638
Weft Q

13P

19T

22B

Fig. 636
Weft O

22P

32T

30B

Fig. 639
Weft R

12P

21T

22B

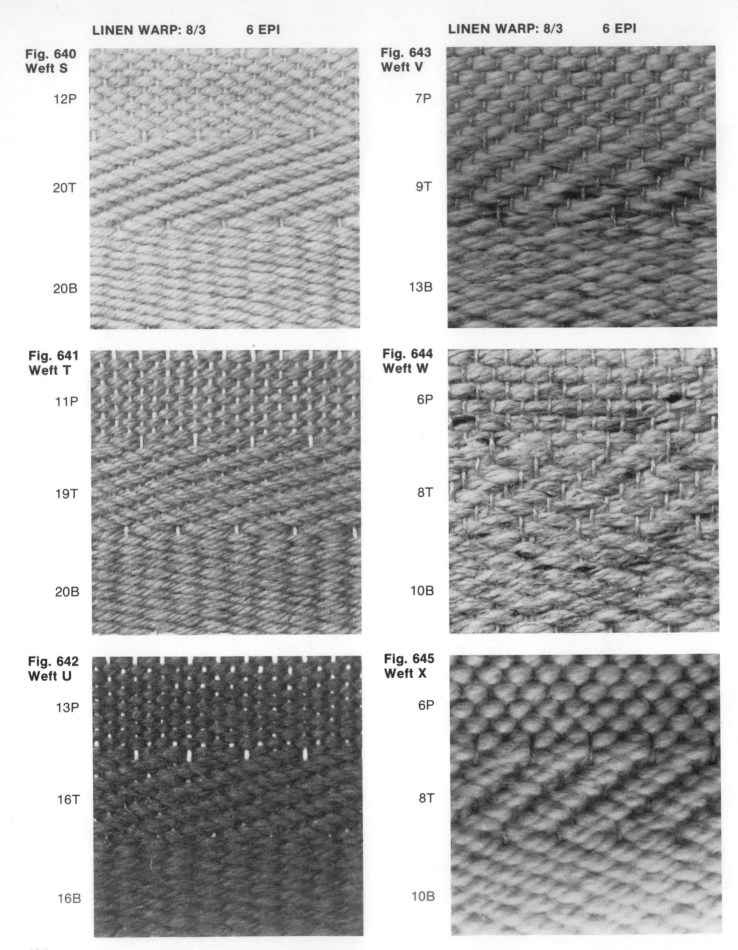

Fig. 640
Weft S

12P

20T

20B

Fig. 641
Weft T

11P

19T

20B

Fig. 642
Weft U

13P

16T

16B

Fig. 643
Weft V

7P

9T

13B

Fig. 644
Weft W

6P

8T

10B

Fig. 645
Weft X

6P

8T

10B

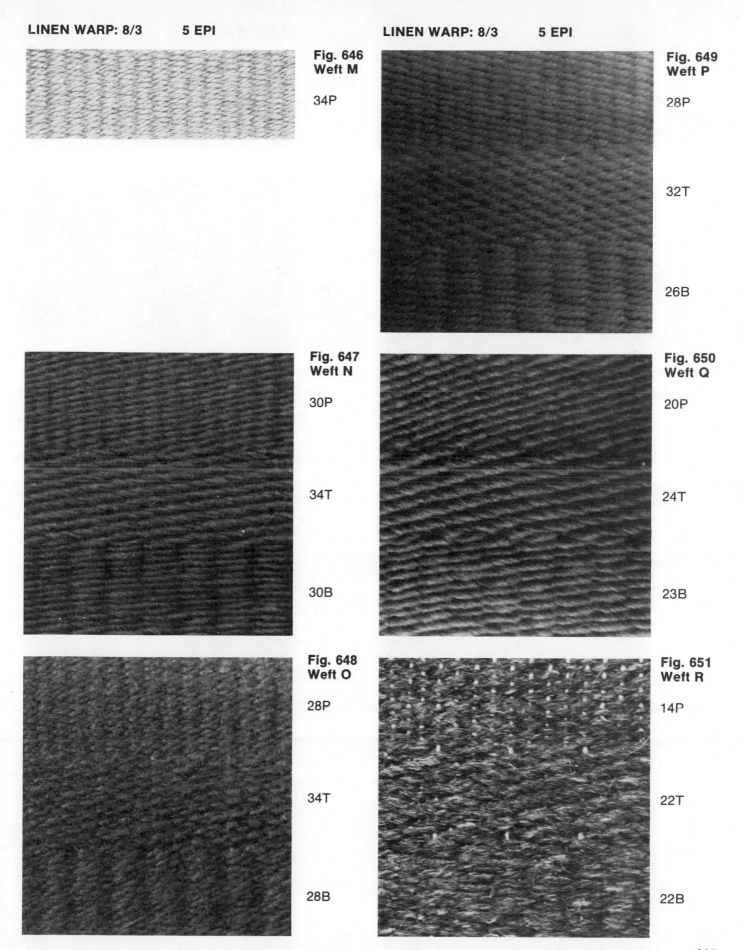

LINEN WARP: 8/3   5 EPI

Fig. 646
Weft M

34P

LINEN WARP: 8/3   5 EPI

Fig. 649
Weft P

28P

32T

26B

Fig. 647
Weft N

30P

34T

30B

Fig. 650
Weft Q

20P

24T

23B

Fig. 648
Weft O

28P

34T

28B

Fig. 651
Weft R

14P

22T

22B

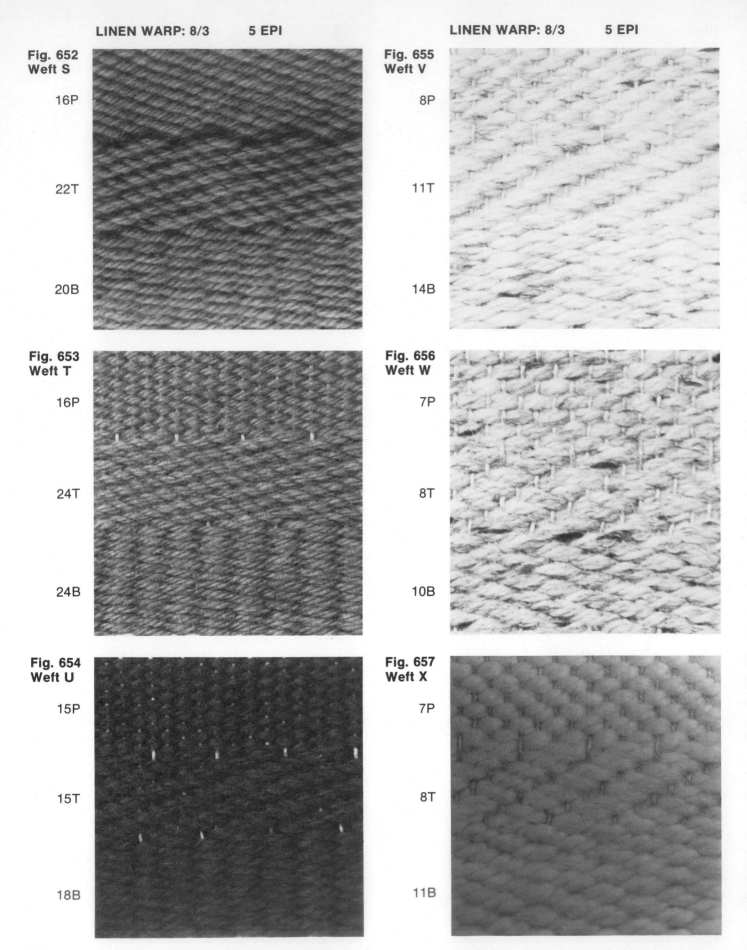

Fig. 652
Weft S

16P

22T

20B

Fig. 653
Weft T

16P

24T

24B

Fig. 654
Weft U

15P

15T

18B

Fig. 655
Weft V

8P

11T

14B

Fig. 656
Weft W

7P

8T

10B

Fig. 657
Weft X

7P

8T

11B

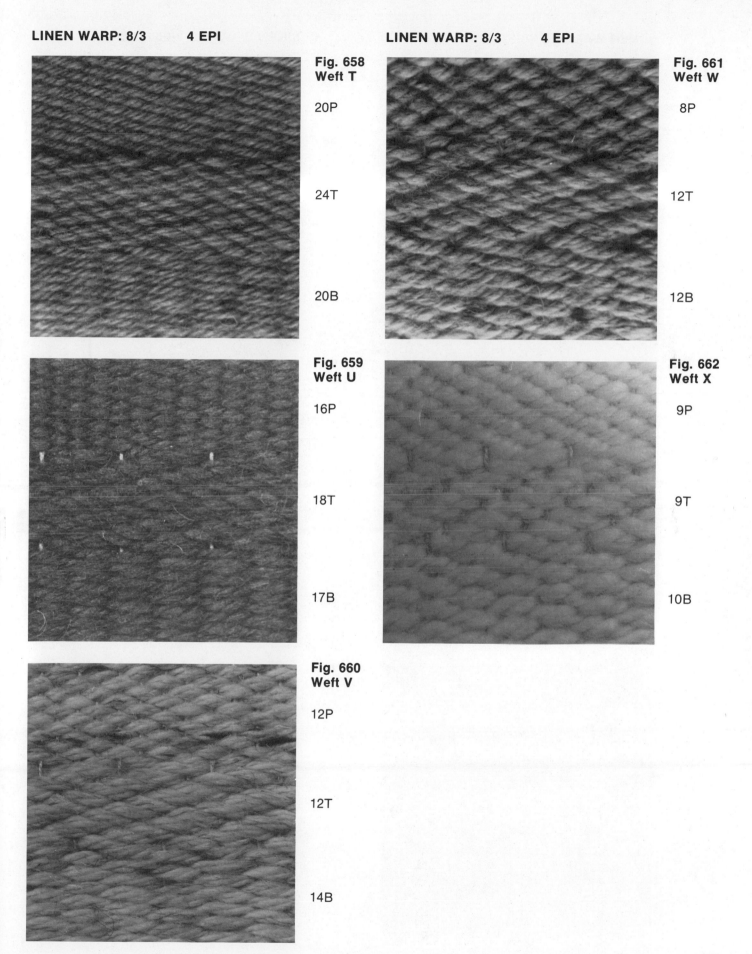

**Fig. 658
Weft T**

20P

24T

20B

**Fig. 661
Weft W**

8P

12T

12B

**Fig. 659
Weft U**

16P

18T

17B

**Fig. 662
Weft X**

9P

9T

10B

**Fig. 660
Weft V**

12P

12T

14B

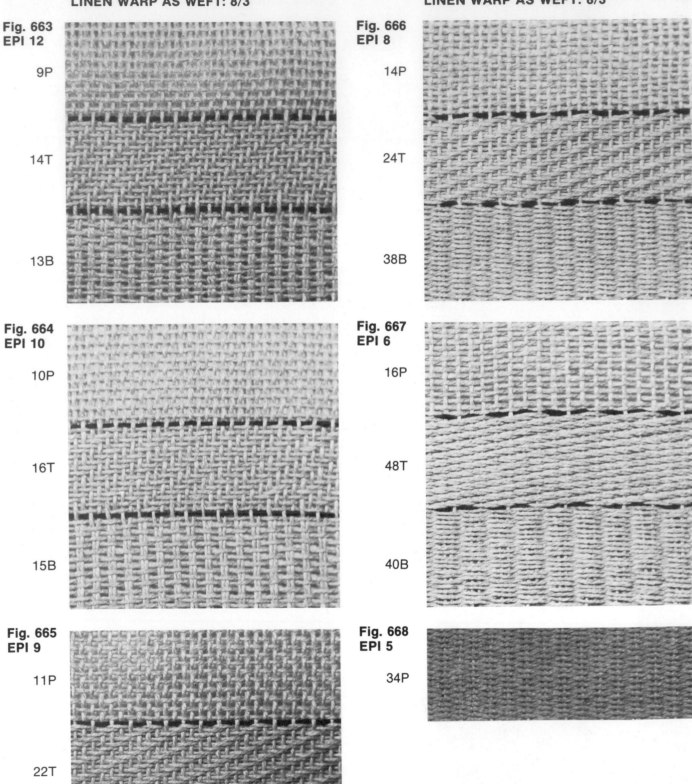

Fig. 663
EPI 12

9P

14T

13B

Fig. 664
EPI 10

10P

16T

15B

Fig. 665
EPI 9

11P

22T

34B

Fig. 666
EPI 8

14P

24T

38B

Fig. 667
EPI 6

16P

48T

40B

Fig. 668
EPI 5

34P

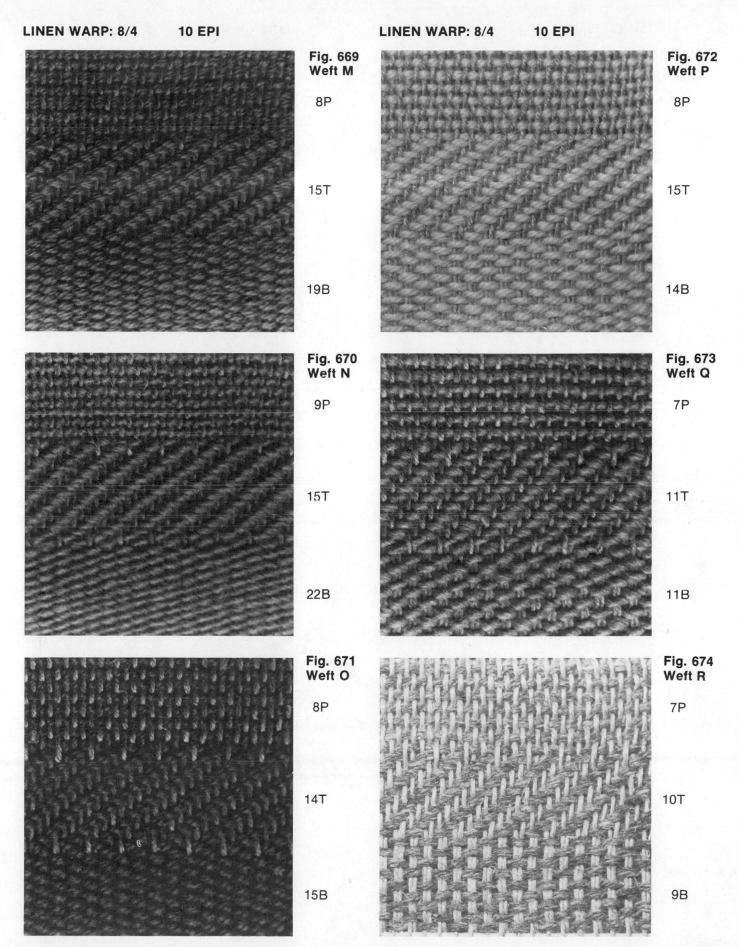

Fig. 669
Weft M

8P

15T

19B

Fig. 672
Weft P

8P

15T

14B

Fig. 670
Weft N

9P

15T

22B

Fig. 673
Weft Q

7P

11T

11B

Fig. 671
Weft O

8P

14T

15B

Fig. 674
Weft R

7P

10T

9B

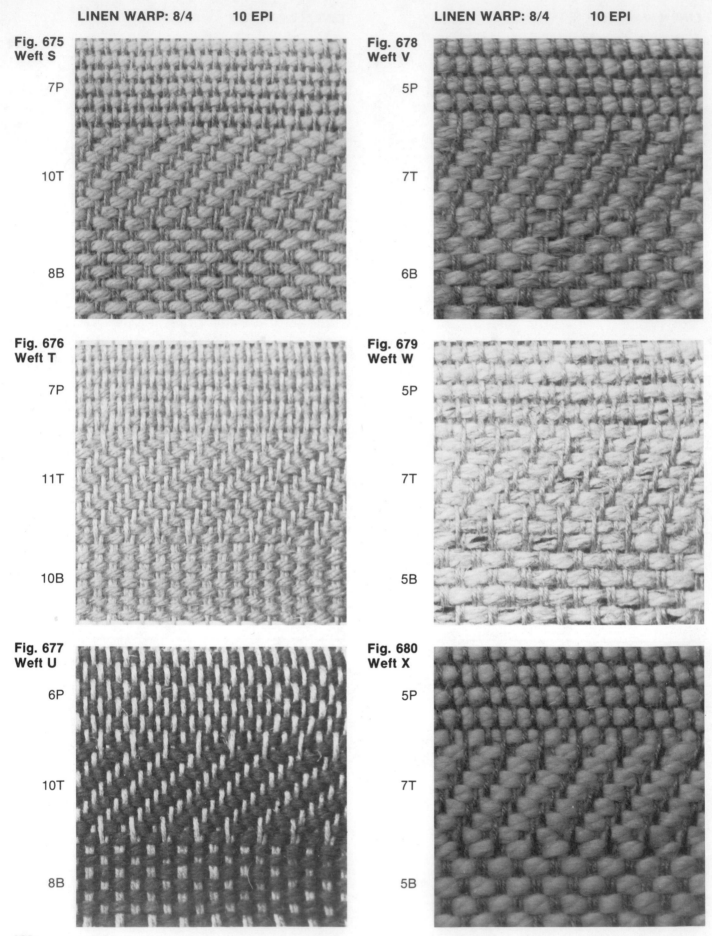

Fig. 675
Weft S

7P

10T

8B

Fig. 678
Weft V

5P

7T

6B

Fig. 676
Weft T

7P

11T

10B

Fig. 679
Weft W

5P

7T

5B

Fig. 677
Weft U

6P

10T

8B

Fig. 680
Weft X

5P

7T

5B

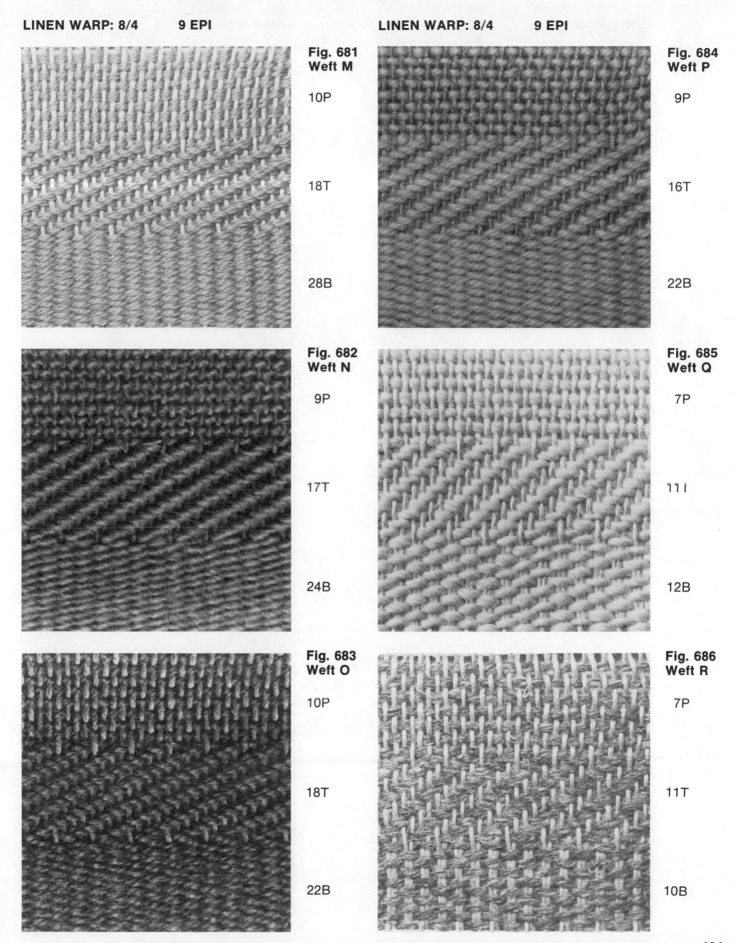

Fig. 681
Weft M

10P

18T

28B

Fig. 684
Weft P

9P

16T

22B

Fig. 682
Weft N

9P

17T

24B

Fig. 685
Weft Q

7P

11 I

12B

Fig. 683
Weft O

10P

18T

22B

Fig. 686
Weft R

7P

11T

10B

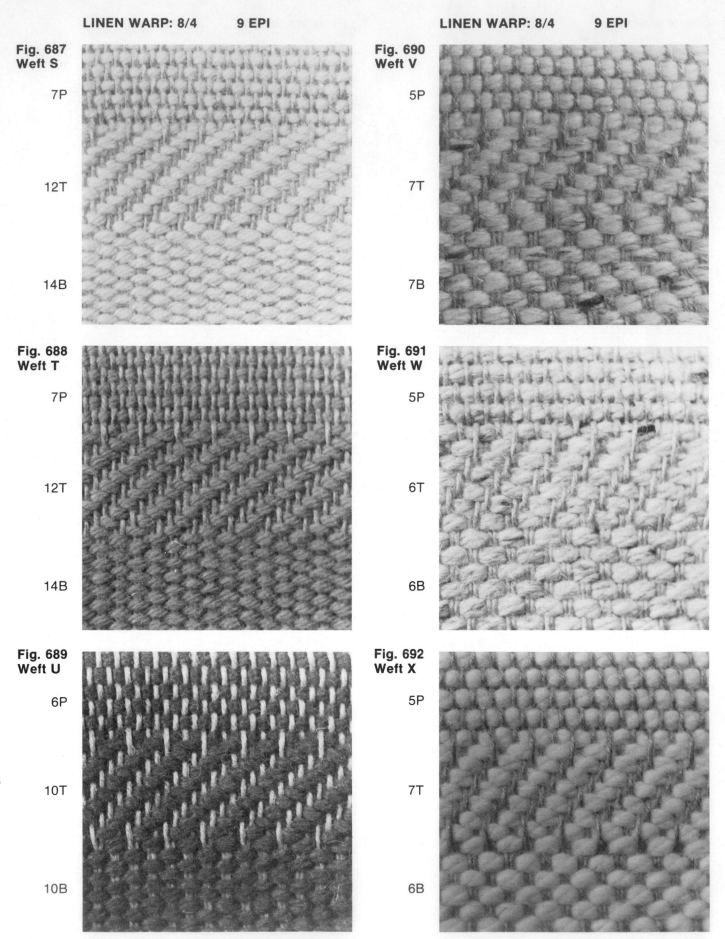

Fig. 687
Weft S

7P

12T

14B

Fig. 688
Weft T

7P

12T

14B

Fig. 689
Weft U

6P

10T

10B

Fig. 690
Weft V

5P

7T

7B

Fig. 691
Weft W

5P

6T

6B

Fig. 692
Weft X

5P

7T

6B

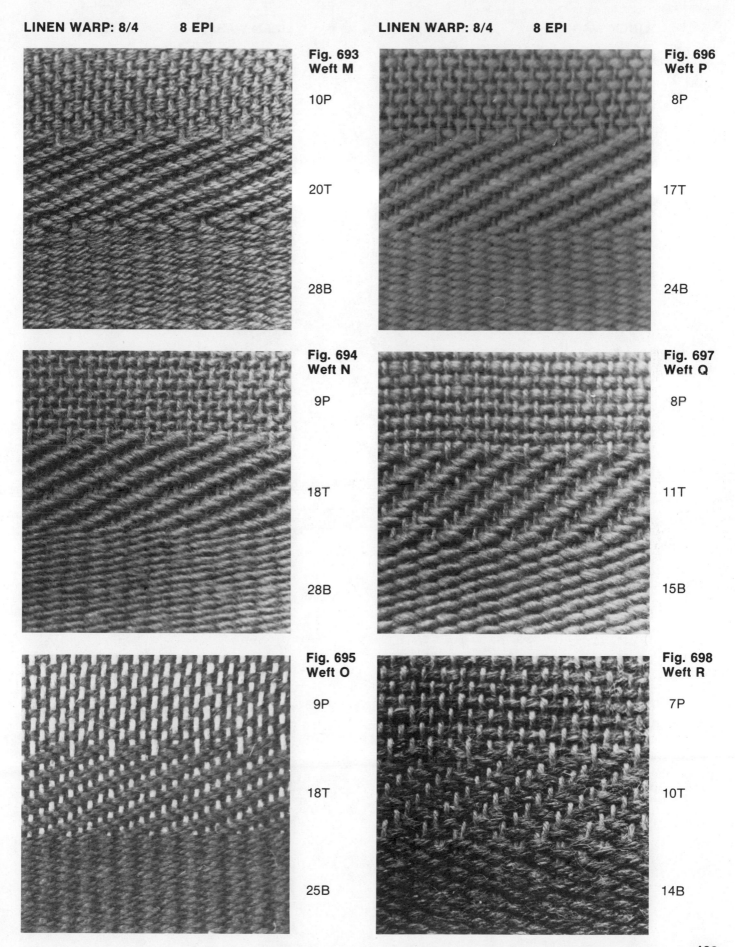

Fig. 693
Weft M

10P

20T

28B

Fig. 696
Weft P

8P

17T

24B

Fig. 694
Weft N

9P

18T

28B

Fig. 697
Weft Q

8P

11T

15B

Fig. 695
Weft O

9P

18T

25B

Fig. 698
Weft R

7P

10T

14B

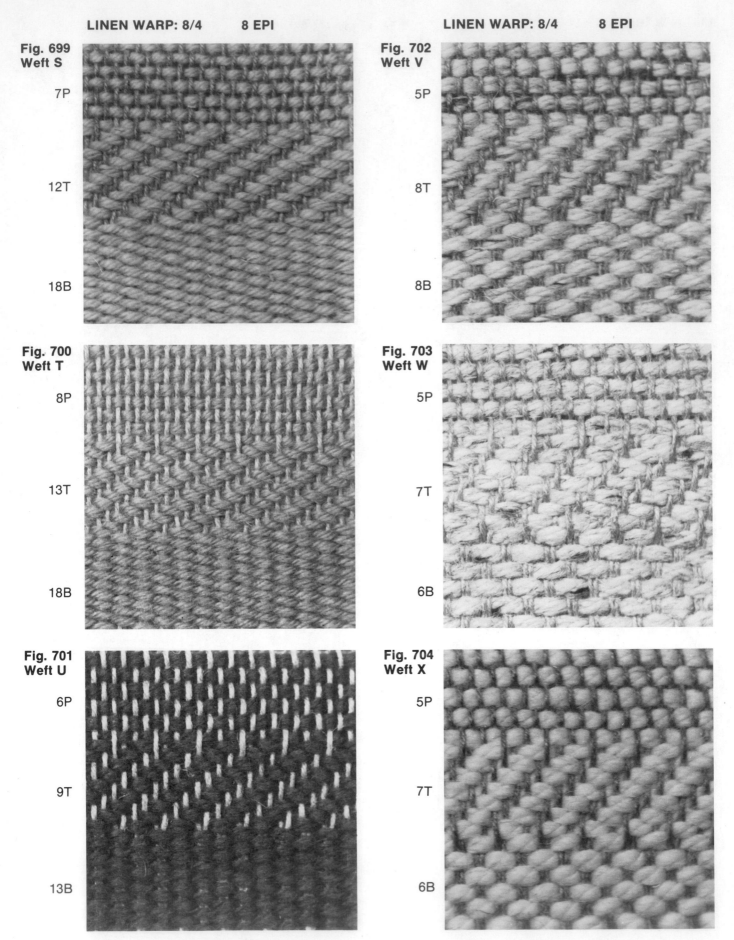

Fig. 699
Weft S

7P

12T

18B

Fig. 702
Weft V

5P

8T

8B

Fig. 700
Weft T

8P

13T

18B

Fig. 703
Weft W

5P

7T

6B

Fig. 701
Weft U

6P

9T

13B

Fig. 704
Weft X

5P

7T

6B

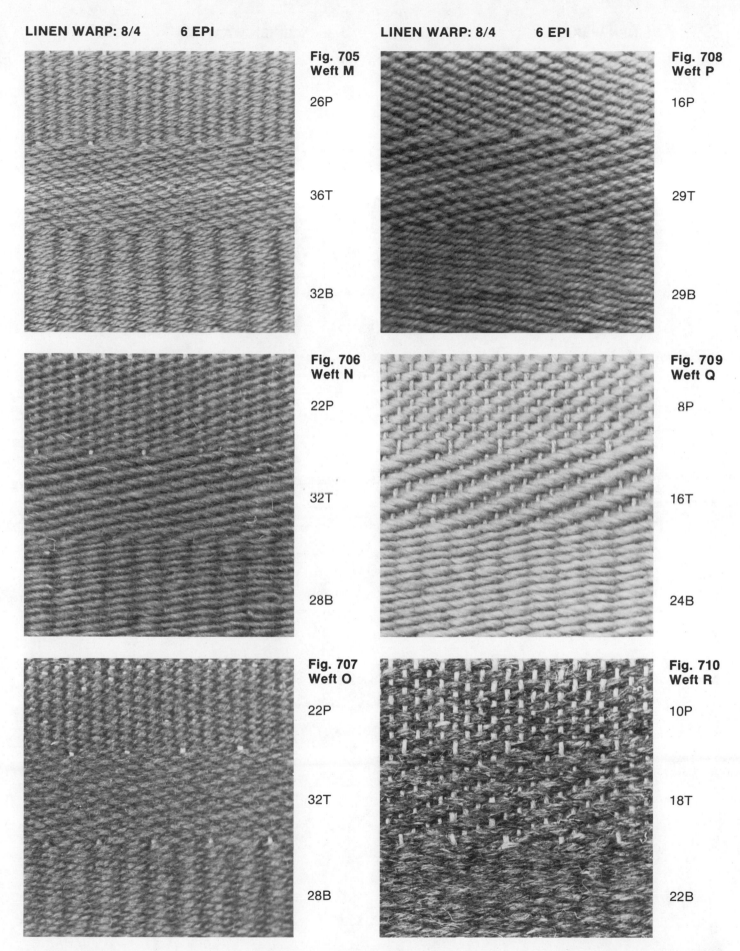

Fig. 705
Weft M

26P

36T

32B

Fig. 708
Weft P

16P

29T

29B

Fig. 706
Weft N

22P

32T

28B

Fig. 709
Weft Q

8P

16T

24B

Fig. 707
Weft O

22P

32T

28B

Fig. 710
Weft R

10P

18T

22B

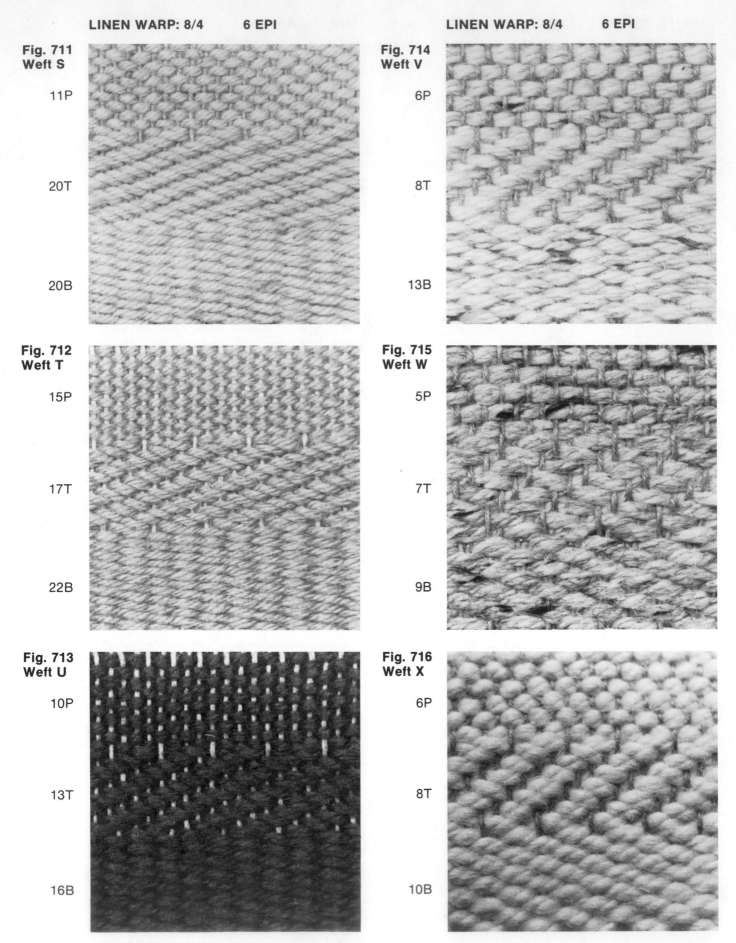

Fig. 711
Weft S

11P

20T

20B

Fig. 714
Weft V

6P

8T

13B

Fig. 712
Weft T

15P

17T

22B

Fig. 715
Weft W

5P

7T

9B

Fig. 713
Weft U

10P

13T

16B

Fig. 716
Weft X

6P

8T

10B

LINEN WARP: 8/4 5 EPI

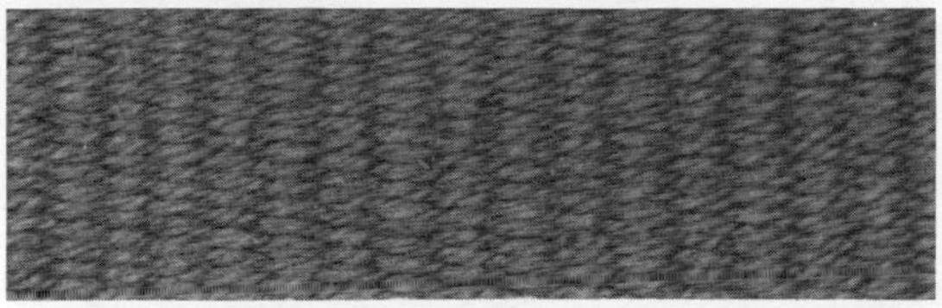

Fig. 717
Weft M

34P

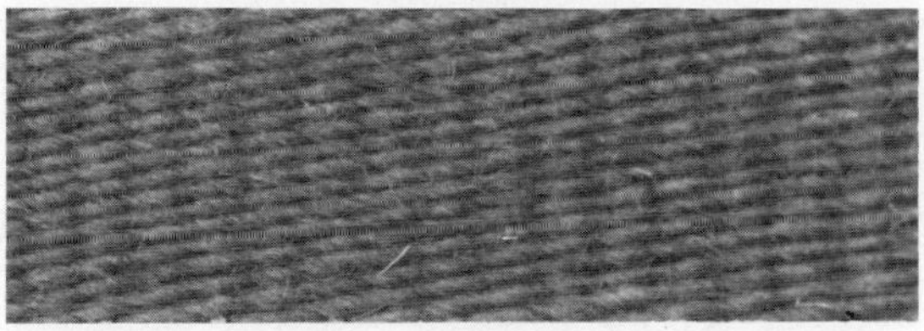

Fig. 718
Weft N

32P

Fig. 719
Weft O

28P

LINEN WARP: 8/4 5 EPI

Fig. 720
Weft P

30P

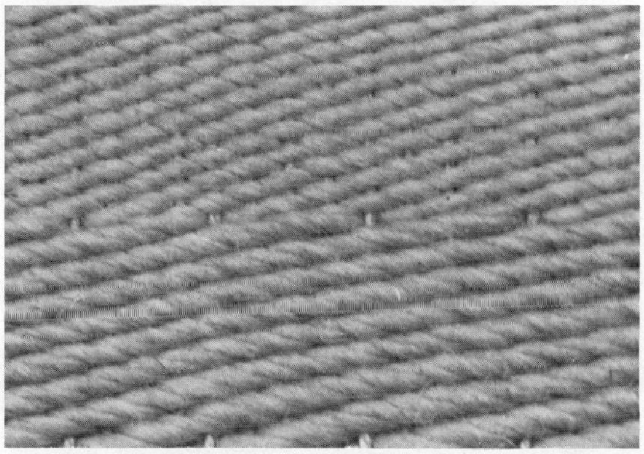

Fig. 721
Weft Q

20P

30T

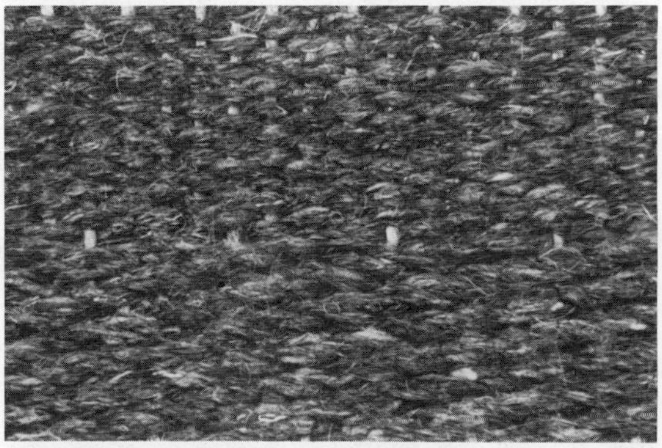

Fig. 722
Weft R

18P

24T

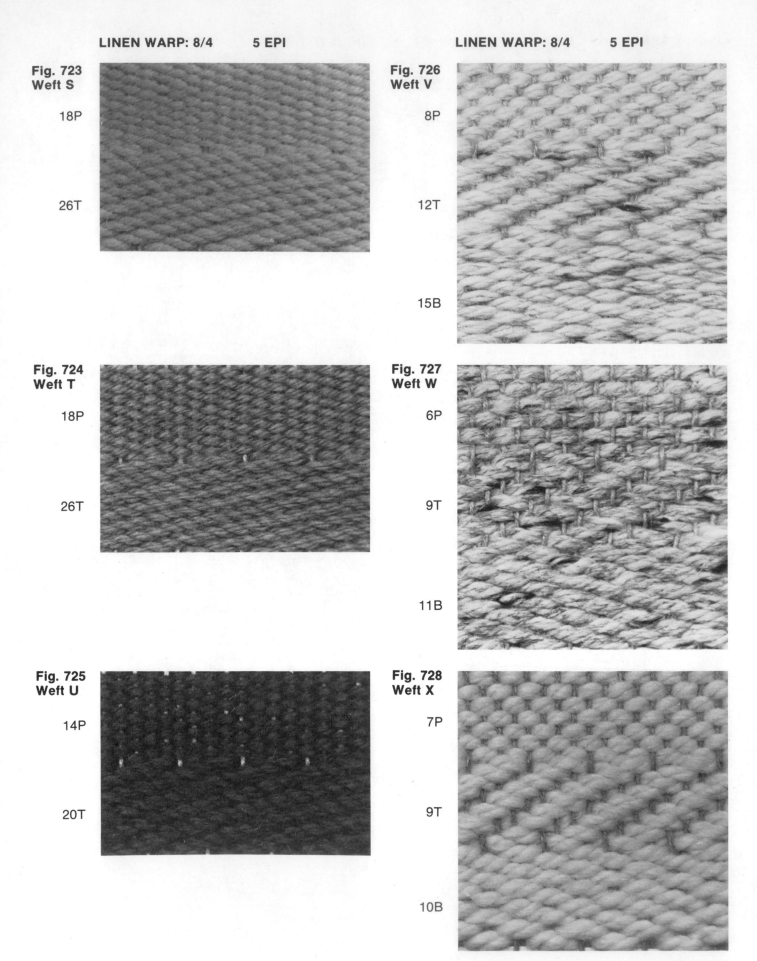

Fig. 723
Weft S

18P

26T

Fig. 724
Weft T

18P

26T

Fig. 725
Weft U

14P

20T

Fig. 726
Weft V

8P

12T

15B

Fig. 727
Weft W

6P

9T

11B

Fig. 728
Weft X

7P

9T

10B

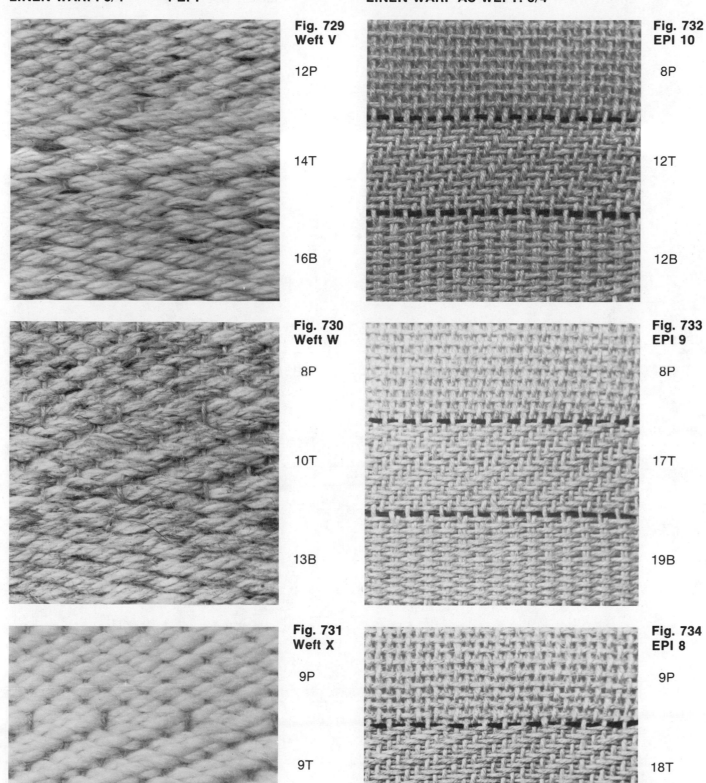

Fig. 729
Weft V

12P

14T

16B

Fig. 732
EPI 10

8P

12T

12B

Fig. 730
Weft W

8P

10T

13B

Fig. 733
EPI 9

8P

17T

19B

Fig. 731
Weft X

9P

9T

11B

Fig. 734
EPI 8

9P

18T

23B

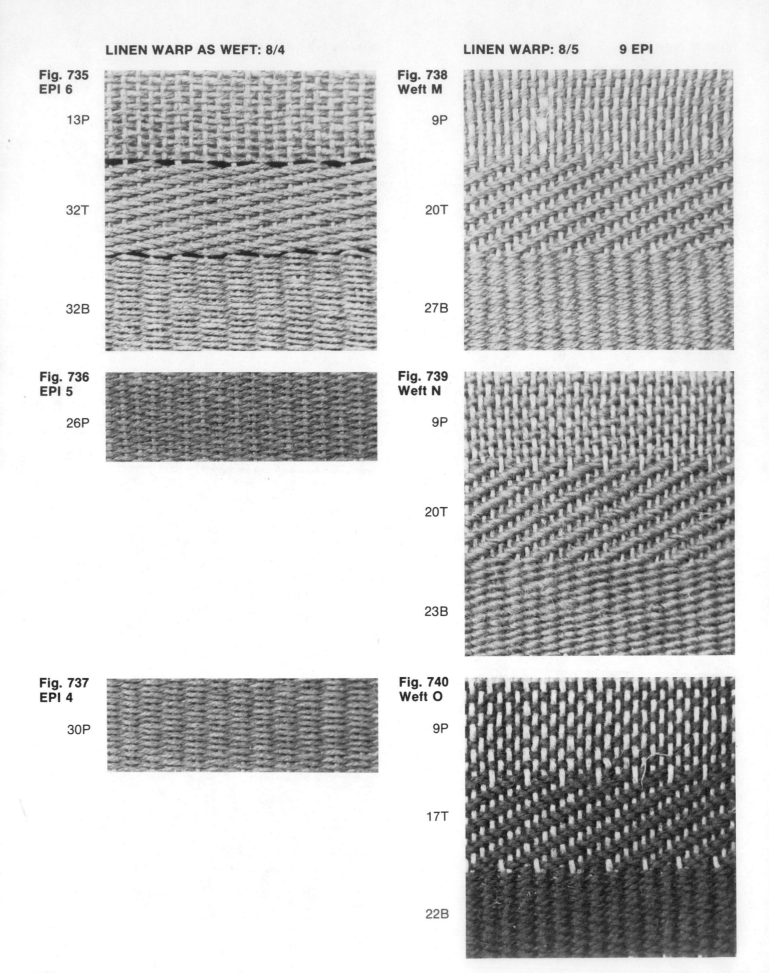

LINEN WARP AS WEFT: 8/4

LINEN WARP: 8/5   9 EPI

Fig. 735
EPI 6

13P

32T

32B

Fig. 736
EPI 5

26P

Fig. 737
EPI 4

30P

Fig. 738
Weft M

9P

20T

27B

Fig. 739
Weft N

9P

20T

23B

Fig. 740
Weft O

9P

17T

22B

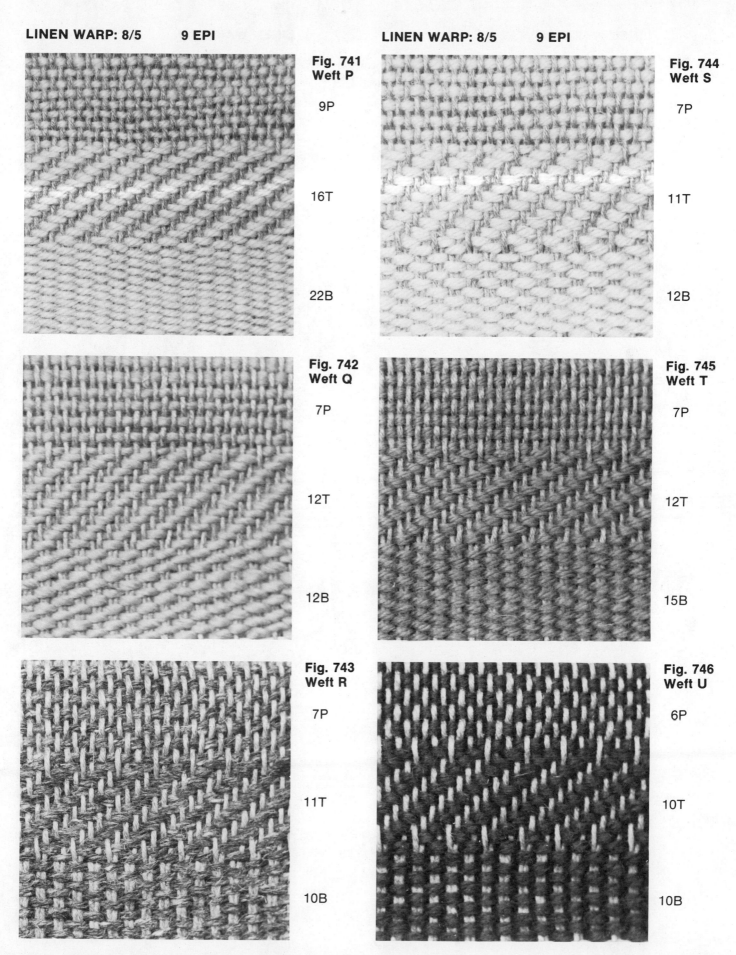

Fig. 741
Weft P

9P

16T

22B

Fig. 744
Weft S

7P

11T

12B

Fig. 742
Weft Q

7P

12T

12B

Fig. 745
Weft T

7P

12T

15B

Fig. 743
Weft R

7P

11T

10B

Fig. 746
Weft U

6P

10T

10B

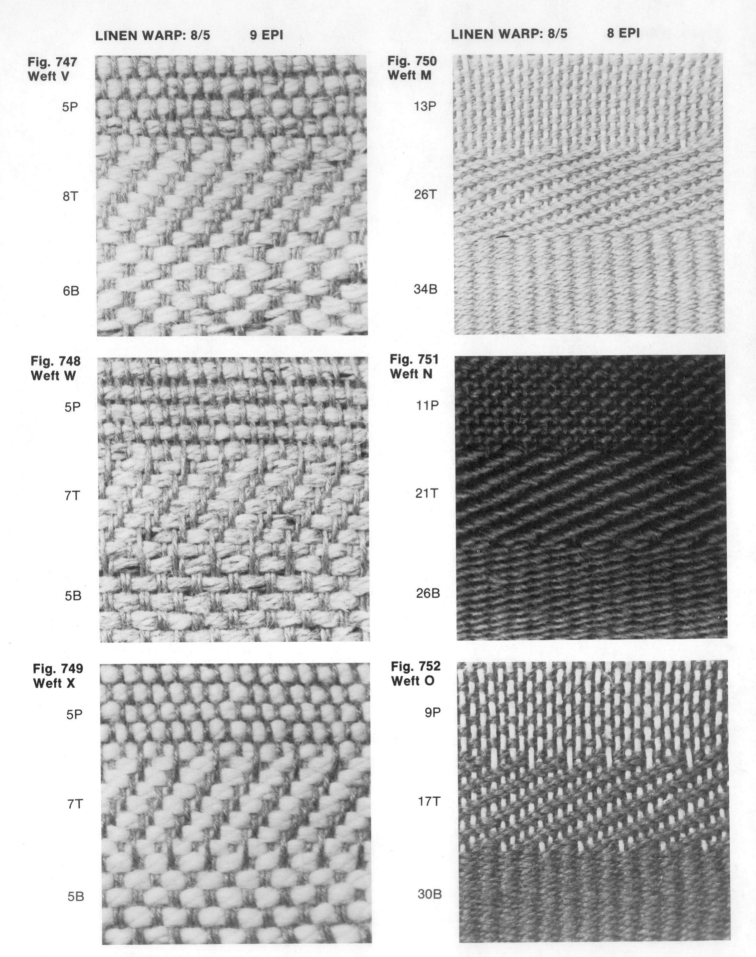

Fig. 747
Weft V

5P

8T

6B

Fig. 750
Weft M

13P

26T

34B

Fig. 748
Weft W

5P

7T

5B

Fig. 751
Weft N

11P

21T

26B

Fig. 749
Weft X

5P

7T

5B

Fig. 752
Weft O

9P

17T

30B

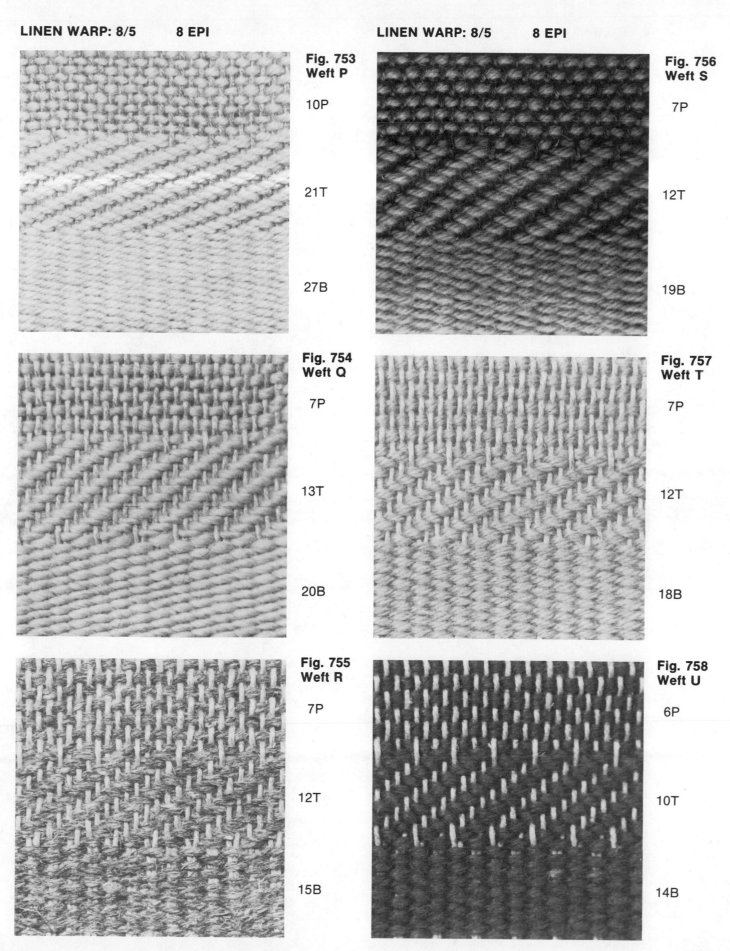

Fig. 753
Weft P

10P

21T

27B

Fig. 756
Weft S

7P

12T

19B

Fig. 754
Weft Q

7P

13T

20B

Fig. 757
Weft T

7P

12T

18B

Fig. 755
Weft R

7P

12T

15B

Fig. 758
Weft U

6P

10T

14B

143

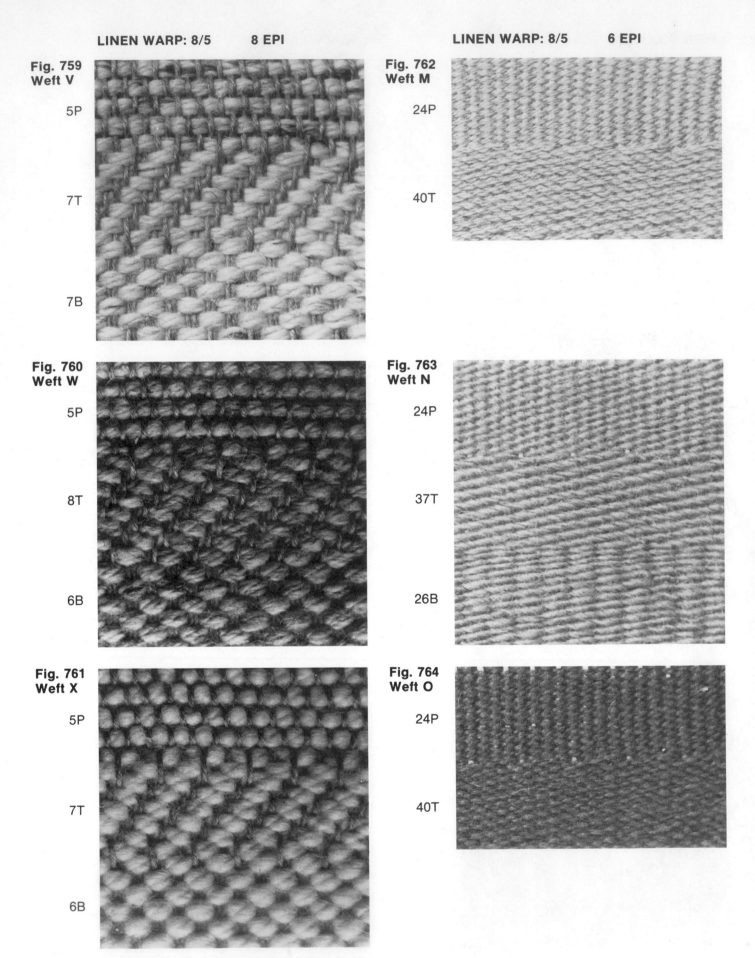

**Fig. 759
Weft V**

5P

7T

7B

**Fig. 762
Weft M**

24P

40T

**Fig. 760
Weft W**

5P

8T

6B

**Fig. 763
Weft N**

24P

37T

26B

**Fig. 761
Weft X**

5P

7T

6B

**Fig. 764
Weft O**

24P

40T

144

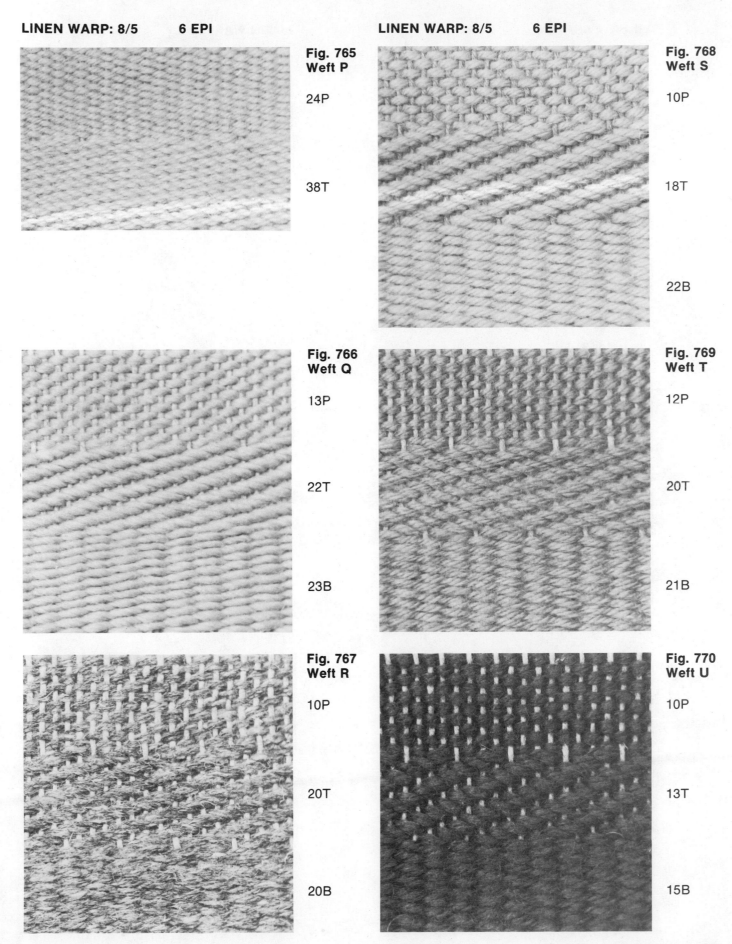

Fig. 765
Weft P

24P

38T

Fig. 768
Weft S

10P

18T

22B

Fig. 766
Weft Q

13P

22T

23B

Fig. 769
Weft T

12P

20T

21B

Fig. 767
Weft R

10P

20T

20B

Fig. 770
Weft U

10P

13T

15B

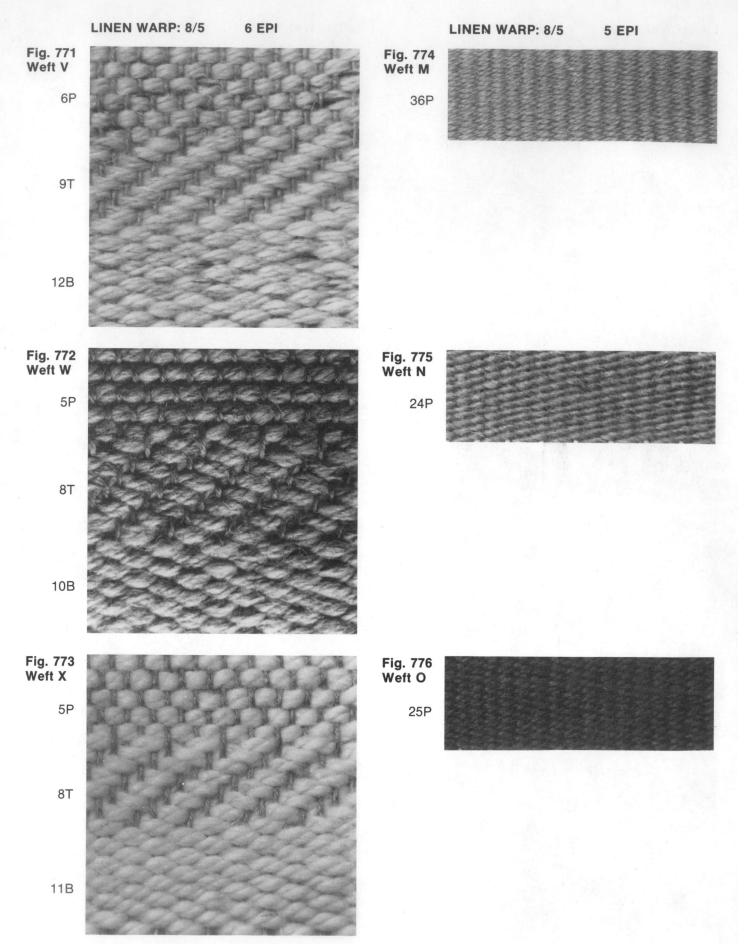

LINEN WARP: 8/5   6 EPI

Fig. 771
Weft V

6P

9T

12B

Fig. 772
Weft W

5P

8T

10B

Fig. 773
Weft X

5P

8T

11B

LINEN WARP: 8/5   5 EPI

Fig. 774
Weft M

36P

Fig. 775
Weft N

24P

Fig. 776
Weft O

25P

LINEN WARP: 8/5 5 EPI

Fig. 777
Weft P

30P

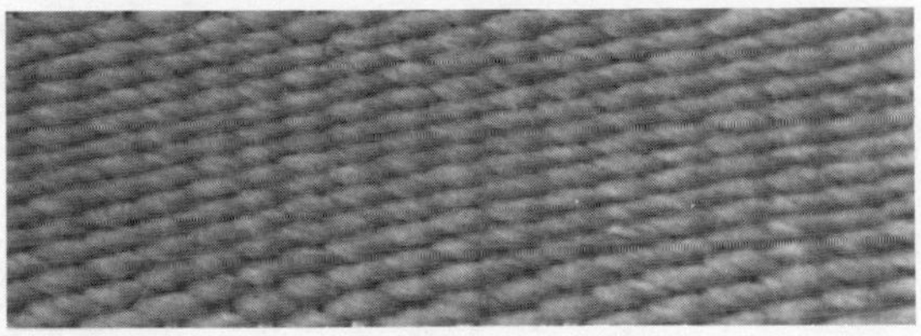

Fig. 778
Weft Q

26P

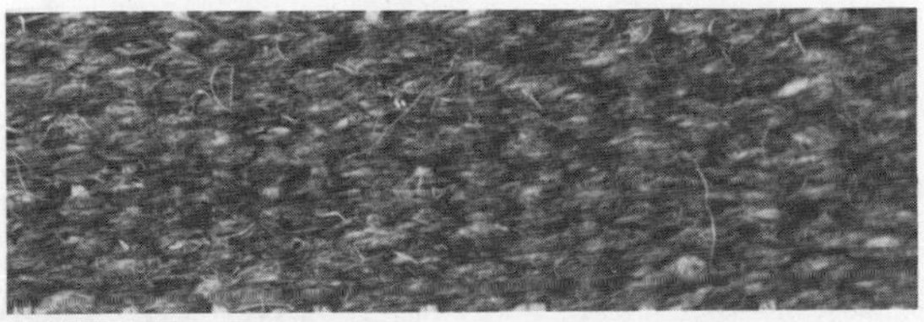

Fig. 779
Weft R

18P

LINEN WARP: 8/5 5 EPI

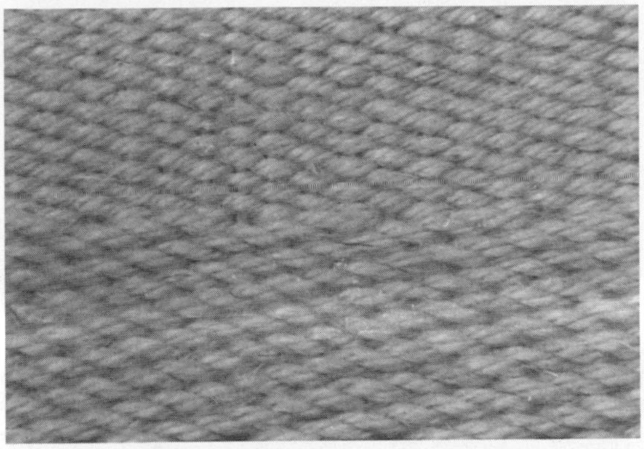

Fig. 780
Weft S

19P

30T

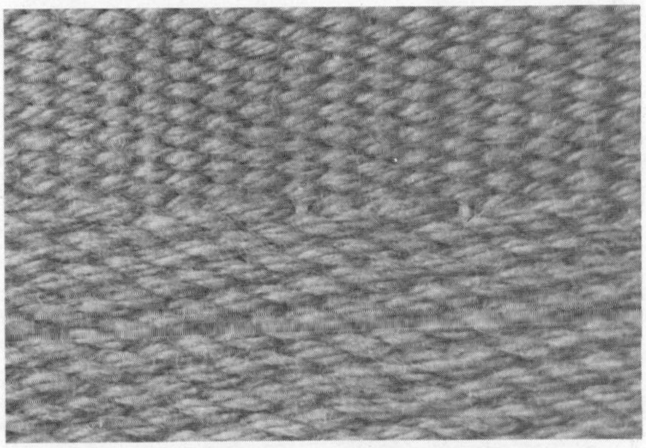

Fig. 781
Weft T

19P

30T

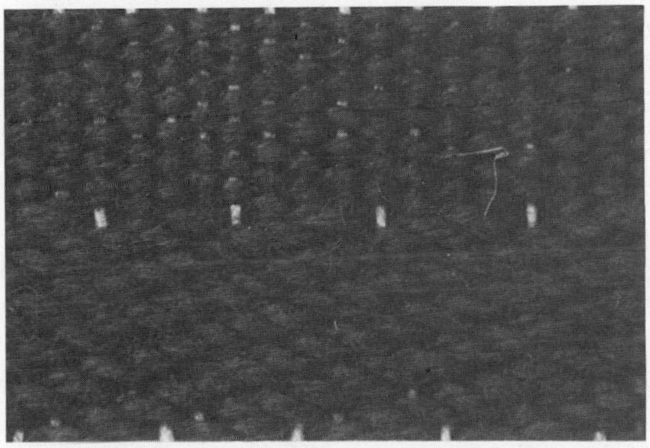

Fig. 782
Weft U

14P

20T

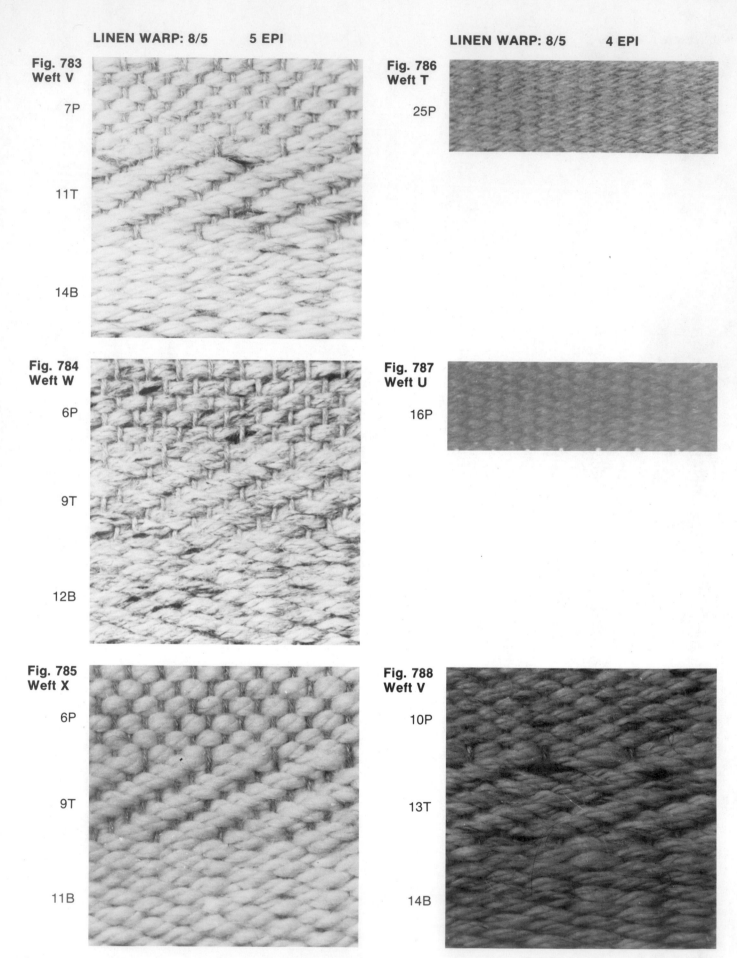

LINEN WARP: 8/5   5 EPI

Fig. 783
Weft V

7P

11T

14B

LINEN WARP: 8/5   4 EPI

Fig. 786
Weft T

25P

Fig. 784
Weft W

6P

9T

12B

Fig. 787
Weft U

16P

Fig. 785
Weft X

6P

9T

11B

Fig. 788
Weft V

10P

13T

14B

LINEN WARP: 8/5   4 EPI

LINEN WARP AS WEFT: 8/5

Fig. 789
Weft W

8P

10T

14B

Fig. 791
EPI 9

8P

13T

12B

Fig. 790
Weft X

8P

8I

12B

Fig. 792
EPI 8

8P

15T

18B

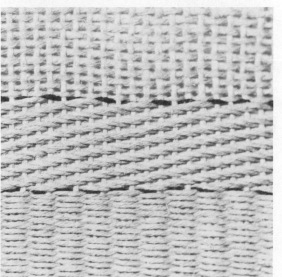

Fig. 793
EPI 6

11P

28T

30B

LINEN WARP AS WEFT: 8/5

Fig. 794
EPI 5

16P

Fig. 795
EPI 4

26P

Supplemental Wefts

With Cotton Warps: Figures 796-873

With Linen Warps: Figures 874-939

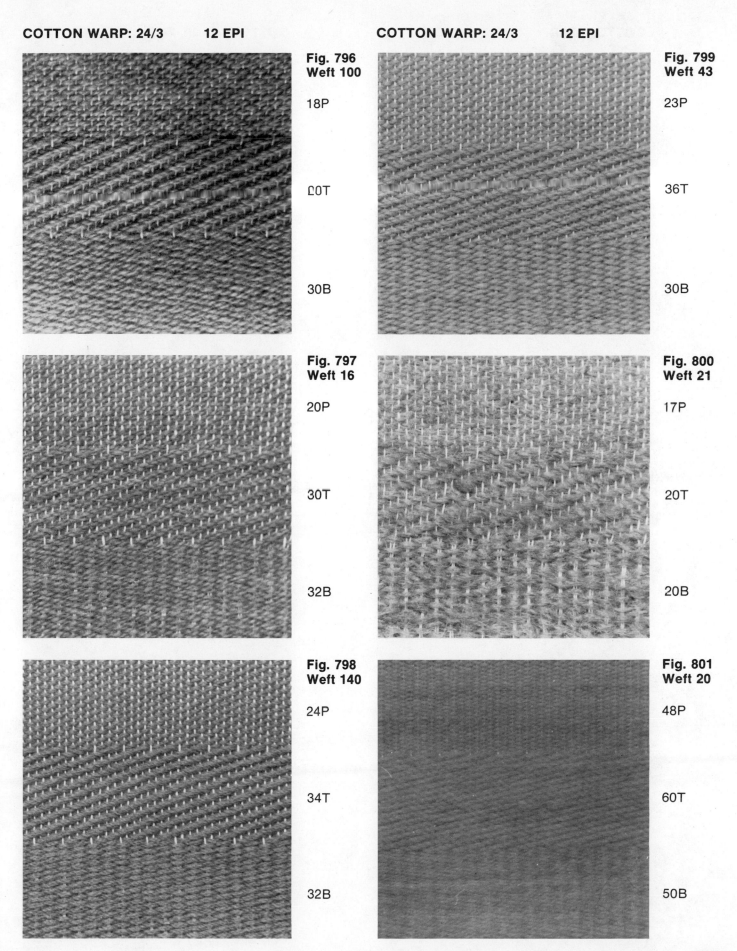

Fig. 796
Weft 100

18P

ℓ0T

30B

Fig. 797
Weft 16

20P

30T

32B

Fig. 798
Weft 140

24P

34T

32B

Fig. 799
Weft 43

23P

36T

30B

Fig. 800
Weft 21

17P

20T

20B

Fig. 801
Weft 20

48P

60T

50B

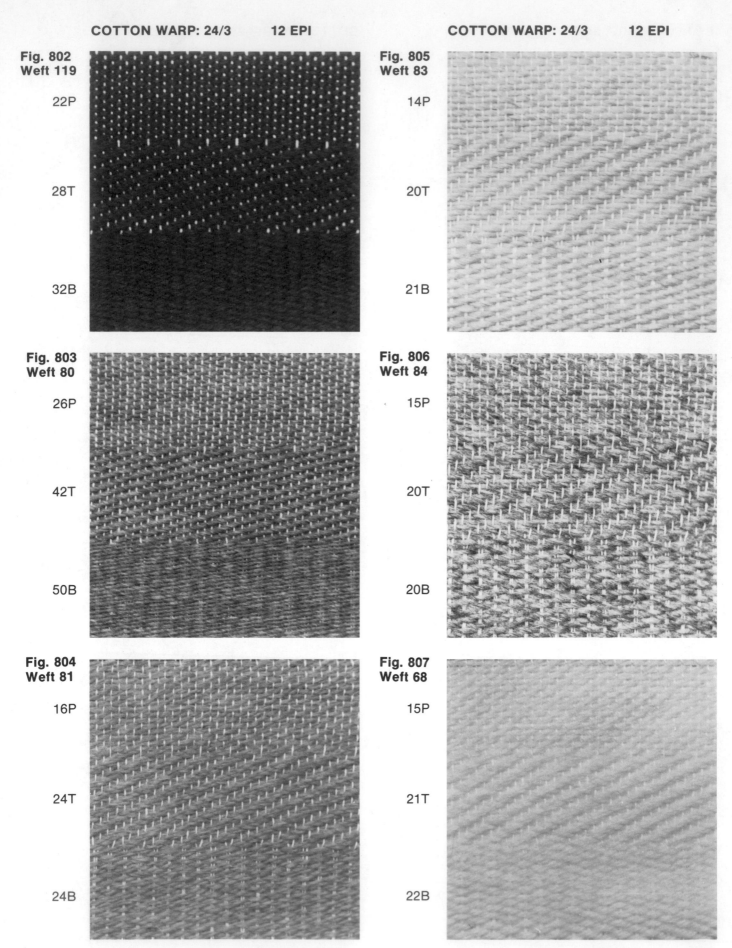

Fig. 802
Weft 119

22P

28T

32B

Fig. 805
Weft 83

14P

20T

21B

Fig. 803
Weft 80

26P

42T

50B

Fig. 806
Weft 84

15P

20T

20B

Fig. 804
Weft 81

16P

24T

24B

Fig. 807
Weft 68

15P

21T

22B

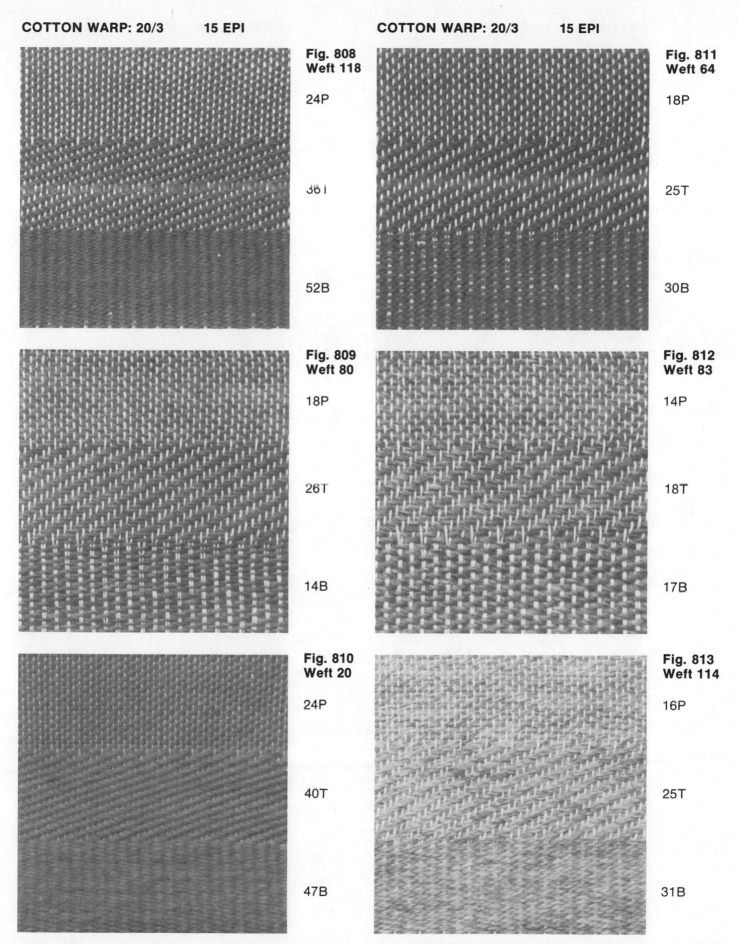

Fig. 808
Weft 118

24P

36T

52B

Fig. 811
Weft 64

18P

25T

30B

Fig. 809
Weft 80

18P

26T

14B

Fig. 812
Weft 83

14P

18T

17B

Fig. 810
Weft 20

24P

40T

47B

Fig. 813
Weft 114

16P

25T

31B

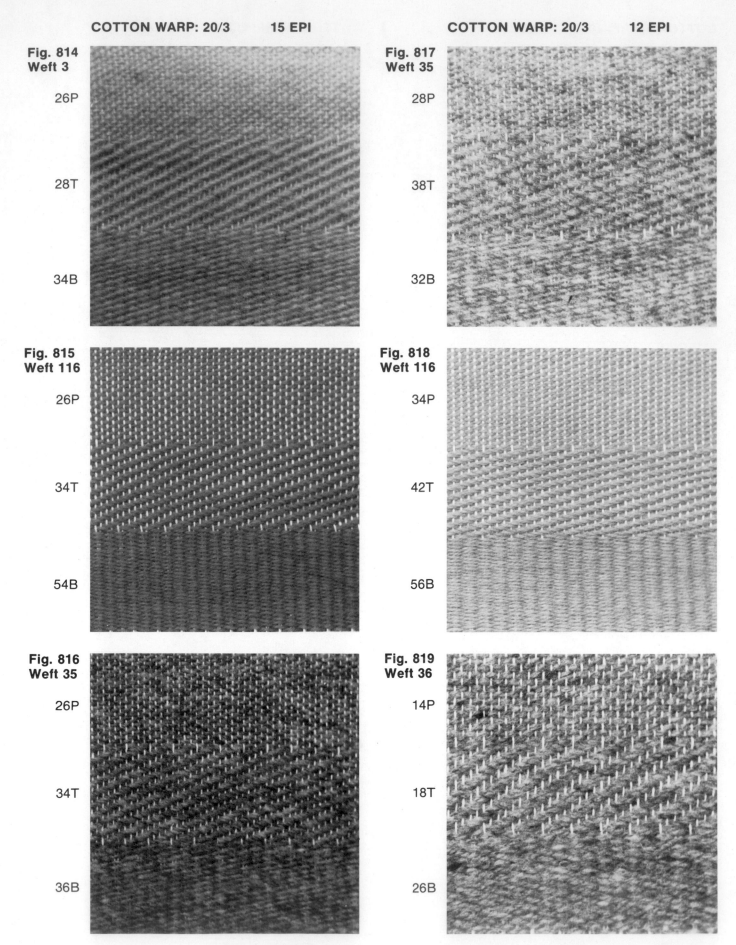

Fig. 814
Weft 3

26P

28T

34B

Fig. 817
Weft 35

28P

38T

32B

Fig. 815
Weft 116

26P

34T

54B

Fig. 818
Weft 116

34P

42T

56B

Fig. 816
Weft 35

26P

34T

36B

Fig. 819
Weft 36

14P

18T

26B

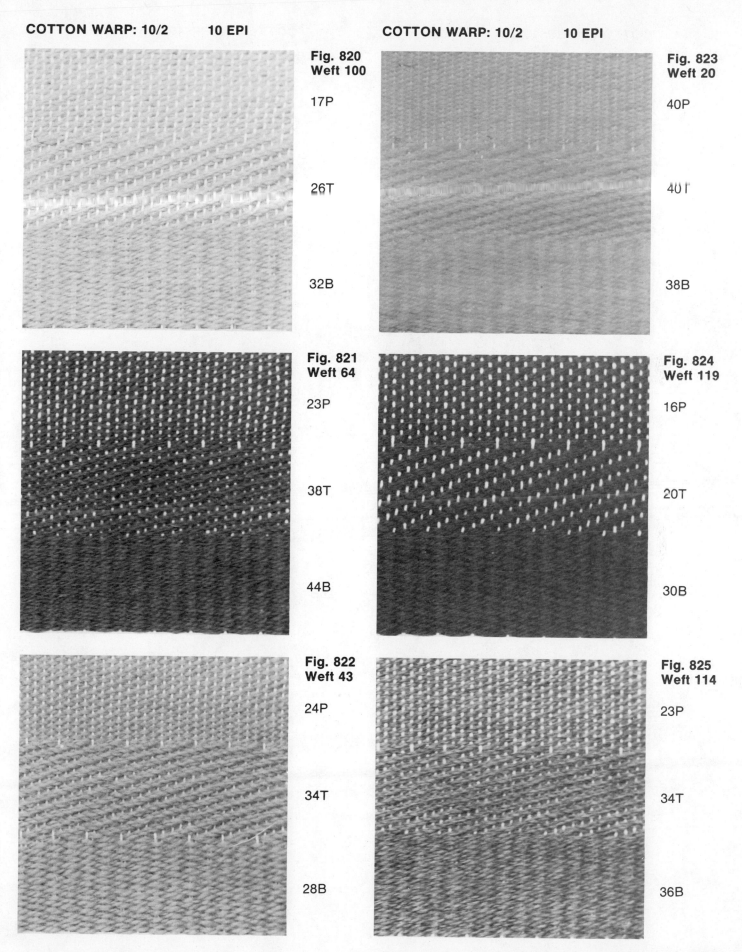

COTTON WARP: 10/2 10 EPI

Fig. 820
Weft 100

17P

26T

32B

COTTON WARP: 10/2 10 EPI

Fig. 823
Weft 20

40P

40T

38B

Fig. 821
Weft 64

23P

38T

44B

Fig. 824
Weft 119

16P

20T

30B

Fig. 822
Weft 43

24P

34T

28B

Fig. 825
Weft 114

23P

34T

36B

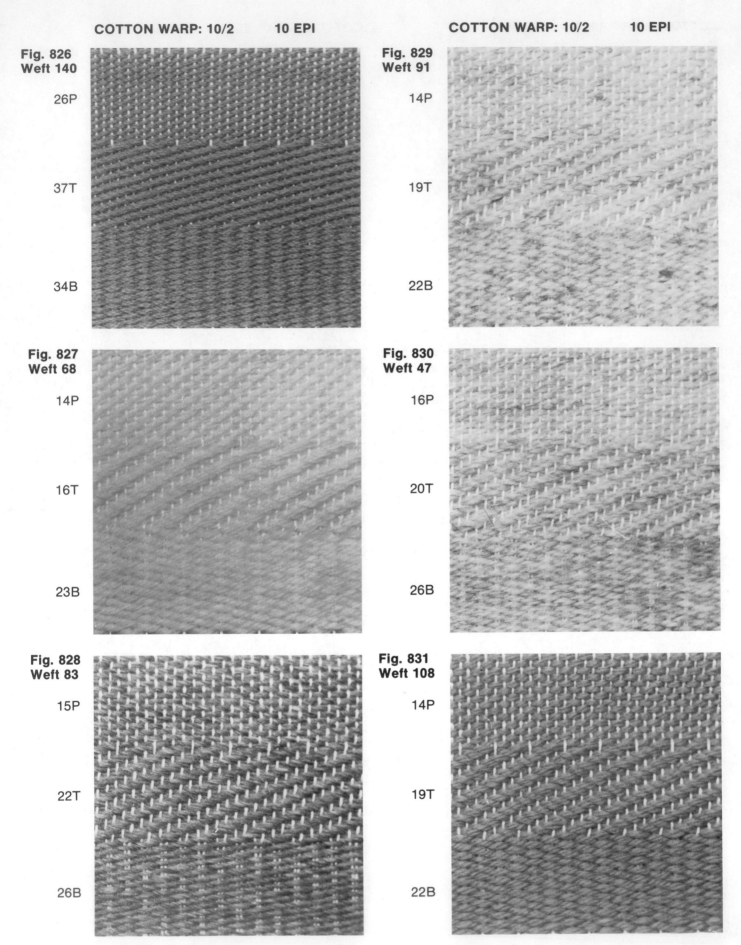

Fig. 826
Weft 140

26P

37T

34B

Fig. 829
Weft 91

14P

19T

22B

Fig. 827
Weft 68

14P

16T

23B

Fig. 830
Weft 47

16P

20T

26B

Fig. 828
Weft 83

15P

22T

26B

Fig. 831
Weft 108

14P

19T

22B

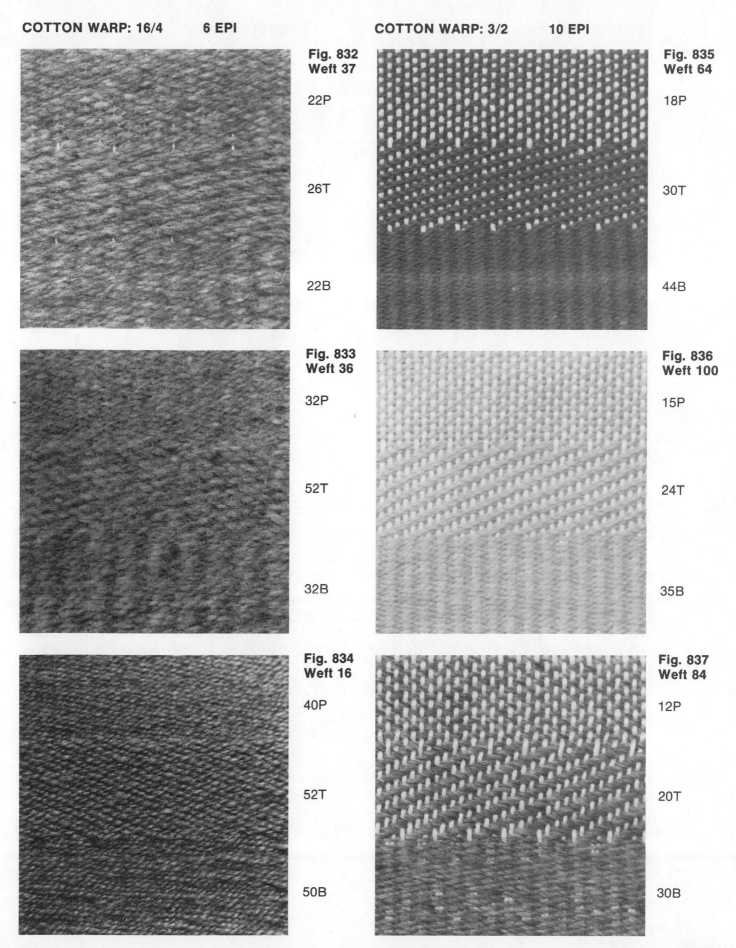

COTTON WARP: 16/4   6 EPI

Fig. 832
Weft 37

22P

26T

22B

Fig. 833
Weft 36

32P

52T

32B

Fig. 834
Weft 16

40P

52T

50B

COTTON WARP: 3/2   10 EPI

Fig. 835
Weft 64

18P

30T

44B

Fig. 836
Weft 100

15P

24T

35B

Fig. 837
Weft 84

12P

20T

30B

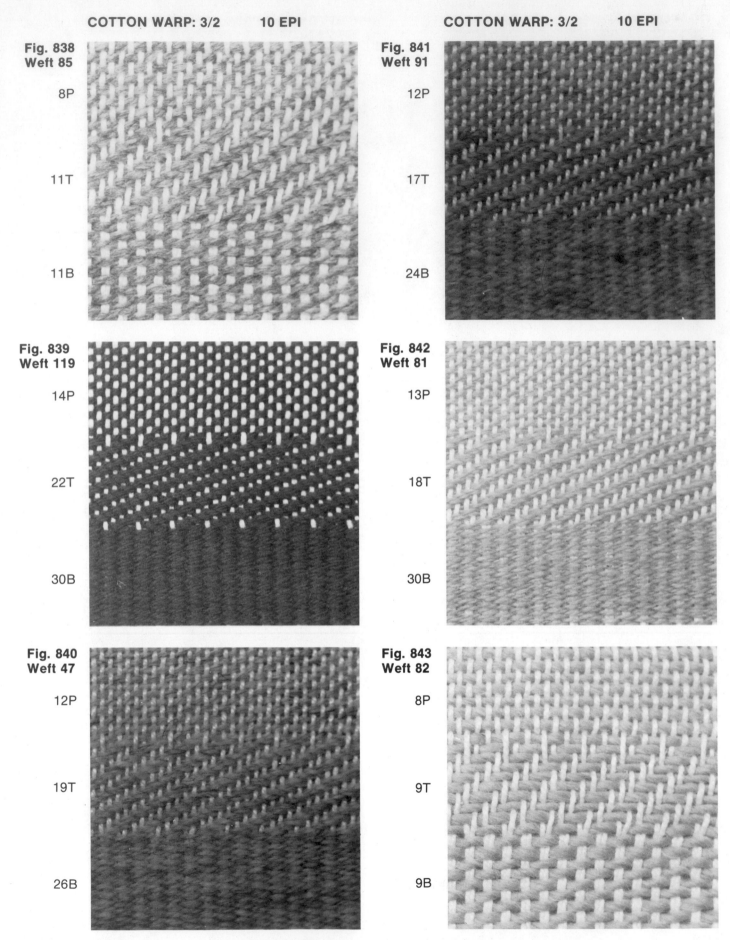

Fig. 838
Weft 85

8P

11T

11B

Fig. 841
Weft 91

12P

17T

24B

Fig. 839
Weft 119

14P

22T

30B

Fig. 842
Weft 81

13P

18T

30B

Fig. 840
Weft 47

12P

19T

26B

Fig. 843
Weft 82

8P

9T

9B

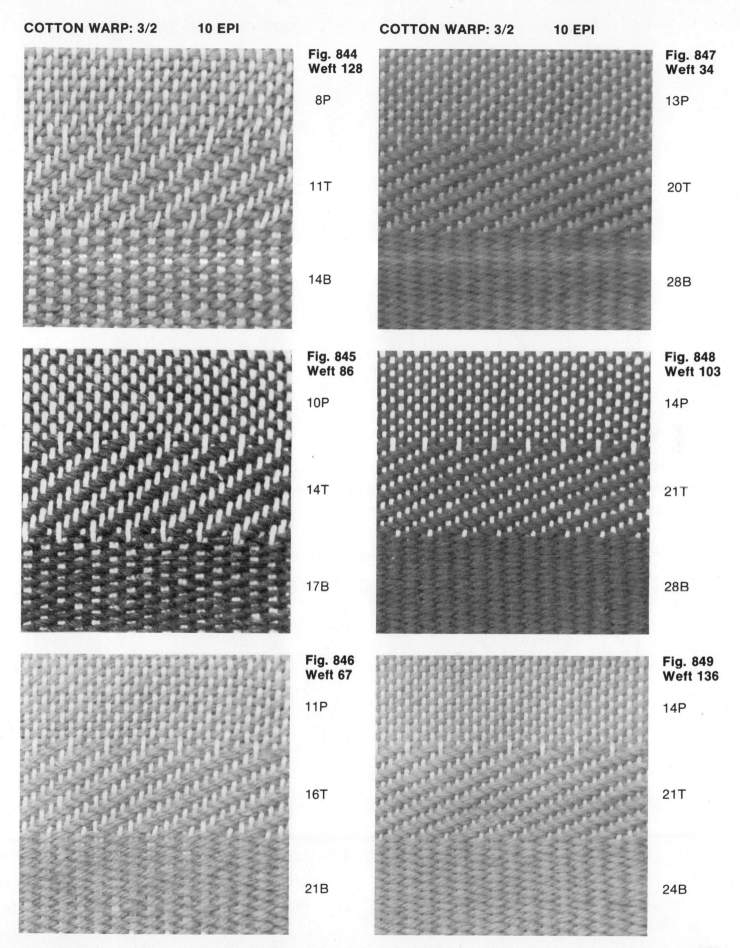

Fig. 844
Weft 128

8P

11T

14B

Fig. 847
Weft 34

13P

20T

28B

Fig. 845
Weft 86

10P

14T

17B

Fig. 848
Weft 103

14P

21T

28B

Fig. 846
Weft 67

11P

16T

21B

Fig. 849
Weft 136

14P

21T

24B

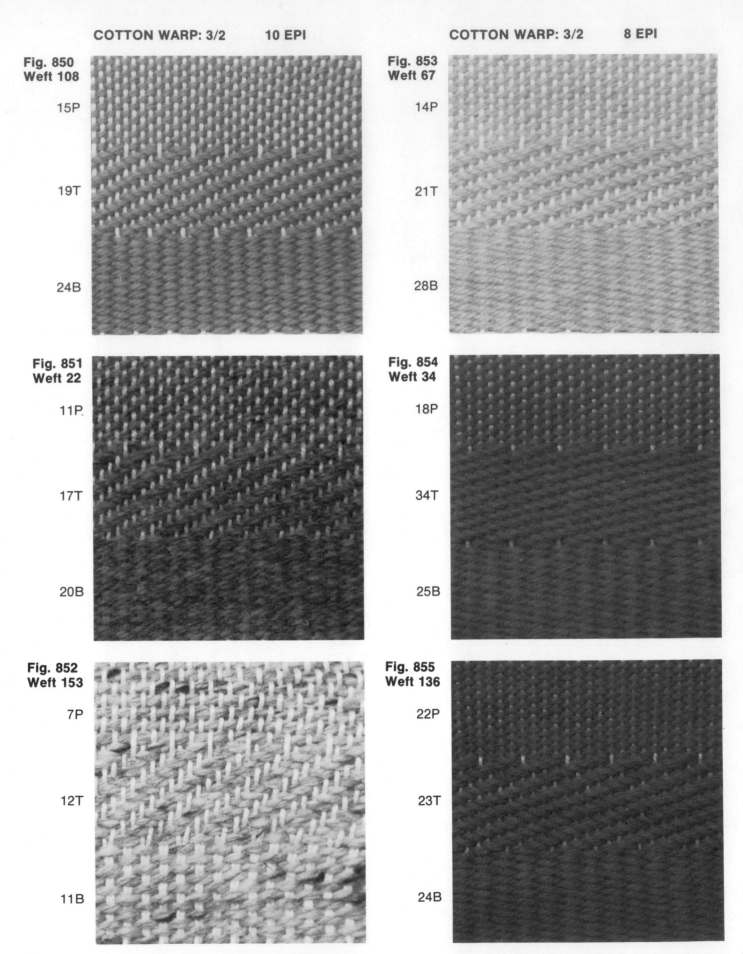

Fig. 850
Weft 108

15P

19T

24B

Fig. 851
Weft 22

11P

17T

20B

Fig. 852
Weft 153

7P

12T

11B

Fig. 853
Weft 67

14P

21T

28B

Fig. 854
Weft 34

18P

34T

25B

Fig. 855
Weft 136

22P

23T

24B

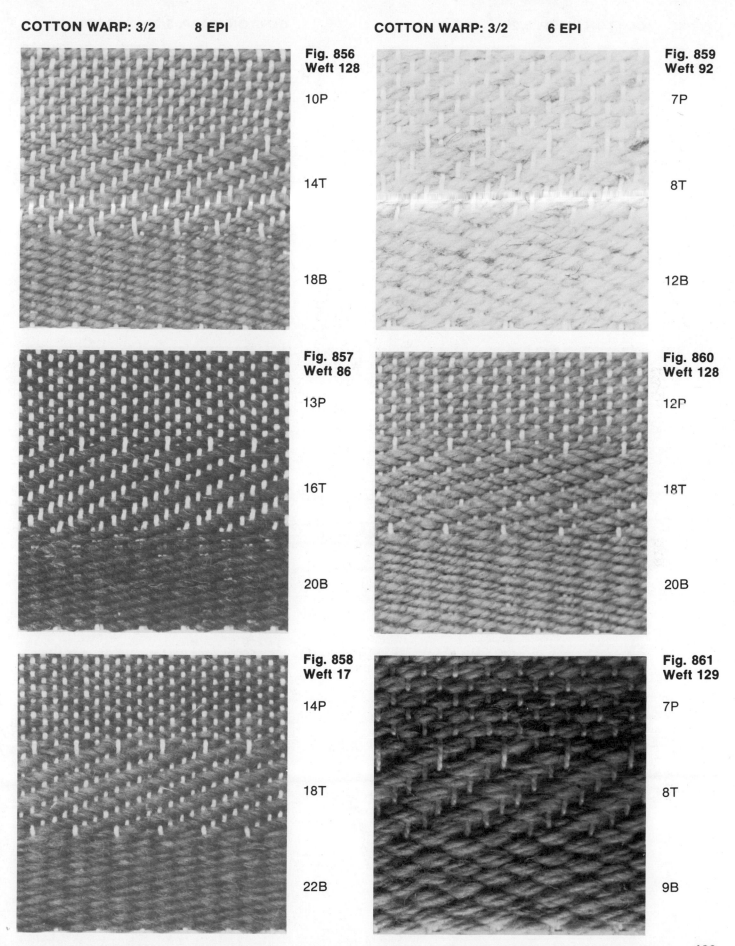

COTTON WARP: 3/2   8 EPI

COTTON WARP: 3/2   6 EPI

Fig. 856
Weft 128

10P

14T

18B

Fig. 857
Weft 86

13P

16T

20B

Fig. 858
Weft 17

14P

18T

22B

Fig. 859
Weft 92

7P

8T

12B

Fig. 860
Weft 128

12P

18T

20B

Fig. 861
Weft 129

7P

8T

9B

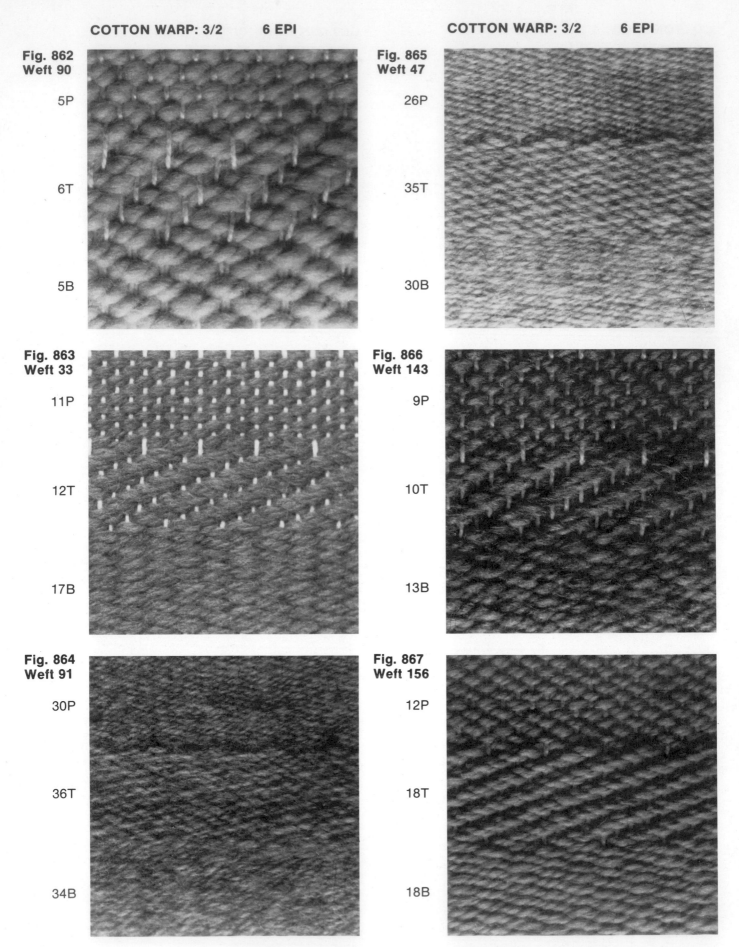

Fig. 862
Weft 90

5P

6T

5B

Fig. 865
Weft 47

26P

35T

30B

Fig. 863
Weft 33

11P

12T

17B

Fig. 866
Weft 143

9P

10T

13B

Fig. 864
Weft 91

30P

36T

34B

Fig. 867
Weft 156

12P

18T

18B

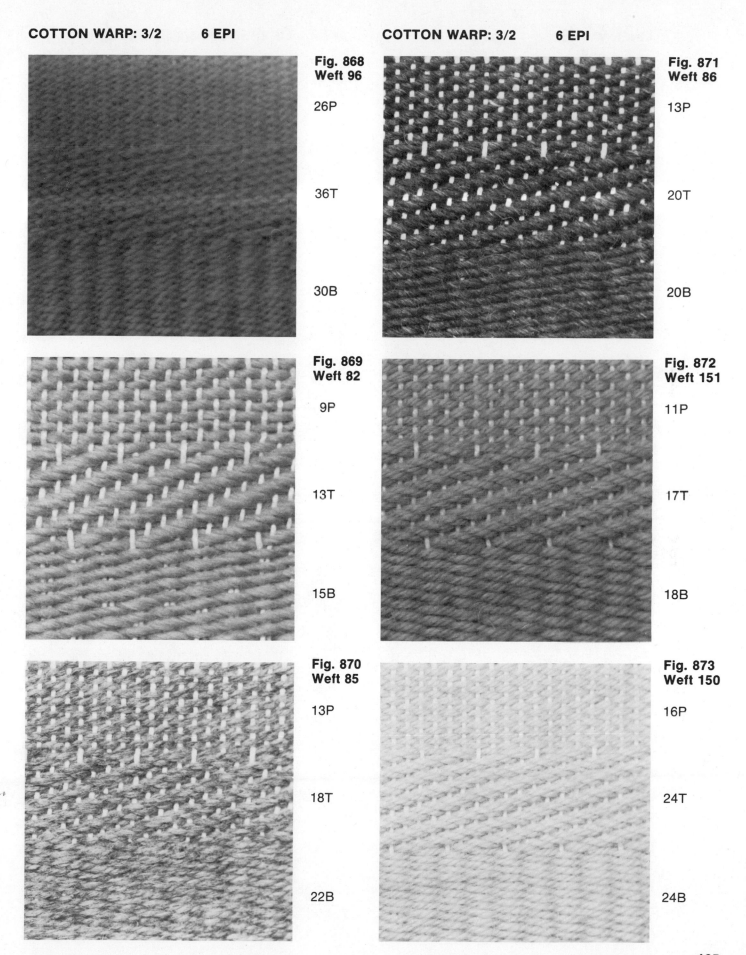

Fig. 868
Weft 96

26P

36T

30B

Fig. 871
Weft 86

13P

20T

20B

Fig. 869
Weft 82

9P

13T

15B

Fig. 872
Weft 151

11P

17T

18B

Fig. 870
Weft 85

13P

18T

22B

Fig. 873
Weft 150

16P

24T

24B

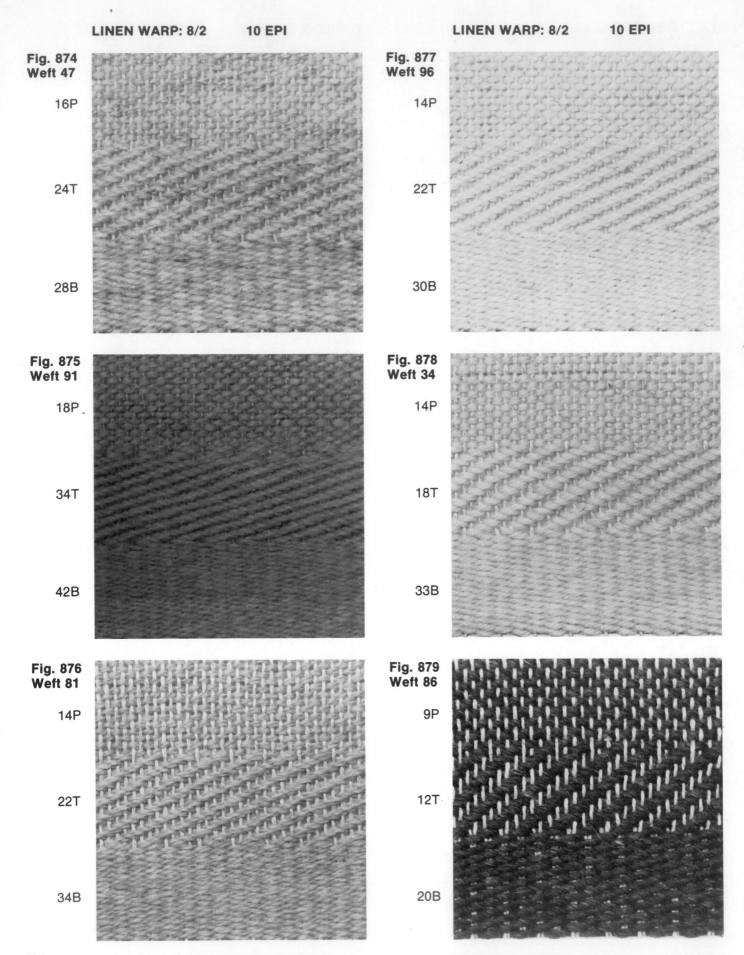

Fig. 874
Weft 47

16P

24T

28B

Fig. 877
Weft 96

14P

22T

30B

Fig. 875
Weft 91

18P

34T

42B

Fig. 878
Weft 34

14P

18T

33B

Fig. 876
Weft 81

14P

22T

34B

Fig. 879
Weft 86

9P

12T

20B

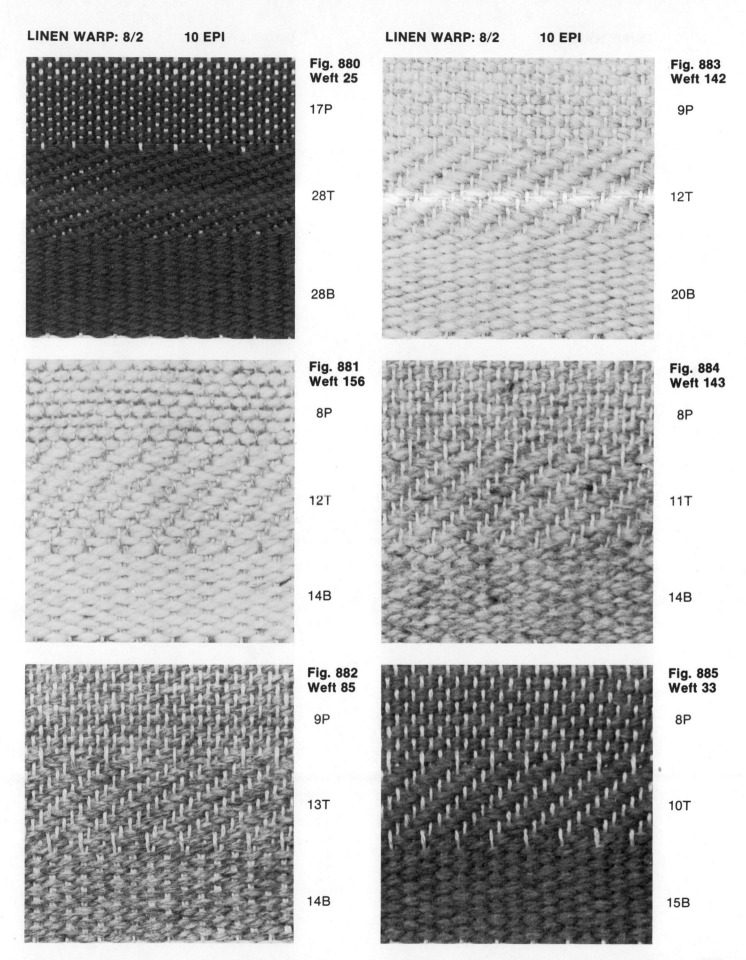

LINEN WARP: 8/2   10 EPI

Fig. 880
Weft 25

17P

28T

28B

LINEN WARP: 8/2   10 EPI

Fig. 883
Weft 142

9P

12T

20B

Fig. 881
Weft 156

8P

12T

14B

Fig. 884
Weft 143

8P

11T

14B

Fig. 882
Weft 85

9P

13T

14B

Fig. 885
Weft 33

8P

10T

15B

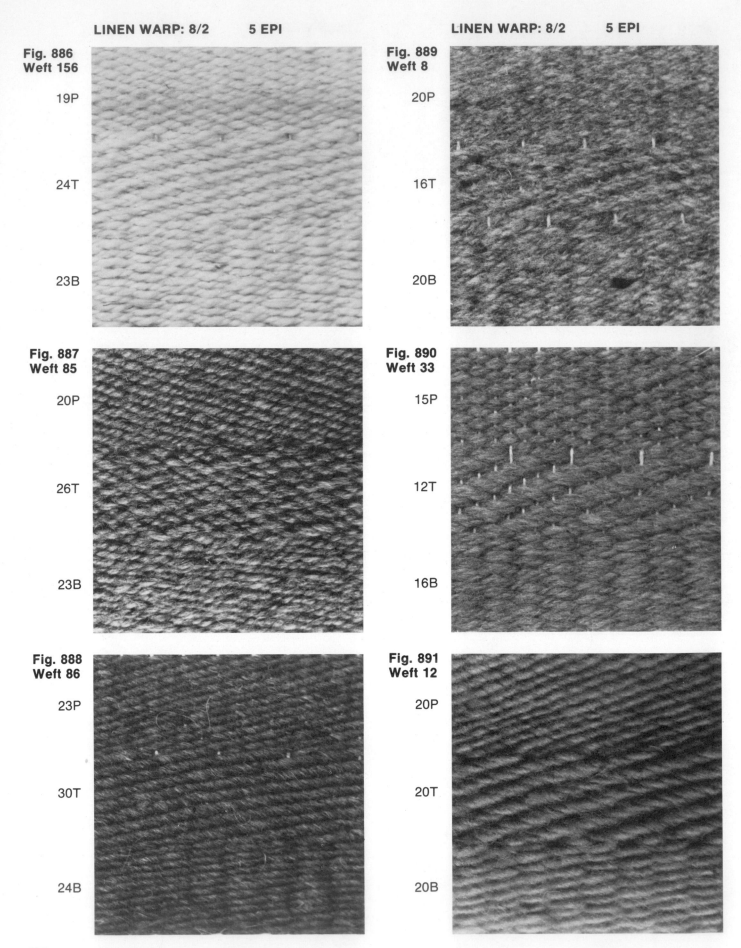

Fig. 886
Weft 156

19P

24T

23B

Fig. 887
Weft 85

20P

26T

23B

Fig. 888
Weft 86

23P

30T

24B

Fig. 889
Weft 8

20P

16T

20B

Fig. 890
Weft 33

15P

12T

16B

Fig. 891
Weft 12

20P

20T

20B

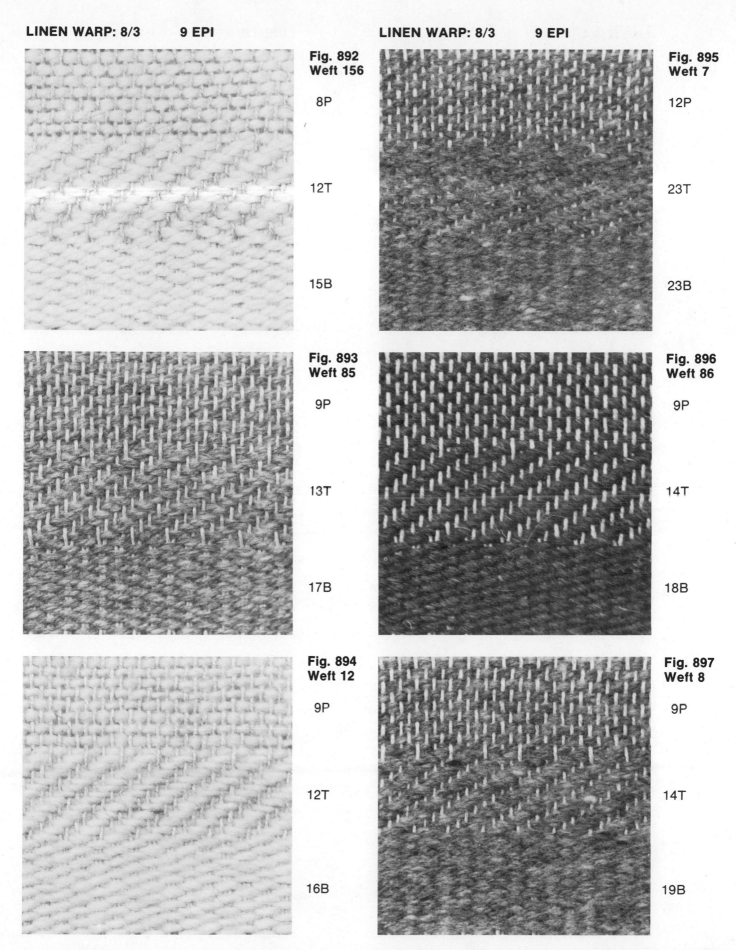

Fig. 892
Weft 156

8P

12T

15B

Fig. 895
Weft 7

12P

23T

23B

Fig. 893
Weft 85

9P

13T

17B

Fig. 896
Weft 86

9P

14T

18B

Fig. 894
Weft 12

9P

12T

16B

Fig. 897
Weft 8

9P

14T

19B

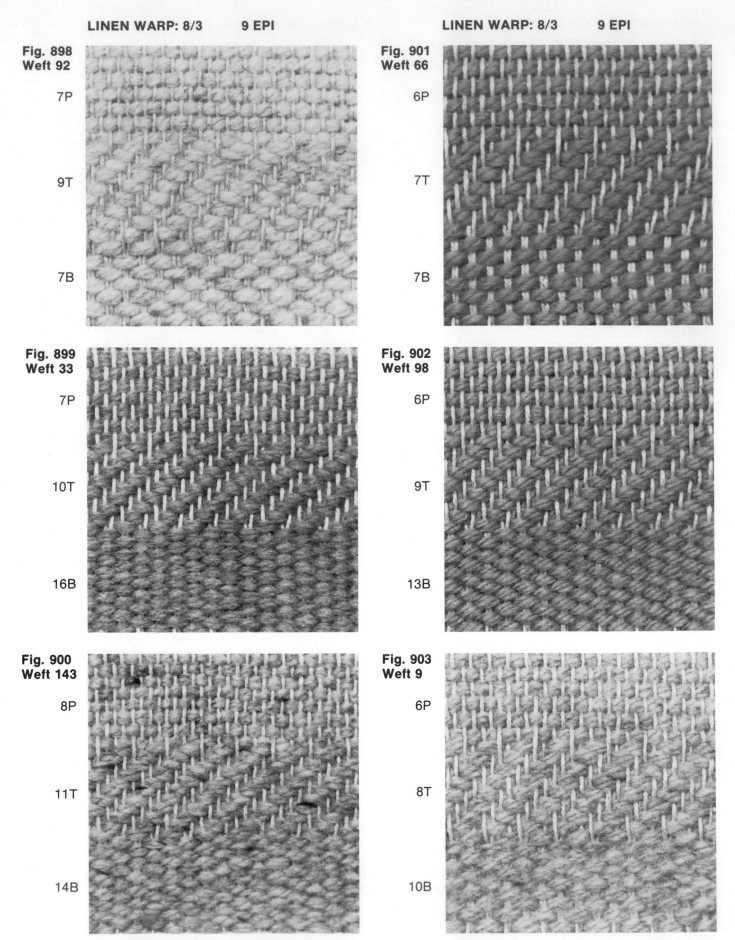

Fig. 898
Weft 92

7P

9T

7B

Fig. 901
Weft 66

6P

7T

7B

Fig. 899
Weft 33

7P

10T

16B

Fig. 902
Weft 98

6P

9T

13B

Fig. 900
Weft 143

8P

11T

14B

Fig. 903
Weft 9

6P

8T

10B

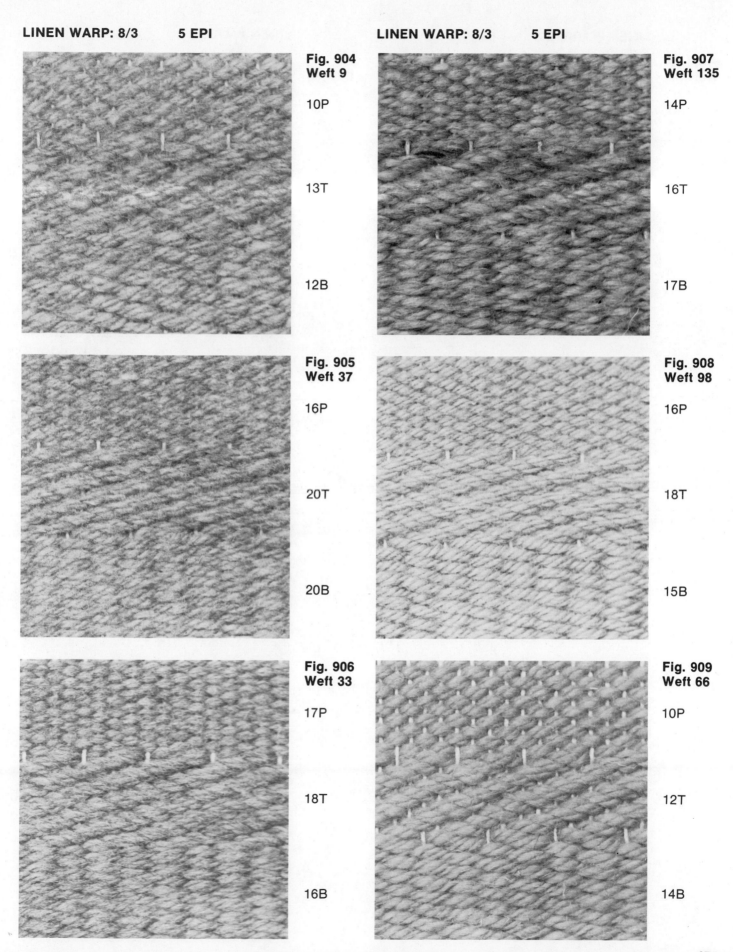

LINEN WARP: 8/3   5 EPI

Fig. 904
Weft 9

10P

13T

12B

Fig. 907
Weft 135

14P

16T

17B

Fig. 905
Weft 37

16P

20T

20B

Fig. 908
Weft 98

16P

18T

15B

Fig. 906
Weft 33

17P

18T

16B

Fig. 909
Weft 66

10P

12T

14B

171

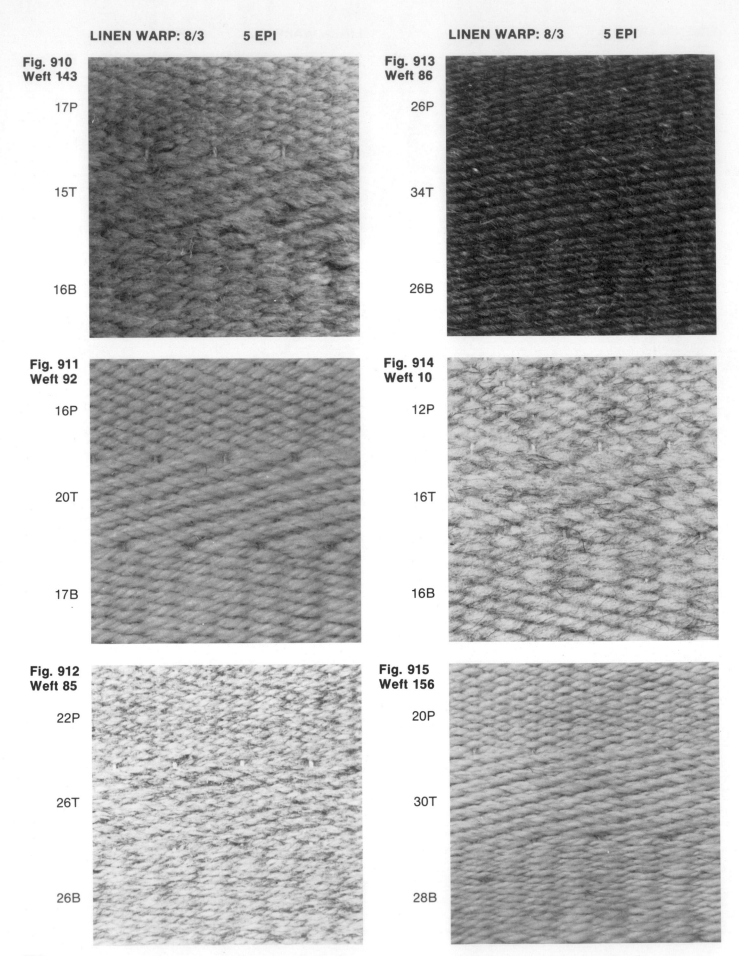

Fig. 910
Weft 143

17P

15T

16B

Fig. 911
Weft 92

16P

20T

17B

Fig. 912
Weft 85

22P

26T

26B

Fig. 913
Weft 86

26P

34T

26B

Fig. 914
Weft 10

12P

16T

16B

Fig. 915
Weft 156

20P

30T

28B

172

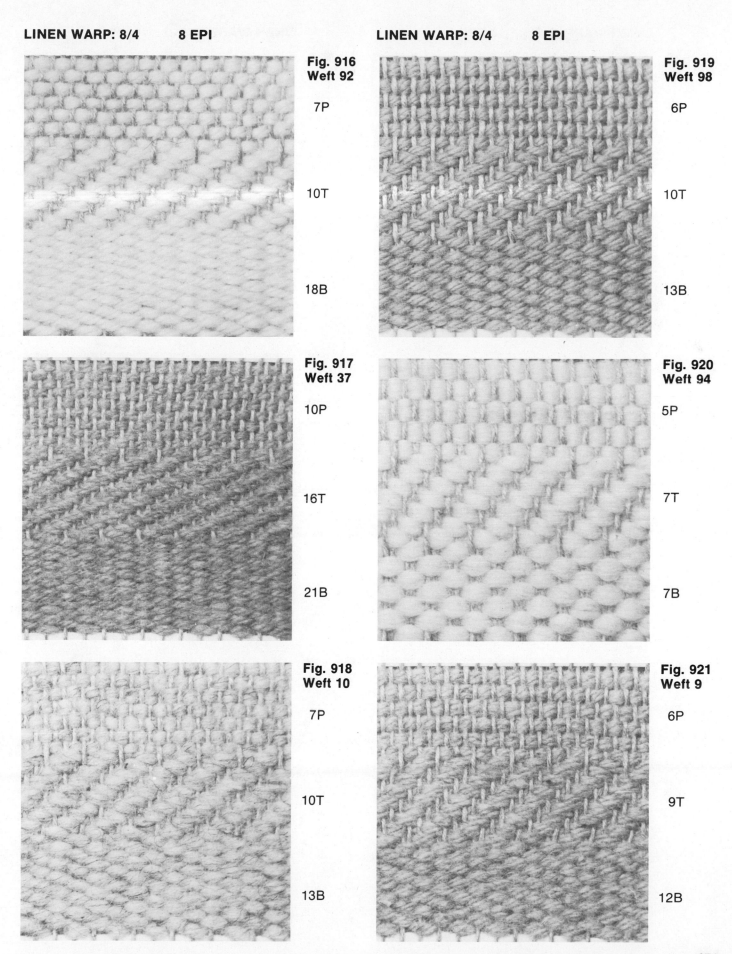

Fig. 916
Weft 92

7P

10T

18B

Fig. 919
Weft 98

6P

10T

13B

Fig. 917
Weft 37

10P

16T

21B

Fig. 920
Weft 94

5P

7T

7B

Fig. 918
Weft 10

7P

10T

13B

Fig. 921
Weft 9

6P

9T

12B

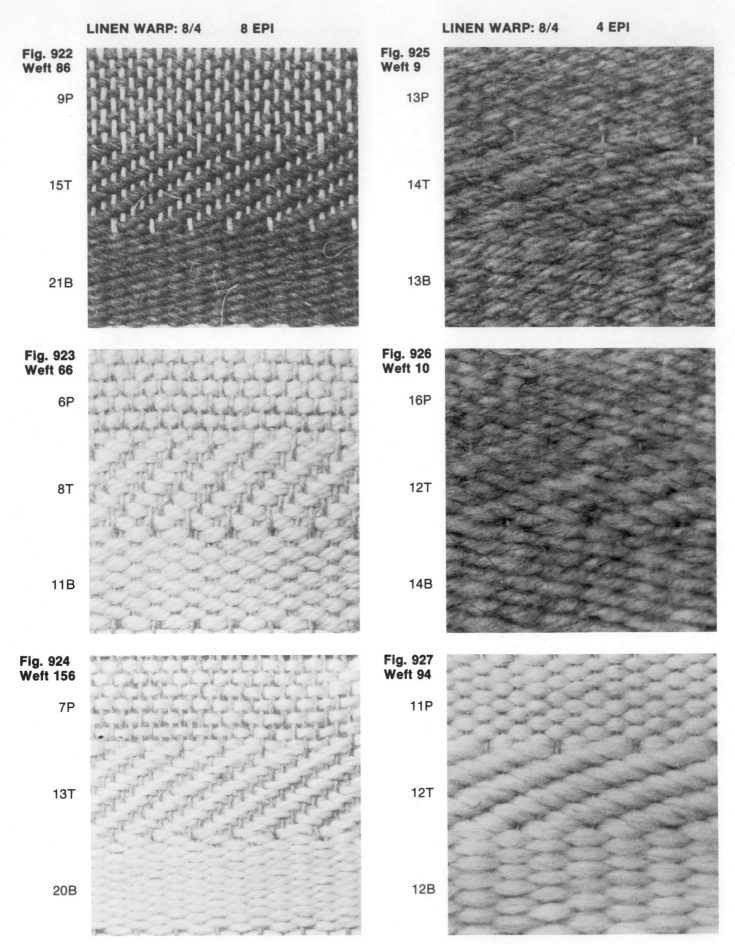

Fig. 922
Weft 86

9P

15T

21B

Fig. 923
Weft 66

6P

8T

11B

Fig. 924
Weft 156

7P

13T

20B

Fig. 925
Weft 9

13P

14T

13B

Fig. 926
Weft 10

16P

12T

14B

Fig. 927
Weft 94

11P

12T

12B

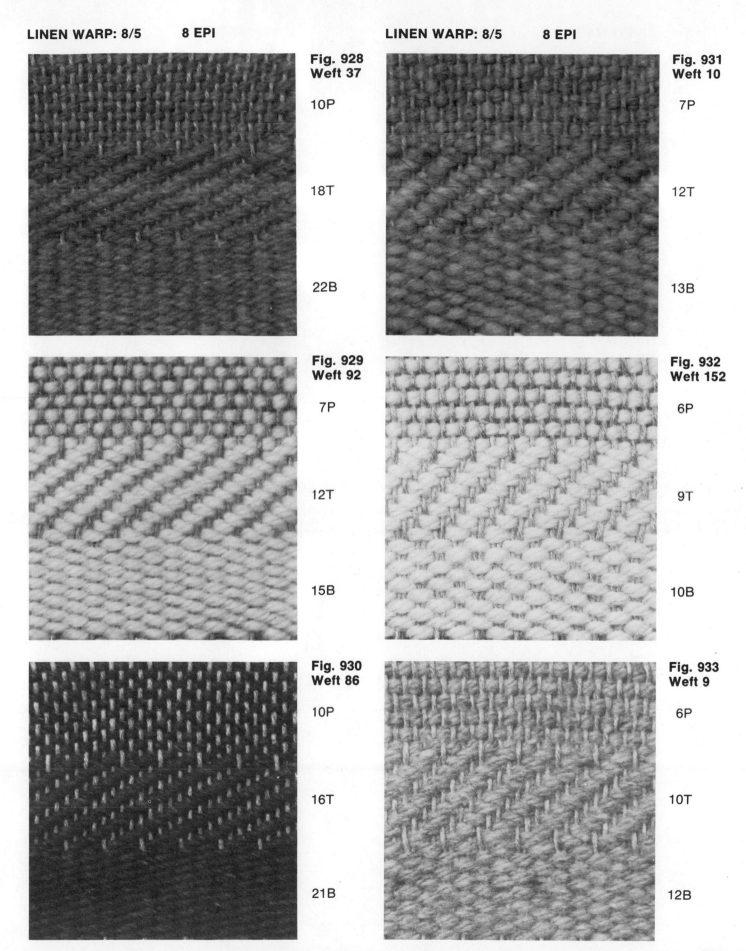

Fig. 928
Weft 37

10P

18T

22B

Fig. 931
Weft 10

7P

12T

13B

Fig. 929
Weft 92

7P

12T

15B

Fig. 932
Weft 152

6P

9T

10B

Fig. 930
Weft 86

10P

16T

21B

Fig. 933
Weft 9

6P

10T

12B

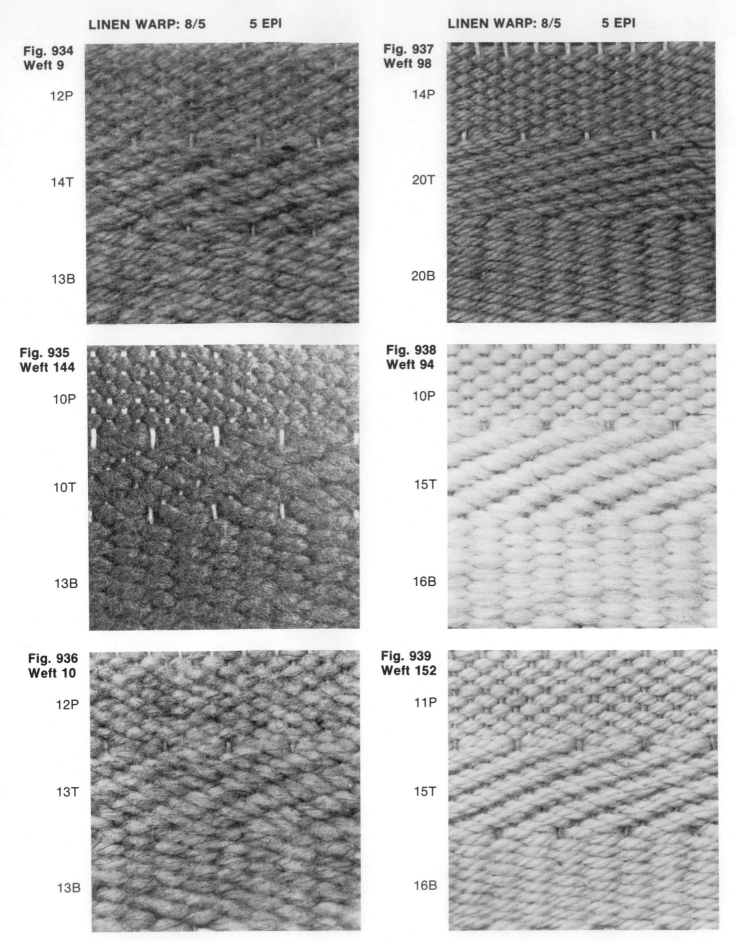

Fig. 934
Weft 9

12P

14T

13B

Fig. 937
Weft 98

14P

20T

20B

Fig. 935
Weft 144

10P

10T

13B

Fig. 938
Weft 94

10P

15T

16B

Fig. 936
Weft 10

12P

13T

13B

Fig. 939
Weft 152

11P

15T

16B

Appendix I: Cotton Warp Yarns

Yardages have been provided by the manufacturers, and are given in yards per pound.

All the manufacturers listed below sell wholesale to retail outlets; those that also sell via mail order are so noted. Enquiries are welcome, and should be sent to the address listed below.

Manufacturers	Figures		Yarns	Yds/Lb
Belding Lily			20/2	8400
Box 88	44-89, 796-807		24/3	6720
Shelby, NC 28150	90-134, 808-819		20/3	5600
Mail Order	135-196, 820-831		10/2	4200
	197-281, 832-834		16/4	3360
	282-346		10/3	2800
	347-435		5/2	2100
			3/2	1260
Cum Textile Industries, Ltd.			2/16	5600
5 Roemersgade		cottolin 2/22		3200
1362 Copenhagen, Denmark	(50% Cotton, 50% Linen)			
Frederick J. Fawcett, Inc.			20/2	8400
129 South Street				
Boston, MA 02111				
Mail Order				
Fort Crailo Yarns Co.			8/2	3360
2 Green Street			8/3	2240
Rensselaer, NY 12144			8/4	1680
Mail Order			8/5	1344
Samples: $2.00			8/6	1120
Robinson Anton Textile Co.			#33	10000
175 Bergen Boulevard			00/3	14000
Fairview, NJ 07022			20/2	8400
Mail Order			16/2	6720
			10/2	4200
Scott's Woolen Mills			16/2	6720
Hecla & Elmdale Streets				
Uxbridge, MA 01569				
Mail Order				
Usdan Kolmes Industries	1-43		20/2	8400
541 W. 37th Street			10/2	4200
New York, NY 10018			5/2	2100
Mail Order	436-502, 835-873		3/2	1260

Appendix II: Linen Warp Yarns

Manufacturers	Figures	Yarns	Yds/Lb
Bockens Linen Rug Warp	503-585, 874-891	8/2	1200
Holma-Helsinglands AB	586-668, 892-915	8/3	800
Forsa, Sweden	669-737, 916-927	8/4	600
	738-795, 928-939	8/5	480
Cum Textile Industries, Ltd.		4/1 tow	1250
5 Roemersgade		16/1	4715
1362 Copenhagen, Denmark			
Frederick J. Fawcett, Inc.		1½ lea	450
129 South Street		8/1	2400
Boston, MA 02111		10/1	3000
Mail Order		14/1	4200
		20/1	6000
		10/2	1350
		10/5	540
		20/2	3000
		40/2	6000
		70/2	10500
		20/11	500
Plymouth Yarn Co.		10/5	600
Box 28		10/2	1500
Bristol, PA 19007			
Scott's Woolen Mills		10/2	1500
Hecla & Elmdale Streets			
Uxbridge, MA 01569			
Mail Order			

Appendix III: Wool Weft Yarns

Yardages and yarn sizes have been provided by the manufacturer and are accurate to within + or − 5%. Certain dyes, however, are heavier than others and there might be less yardage per unit weight due to dyestuff and finishing procedures than other colors of the same spin. Yarns spun on the worsted system will have different results from yarns spun on the woolen system, even if the yards per unit weight are the same.

Yardages are given in yards per pound, unless otherwise noted as yards per kilo.

All listed manufacturers sell wholesale to retail outlets. Those that also sell via mail order are so noted, with the charge for samples, if applicable. Enquiries are welcome, and should be sent to the address listed.

ABBREVIATIONS:	VW	= Virgin Wool	Lt	= Light	SE	= Single ends, not plied
	KW	= Knitting Worsted	Med	= Medium	Y/K	= Yards per Kilo
	Wd	= Worsted Spun	Hvy	= Heavy	M/K	= Meters per Kilo
	W	= Woolen Spun	Wgt	= Weight		

* See Figures 1-502
** See Figures 503-795

Manufacturers	Wefts	Yarns	Yds/Unit	Figures
Appleton Bros. of London	1.	Crewel - 2 Ply	3840	
Main Street	D, 2.	Tapestry - 4 Ply	1280	*
Little Compton, RI 02837				
Bartlettyarns, Inc.	3.	Softspun - SE	1880	814
Harmony, ME 04942	4.	Homespun - SE	1880	
Mail Order	5.	Lt. Warp - SE	1600	
Samples: $.50	6.	Hvy. Warp - SE	1400	
	7.	Fisherman - 2 Ply	840	895
	8.	Fisherman - 3 Ply	590	889, 897
	9.	Extra Hvy. Rug - 4 Ply	288	903, 904, 921, 925, 933, 934
	10.	Bulky - SE	340	914, 918, 926, 931, 936
	11.	Baby Bulky - SE	560	
	12.	Primitive, Navajo Type - SE	560	891, 894
Bergå AB	C, 13.	Filtgarn - 6/2	3300 y/k	*
Arkhyttan	14.	Ryagarn 2/2	1100 y/k	
S - 783 02 Stora Skedvi	15.	Hargarn 1/1	1100 y/k	
Sweden	16.	Gobelänggarn 5.5/2	5400 y/k	797, 834
	17.	Gute 1.5/1	1650 y/k	858
Bernat, Emile & Sons	18.	Tapestria - 4 Ply	913	
Depot & Mendon Street	E, 19.	Sesame Wd. - 4 Ply	1080	*
Uxbridge, MA 10569	20.	Sesame Sport - 3 Ply	2030	801, 810, 823
	21.	Mohair - SE	900	800
	22.	Blarney Spun - 3 Ply	700	851
Briggs & Little Woolen	23.	Warp & Weft - 1/12	2200	
Mills, Ltd.	24.	Warp & Weft - 2/12	1100	
Harvey Station				
York Mills, N.B.				
Canada EOH 1HO				
Mail Order				
Brunswick Worsted Mills	F, 25.	Germantown K.W. - 4 Ply	1000	*, 880
230 Fifth Avenue	26.	Pomfret Sport - 4 Ply	1600	
New York, NY 10001	27.	Fairhaven Fingering - 3 Ply	2800	
	28.	Natural Irish - 3 Ply	720	
	29.	Persian - 3/2/8	780	
	30.	Monhegan Bulky - 4 Ply	480	
	31.	Monhegan - 4 Ply	1060	
	32.	Monhegan Sport - 4 Ply	1600	
	33.	Aspen - 4 Ply	480	863, 885, 890, 899, 906
	34.	Tapestry - 4 Ply	512	847, 854, 878

Manufacturers	Wefts	Yarns	Yds/Unit	Figures
Chester Farms	35.	Fisherman's 1 Ply	1800	816, 817
RD 2, Box 456	36.	Fisherman's 2 Ply	840	819, 833
Gordansville, VA 22942	37.	Fisherman's 3 Ply	580	832, 905, 917, 928
Mail Order	38.	Bulky - 4 Ply	500	
Samples: $.50 + SASE				
Christopher Sheep Farm	39.	Fisherman's 1 Ply	1600	
RFD #2	40.	Fisherman's 2 Ply	840	
Richmond, ME 04357	41.	Fisherman's 3 Ply	580	
Mail Order				
J & H Clasgens Co.	42.	Wool Warp - 2/18	5040	
New Richmond, OH 45157				
Mill Store				
Mail Order				
Samples: $1.00				
Coats & Clark	43.	Red Heart - 2/8 Wd.	1976	799, 822
Box 1966				
Stamford, CI 06904				
Columbia Minerva	G, M, 44.	Persian - 3/2/8	800	* **
295 Fifth Avenue				
New York, NY 10016				
Condon, Wm & Sons	45.	1/8	2100	
Box 129	46.	2/9 Fine	1100	
Charlottetown, P.E.I.	47.	2/6 Med.	800	830, 840, 865, 874
Canada CIA 7K3	48.	3/6 Med. Hvy.	450	
Mail Order	49.	hvy. 5 Ply	300	
Conlin Yarns	50.	2¼ Run - SE	3600	
Box 11818	51.	Knitting/Tapestry - 4 Ply	1120	
Philadelphia, PA 19128				
Mail Order				
Craftsmen's Mark Yarns	52.	12 Cheviot - SE	3072	
Trofnunt 630	53.	0's Med. Wgt. - SE	2048	
Denbigh LLI6 5 UD	54.	5's Hvy. Wgt. - SE	1280	
North Wales, U. K.	55.	Rug - 2/5	640	
Mail Order only	56.	Treble Ply - 3/2/5	240	
Samples: $3.50	57.	Wd. Warp - 2 Ply	700	
Cum Textile Ind., Inc.	58.	5.5/1	2710	
5 Roemersgade	59.	Swedish - 7/2	1640	
1362 Copenhagen	B, 60.	Wd. 20/2	4920	*
Denmark	H, N, 61.	Mattgarn - 1 Ply	620	* **
	J, O, 62.	Asbo Rya - 2 Ply	570	* **
	63.	Homespun - 1 Ply	1510	
	64.	Gobelin - 2 Ply	1780	811, 821, 835
Dartmouth House	65.	Persian - 3/2/8	800	
The Robert Joseph Co.	66.	Rug - 3/16	256	901, 909, 923
145 W. 4th Street	67.	Rug - 4/45	720	846, 853
Cincinnati, OH 45202				
Mail Order				
Samples: $2.00				
Dollfus-Mieg & Cie (DMC)	68.	Tapestry	1600 M/K	807, 827
Mulhouse, France				
Frederick J. Fawcett, Inc.	69.	Wd. 2/20	5600	
129 South Street	70.	Wd. 3/12	2160	
Boston, MA 02111				
Mail Order				

Manufacturers	Wefts	Yarns	Yds/Unit	Figure
Fort Crailo Yarns Co. 2 Green Street Rennsalaer, NY 12144 Mail Order Samples: $2.00	71. 72. 73. 74.	Rya - 2 Ply Crailo Spun - SE Litespun - 2 Ply Crailo Zephyr Wd. - 2 Ply	600 700 1700 4900	
Greentree Ranch Wools 163 N. Carter Lake Road Loveland, CO 80537 Mail Order	75. 76. 77. 78. 79.	Alpen wool, Lt. - Cored Alpen wool, Med. - Cored Alpen wool, Hvy. - Cored Lt. Fancy - Cored Wool fringe	36 21 16 75 96	
Harrisville Designs Box 51A Harrisville, NH 03450 Mail Order Samples: $2.00	80. 81. Q, 82. 83. 84. 85. 86. 87.	Dyed V. W. - 1 Ply Dyed V. W. - 2 Ply Designer yarns - SE Heathers - SE Naturals - 1 Ply Naturals - 2 Ply Hampshire - 1 Ply Cable - Cored	2000 1000 500 1250 Y/K 1000 500 400 20	803, 809 804, 842, 876 **, 843, 869 805, 812, 828 806, 837 838, 870, 882, 887, 893, 912 845, 857, 871, 879, 888, 896, 913, 922, 930
Henry's Attic 5 Mercury Avenue Monroe, NY 10950 Mail Order Samples: $5.00	88. 89. X, 90. 91. 92. 93.	Moby Dick - Cored Toros II Double Loop Mule Spun - 2 Ply, W Crown Colony Rug - 2 Ply Crown Colony Rug - 3 Ply Crown Colony Rug - 4 Ply	35 300 150 1040 350 640	**, 862 829, 841, 864, 875 859, 898, 911, 916, 929
La Mieux, Filature Inc. St. Ephrem Beauce, Quebec Canada Mail Order	94. 95. 96. 97. 98. 99. 100. 101.	Rouet - 4 Ends Carded Wool Ruban - Combed Wool Quebecoise - 2 Ply Quebecoise - 3 Ply Villagoise - 4 Ply Minerve - SE Beauceronne - 2 Ply Rustique - SE	300 20 1100 750 300 690 1800 2000	920, 927, 938 868, 877 902, 908, 919, 937 796, 820, 836
Lion Brand Yarn Co. 1270 Broadway New York, NY 10001	102. 103.	Woolana - 2 Ply Knitting Wd. - 4 Ply	675 Y/K 1100	848
Manos del Uruguay 35 W. 36th Street New York, NY 10018 Mail Order	104. 105. 106. 107.	Type 1 - Handspun SE Type 2 - Handspun SE Type 3 - 2 Ply Type 4 - SE	1200 700 700 100	
Melrose Yarn Co. 1305 Utica Avenue Brooklyn, NY 11203 Att: Customer Service	108. 109.	Woolympia - 4 Ply Naturella - 3 Ply	1080 1500 Y/K	831, 850
Mexiskeins Box 4123 Missoula, MO 59801	110. 111. 112. 113.	Fine - SE Medium - SE Heavy - SE Wool Warp - SE	493 113 50 1000	
Novitex Box 6632 Providence, RI 02940	114.	Wd. 6/2	1680	813, 825
Oregon Worsted Co. Box 02098, Department L Portland, OR 97202	115. 116.	Maypole Willamette 20/2 Maypole Nahalem 3/12	5600 2160	815, 818

Manufacturers	Wefts	Yarns	Yds/Unit	Figures
Paternayan Bros. Inc.		117. Persian 3/2/8½	710	
312 E. 95th Street		118. Paterna Crewel - 2 Ply	3000	808
New York, NY 10028		119. Paterna Tapestry	1000	802, 824, 839
	J, T, 120.	Shag Rug - 4 Ply	360	* **
	K, U, 121.	Paterna Rug - 3 Ply	250	* **
Plymouth Yarn Co.		122. Natural Wool Roving	175	
Box 28		123. Persian - 3/2/8	700	
Bristol, PA 19007		124. Nordika - 2 Ply	432	
		125. Berber - 4 Ply	210	
		126. Indiecita Alpaca - 3 Ply	1500	
		127. Indiecita Alpaca - 4 Ply	850	
Scott's Woolen Mill		128. Bulgari - 2 Ply	430	844, 856, 860
Hecla & Elmdale Streets	V, 129.	Berber - 4 Ply	210	**, 861
Uxbridge, MA 01569		130. Wd. 2/11	3080	
Mill Store		131. Wd. 2/13	3640	
Mail Order		132. Wd. 2/14	3900	
		133. Wd. 2/15	4200	
		134. Wd. 2/24	6700	
Solar Spun		135. Rug Wool	326	907
Box 164				
Jenkintown, PA				
Mail Order				
Spinnerin Yarn Co.		136. Marvel Twist K.W. - 4 Ply	2750 Y/K	849, 855
230 Fifth Avenue		137. Fisherman's yarn - 3 Ply	2750 Y/K	
New York, NY 10001		138. Pippin sport - 3 Ply	2100 Y/K	
Att: Mr. R. Mattes		139. Clou - 2 Ply	2100 Y/K	
U.S. Distributor of		140. Livia - 4 Ply	3300 Y/K	798, 826
Schaffhouse Yarns		141. Homespun - SE	900 Y/K	
		142. Viking - SE	1050 Y/K	883
		143. Big Sky - 2 Ply	1050 Y/K	866, 884, 900, 910
		144. Smyrna - 2 Ply	440 Y/K	935
Tahki Imports, Ltd.		145. Donegal Tweed Super Hvy.	500	
62 Madison Street		146. Donegal Tweed Homespun -SE	900	
Hackensack, NJ 07601		147. Donegal Tweed K. W.	800	
		148. Soho - SE	500	
		149. Stimoni Greek Warp - SE	974	
George Wells	P, 150.	Lt. Wgt. Rug - 3 Ply	640	**, 873
The Ruggery	S, 151.	Med. Wgt. Rug - 4 Ply	400	**, 872
Glen Head, L. I.		152. Hvy. Wgt. Rug - 3 Ply	256	932, 939
NY 11545				
Mail Order				
Wilde Yarns		153. Natural Berber - 2 Ply	864	852
3705 Main Street	R, 154.	Natural Berber - 4 Ply	432	**
Philadelphia, PA		155. Natural Berber - 6 Ply	288	
19127		156. Natural white - 2 Ply	480	867, 881, 886, 892, 915, 924
Mail Order		157. Natural white - 4 Ply	240	
		158. Natural white - 6 Ply	160	
		159. Hvy. Berber - 3 Ply	576	
	L, W, 160.	Hvy. Berber - 4 Ply	160	* **
Yorkshire Yarn Co.		161. Yorkshire Tweed - SE	138	
1121 California Street				
Denver, CO 80204				

Many of the yarns in this listing are similar to each other in yardage, spin, and hand, and can — for the most part — be interchanged with each other as dictated by availability. It would be helpful to compare the Figures to select that which is the most pleasing.

Index I: Cotton Warps

Refer to Table III for complete information on wefts.

WARP: 20/2

WEFT	20 EPI				15 EPI				12 EPI				10 EPI			
	FIG	P	T	B	FIG	P	T	B	FIG	P	T	B	FIG	P	T	B
A	1	42	96	146	10	100	150	146	21	150	212	176	32	150	200	172
B	2	42	62	100	11	76	112	100	22	90	120	110	33	86	104	76
C	3	14	24	28	12	22	30	34	23	26	34	44	34	26	32	40
D	4	15	26	30	13	19	34	46	24	20	32	38	35	26	40	36
E	5	13	22	22	14	18	22	28	25	17	26	26	36	24	23	24
F	6	11	19	15	15	14	24	26	26	18	30	24	37	24	24	24
G	7	9	12	15	16	14	16	15	27	14	20	22	38	14	19	21
H	8	10	12	11	17	11	17	16	28	12	16	20	39	14	15	20
I	9	10	13	10	18	12	16	14	29	14	18	16	40	14	16	20
J	-	-	-		19	10	11	9	30	9	12	12	41	8	10	10
K	-	-	-		20	6	8	7	31	7	8	8	42	6	8	8
L	-	-	-		-	-	-		-	-	-		43	5	6	6

WARP: 24/3

WEFT	20 EPI				15 EPI				12 EPI				10 EPI			
	FIG	P	T	B	FIG	P	T	B	FIG	P	T	B	FIG	P	T	B
A	44	21	32	40	53	33	64	80	62	60	128	94	71	64	120	90
B	45	22	40	64	54	50	70	74	63	86	108	88	72	90	96	98
C	46	13	20	17	55	16	22	30	64	20	28	34	73	27	38	40
D	47	12	19	19	56	15	26	24	65	18	32	38	74	28	46	37
E	48	11	17	20	57	14	16	20	66	18	28	28	75	18	24	26
F	49	10	16	18	58	13	18	18	67	17	23	24	76	18	26	26
G	50	9	12	12	59	11	14	14	68	14	18	16	77	14	17	21
H	51	10	13	11	60	11	13	15	69	14	15	18	78	14	17	20
I	52	9	12	10	61	9	13	13	70	12	15	14	79	13	17	19
J	-	-	-		-	-	-		-	-	-		80	9	10	11
K	-	-	-		-	-	-		-	-	-		-	-	-	
L	-	-	-		-	-	-		-	-	-		-	-	-	

WARP: 20/3

WEFT	20 EPI				15 EPI				12 EPI				10 EPI			
	FIG	P	T	B	FIG	P	T	B	FIG	P	T	B	FIG	P	T	B
A	90	20	30	32	99	28	52	66	108	34	68	70		-	-	-
B	91	20	32	50	100	38	76	80	109	82	100	80		-	-	-
C	92	13	18	19	101	14	21	26	110	17	24	30	118	20	34	38
D	93	12	18	16	102	15	22	28	111	16	28	32	119	22	38	34
E	94	10	14	12	103	13	17	24	112	15	22	27	120	22	30	28
F	95	9	14	14	104	12	16	19	113	14	19	24	121	19	24	24
G	96	9	12	9	105	11	15	15	114	12	15	19	122	14	18	22
H	97	10	13	9	106	10	14	14	115	12	15	17	123	15	18	23
I	98	9	12	9	107	10	13	12	116	11	16	17	124	13	17	19
J	-	-	-		-	-	-		117	9	11	11	125	9	11	12
K	-	-	-		-	-	-		-	-	-		126	6	8	8
L	-	-	-		-	-	-		-	-	-		-	-	-	

WARP: 10/2

WEFT	20 EPI				15 EPI				12 EPI				10 EPI			
	FIG	P	T	B	FIG	P	T	B	FIG	P	T	B	FIG	P	T	B
A	135	18	24	26	144	22	40	40	154	26	48	56	165	32	64	68
B	136	20	34	49	145	36	50	66	155	62	86	76	166	80	88	80
C	137	13	18	16	146	15	20	22	156	18	26	28	167	21	36	34
D	138	12	17	17	147	14	20	22	157	17	23	28	168	20	31	32
E	139	10	16	17	148	14	20	22	158	15	22	24	169	18	20	23
F	140	10	16	14	149	12	15	17	159	14	18	24	170	16	19	25
G	141	9	12	11	150	11	15	14	160	12	15	18	171	12	14	21
H	142	9	13	11	151	11	14	12	161	11	15	16	172	15	20	20
I	143	8	11	10	152	9	14	11	162	11	15	16	173	12	18	22
J	-	-	-		153	7	9	8	163	8	9	9	174	10	11	9
K	-	-	-		-	-	-		164	6	8	8	175	7	9	8
L	-	-	-		-	-	-		-	-	-		176	6	6	6

WARP: 24/3   8 EPI

WEFT		FIG	P	T	B
	A		-	-	-
	B		-	-	-
	C	81	32	44	40
	D	82	34	48	40
	E	83	20	26	30
	F	84	18	20	22
	G	85	16	18	24
	H	86	15	22	26
	I	87	15	18	22
	J	88	9	12	14
	K	89	7	8	10
	L		-	-	-

WARP: 20/3   8 EPI

WEFT		FIG	P	T	B
	A		-	-	-
	B		-	-	-
	C		-	-	-
	D		-	-	-
	E	127	28	36	28
	F	128	24	24	26
	G	129	19	24	24
	H	130	19	23	28
	I	131	14	20	24
	J	132	10	12	15
	K	133	8	9	10
	L	134	6	8	7

WARP: 10/2   8 EPI   7½ EPI

WEFT		FIG	P	T	B	FIG	P	T	B
	A		-	-	-		-	-	-
	B		-	-	-		-	-	-
	C	177	34	40	42	187	32	40	42
	D	178	34	38	34	188	38	40	40
	E	179	21	24	23	189	25	27	25
	F	180	21	21	23	190	26	24	24
	G	181	17	23	25	191	18	19	21
	H	182	14	22	24	192	20	24	28
	I	183	14	20	23	193	16	18	24
	J	184	9	12	13	194	9	11	16
	K	185	8	9	9	195	8	9	14
	L	186	6	6	6	196	6	6	6

WARP: 16/4

WEFT	15 EPI FIG	P	T	B	12 EPI FIG	P	T	B	10 EPI FIG	P	T	B	8 EPI FIG	P	T	B
A	197	17	32	52	209	18	40	54	221	44	84	86	233	54	96	78
B	198	34	60	76	210	50	106	94	222	82	132	90	234	100	120	98
C	199	12	24	24	211	17	30	39	223	24	42	44	235	28	40	38
D	200	13	20	20	212	15	24	30	224	22	36	40	236	24	47	41
E	201	12	19	22	213	14	20	24	225	19	26	26	237	22	30	30
F	202	12	17	24	214	14	20	24	226	16	22	26	238	20	25	24
G	203	9	14	12	215	11	17	22	227	13	22	25	239	16	20	22
H	204	9	12	17	216	10	14	16	228	11	17	14	240	13	18	24
I	205	10	14	14	217	11	13	15	229	12	17	22	241	13	18	22
J	206	8	10	9	218	7	10	10	230	9	11	13	242	10	12	14
K	207	7	9	7	219	6	8	7	231	7	8	8	243	7	9	10
L	208	6	6	7	220	5	6	6	232	6	7	6	244	6	7	6

WARP: 10/3

WEFT	15 EPI FIG	P	T	B	12 EPI FIG	P	T	B	10 EPI FIG	P	T	B	8 EPI FIG	P	T	B
A	282	20	30	40	292	24	50	60	303	25	48	60	315	60	92	70
B	283	28	50	74	293	50	108	84	304	84	92	84		-	-	-
C	284	13	23	28	294	18	30	34	305	18	28	34	316	22	36	36
D	285	12	22	24	295	18	28	30	306	20	28	34	317	34	49	46
E	286	11	17	19	296	12	20	24	307	13	19	26	318	22	30	30
F	287	10	14	12	297	12	20	24	308	15	23	25	319	20	30	28
G	288	10	13	11	298	11	16	18	309	12	16	19	320	20	24	27
H	289	9	12	12	299	11	15	17	310	12	16	18	321	17	22	28
I	290	9	13	12	300	10	13	15	311	10	16	17	322	14	20	21
J	291	8	10	9	301	7	10	10	312	8	10	12	323	10	12	12
K		-	-	-	302	6	8	8	313	7	8	8	324	8	9	12
L		-	-	-		-	-	-	314	6	6	7	325	6	8	6

WARP: 5/2

WEFT	15 EPI FIG	P	T	B	12 EPI FIG	P	T	B	10 EPI FIG	P	T	B	8 EPI FIG	P	T	B
A	347	17	35	38	359	18	32	38	371	22	44	50	383	27	68	58
B	348	35	84	110	360	70	148	130	372	90	120	120	384	100	140	110
C	349	14	26	36	361	14	24	34	373	20	36	44	385	30	52	50
D	350	14	26	32	362	14	30	38	374	24	46	48	386	18	40	42
E	351	12	20	22	363	16	30	30	375	26	30	30	387	18	30	24
F	352	11	18	22	364	12	24	24	376	16	26	30	388	16	28	24
G	353	10	14	14	365	10	16	18	377	10	20	26	389	11	21	24
H	354	8	12	12	366	10	16	16	378	12	18	20	390	11	18	21
I	355	9	13	12	367	10	16	18	379	11	16	26	391	11	21	24
J	356	7	9	8	368	8	11	10	380	9	12	15	392	8	11	11
K	357	5	7	6	369	6	8	7	381	6	8	8	393	11	8	7
L	358	4	5	4	370	4	5	4	382	5	5	6	394	5	5	5

WARP: 3/2

WEFT	15 EPI FIG	P	T	B	12 EPI FIG	P	T	B	10 EPI FIG	P	T	B	8 EPI FIG	P	T	B
A	436	12	16	13	445	12	18	20	456	16	24	32	468	24	40	40
B	437	18	31	36	446	26	54	70	457	80	-	-		-	-	-
C	438	12	18	18	447	12	19	18	458	14	30	36	469	33	50	43
D	439	12	18	18	448	14	19	21	459	16	30	38	470	30	50	42
E	440	10	15	13	449	12	18	20	460	17	23	29	471	24	38	30
F	441	10	15	13	450	12	18	15	461	14	20	23	472	17	30	26
G	442	9	12	10	451	9	14	12	462	11	16	19	473	14	18	24
H	443	9	10	8	452	10	16	15	463	10	16	22	474	12	20	24
I	444	8	11	10	453	9	12	12	464	11	18	23	475	15	20	27
J		-	-	-	454	8	9	9	465	8	10	11	476	9	11	11
K		-	-	-	455	6	9	7	466	6	8	9	477	7	8	10
L		-	-	-		-	-	-	467	6	7	6	478	6	8	8

WARP: 16/4

WEFT	7½ EPI FIG	P	T	B	6 EPI FIG	P	T	B	5 EPI FIG	P	T	B	4 EPI FIG	P	T	B
A	245	58	96	76	256	64	88	80	267	80	108	100		-	-	-
B	-	-	-						-	-	-			-	-	-
C	246	34	44	42	257	40	52	77						-	-	-
D	247	28	36	38	258	32	44	38	-	-	-			-	-	-
E	248	24	32	30	259	28	30	28	268	28	32	28		-	-	-
F	249	22	26	26	260	26	28	28	269	26	28	24		-	-	-
G	250	14	20	22	261	18	24	24	270	24	32	26	276	26	24	24
H	251	14	18	24	262	20	22	26	271	22	30	26	277	28	32	30
I	252	12	17	20	263	18	28	22	272	20	24	24	278	24	28	26
J	253	10	12	14	264	11	14	16	273	10	14	16	279	16	20	20
K	254	8	8	8	265	8	9	9	274	10	10	14	280	12	10	12
L	255	6	7	6	266	7	8	7	275	7	7	7	281	8	8	9

WARP: 10/3

WEFT	7½ EPI FIG	P	T	B	6 EPI FIG	P	T	B	5 EPI FIG	P	T	B
A	326	71	-	-		-	-	-		-	-	-
B	-	-	-		-	-	-		-	-	-
C	327	44	-	-		-	-	-		-	-	-
D	-	-	-		-	-	-		-	-	-
E	328	32	39	34		-	-	-		-	-	-
F	329	28	30	24		-	-	-		-	-	-
G	330	20	28	28	336	28	32	24		-	-	-
H	331	20	24	28	337	21	36	28	342	30	36	28
I	332	16	24	26	338	26	34	26	343	24	28	28
J	333	10	14	16	339	12	14	18	344	16	18	20
K	334	7	9	9	340	9	11	12	345	10	11	14
L	335	6	7	7	341	6	8	8	346	7	9	10

WARP: 5/2

WEFT	7½ EPI FIG	P	T	B	6 EPI FIG	P	T	B	5 EPI FIG	P	T	B	4 EPI FIG	P	T	B
A	395	28	68	58	407	40	72	66	418	54	88	66	427	70	96	80
B	396	94	128	100	-	-	-		-	-	-					
C	397	32	42	42	408	40	62	50		-	-	-		-	-	-
D	398	22	52	40	409	34	48	40	-	-	-			-	-	-
E	399	18	36	26	410	26	32	30	419	28	36	28	428	30	38	28
F	400	20	28	25	411	26	28	24	420	26	30	28	429	26	24	24
G	401	13	23	24	412	20	28	24	421	22	30	26	430	26	32	24
H	402	11	18	22	413	14	24	20	422	22	28	24	431	22	28	24
I	403	12	23	21	414	14	26	24	423	26	36	28	432	24	32	24
J	404	8	11	14	415	9	16	15	424	14	16	18	433	14	16	20
K	405	7	9	10	416	7	9	9	425	9	13	14	434	11	12	14
L	406	5	7	5	417	6	6	6	426	6	7	8	435	6	8	10

WARP: 3/2

WEFT	7½ EPI FIG	P	T	B	6 EPI FIG	P	T	B	5 EPI FIG	P	T	B	4 EPI FIG	P	T	B
A	479	24	-	-	488	32	-	-		-	-	-		-	-	-
B	-	-	-		-	-	-		-	-	-		-	-	-
C	-	-	-		-	-	-		-	-	-		-	-	-
D	-	-	-		-	-	-		-	-	-		-	-	-
E	480	24	-	-	489	36	-	-		-	-	-		-	-	-
F	481	22	30	27	490	34	-	-		-	-	-		-	-	-
G	482	16	27	24	491	24	-	-		-	-	-		-	-	-
H	483	15	19	27	492	13	40	32		-	-	-		-	-	-
I	484	17	24	25	493	20	30	28		-	-	-		-	-	-
J	485	9	12	15	494	11	16	19	497	18	20	20	500	20	24	20
K	486	8	8	14	495	9	9	12	498	11	13	15	501	15	17	15
L	487	6	6	7	496	6	7	7	499	7	8	11	502	9	11	11

Index II: Linen Warps

Refer to Table IV for complete information on wefts.

WARP: 8/2

WEFT	12 EPI FIG	P	T	B	10 EPI FIG	P	T	B	9 EPI FIG	P	T	B	8 EPI FIG	P	T	B
M	503	10	18	25	515	11	18	25	527	14	26	26	539	18	30	28
N	504	11	16	18	516	13	20	24	528	14	24	24	540	16	26	28
O	505	10	17	18	517	11	19	24	529	14	21	26	541	16	28	30
P	506	10	16	13	518	11	16	20	530	13	18	23	542	14	20	25
Q	507	8	12	10	519	8	12	14	531	10	12	17	543	10	14	20
R	508	8	10	9	520	8	11	11	532	8	11	18	544	8	13	16
S	509	7	10	9	521	8	11	10	533	9	13	17	545	10	14	18
T	510	7	10	7	522	7	10	11	534	8	11	14	546	9	13	16
U	511	6	8	6	523	6	9	9	535	7	11	13	547	8	11	13
V	512	5	7	5	524	5	7	6	536	6	8	8	548	6	8	11
W	513	5	5	5	525	5	6	6	537	5	7	7	549	6	7	6
X	514	4	6	5	526	5	6	6	538	5	6	6	550	5	7	7

WARP: 8/3

WEFT	12 EPI FIG	P	T	B	10 EPI FIG	P	T	B	9 EPI FIG	P	T	B	8 EPI FIG	P	T	B
M	586	9	15	13	598	9	15	23	610	12	26	30	622	14	26	29
N	587	9	14	14	599	10	15	24	611	12	20	24	623	16	30	34
O	588	9	12	12	600	9	14	15	612	11	19	24	624	12	20	30
P	589	8	12	11	601	9	14	17	613	11	16	22	625	10	20	28
Q	590	7	10	8	602	7	12	12	614	8	12	16	626	9	14	22
R	591	7	9	7	603	7	9	9	615	8	10	15	627	9	13	17
S	592	7	9	7	604	7	10	9	616	7	12	15	628	9	14	20
T	593	7	9	8	605	6	9	9	617	7	11	14	629	9	15	18
U	594	6	9	7	606	6	8	8	618	7	10	12	630	7	10	14
V	595	5	7	5	607	5	7	6	619	6	7	6	631	5	8	8
W	596	5	5	5	608	5	5	5	620	5	6	5	632	5	7	7
X	597	4	6	4	609	4	5	5	621	5	6	5	633	5	7	7

WARP: 8/4

WEFT	10 EPI FIG	P	T	B	9 EPI FIG	P	T	B	8 EPI FIG	P	T	B
M	669	8	15	19	681	10	18	28	693	10	20	28
N	670	9	15	22	682	9	17	24	694	9	18	28
O	671	8	14	15	683	10	18	22	695	9	18	25
P	672	8	15	14	684	9	16	22	696	8	17	24
Q	673	7	11	11	685	7	11	12	697	8	11	15
R	674	7	10	9	686	7	11	10	698	7	10	14
S	675	7	10	8	687	7	12	14	699	7	12	18
T	676	7	11	10	688	7	12	14	700	8	13	18
U	677	6	10	8	689	6	10	10	701	6	9	13
V	678	5	7	6	690	5	7	7	702	5	8	8
W	679	5	7	5	691	5	6	6	703	5	7	6
X	680	5	7	5	692	5	7	6	704	5	7	6

WARP: 8/5

WEFT	9 EPI FIG	P	T	B	8 EPI FIG	P	T	B
M	738	9	20	27	750	13	26	34
N	739	9	20	23	751	11	21	26
O	740	9	17	22	752	9	17	30
P	741	9	16	22	753	10	21	27
Q	742	7	12	12	754	7	13	20
R	743	7	11	10	755	7	12	15
S	744	7	11	12	756	7	12	19
T	745	7	12	15	757	7	12	18
U	746	6	10	10	758	6	10	14
V	747	5	8	6	759	5	7	7
W	748	5	7	5	760	5	8	6
X	749	5	7	5	761	5	7	6

WARP: 8/2

WEFT		6 EPI				5 EPI				4 EPI				WARP AS WEFT				
		FIG	P	T	B	FIG	P	T	B	FIG	P	T	B	FIG	EPI	P	T	B
	M	551	28	38	28	563	30	-	-		-	-	-	580	12	11	22	33
	N	552	26	36	28	564	32	36	30		-	-	-	581	10	14	28	40
	O	553	24	30	28	565	26	36	30		-	-	-	582	9	17	40	48
	P	554	15	24	24	566	26	30	24		-	-	-	583	8	20	56	52
	Q	555	12	14	20	567	20	26	22		-	-	-	584	6	36	-	-
	R	556	12	16	18	568	16	24	23		-	-	-	585	5	48	-	-
	S	557	12	16	18	569	16	19	17		-	-	-					
	T	558	11	14	17	570	16	18	18	575	16	24	20					
	U	559	9	11	14	571	14	14	14	576	14	14	14					
	V	560	6	8	10	572	8	10	12	577	8	12	12					
	W	561	6	7	6	573	6	9	11	578	7	8	12					
	X	562	6	7	8	574	6	8	8	579	10	9	8					

WARP: 8/3

WEFT		6 EPI				5 EPI				4 EPI				WARP AS WEFT				
		FIG	P	T	B	FIG	P	T	B	FIG	P	T	B	FIG	EPI	P	T	B
	M	634	24	36	30	646	34	-	-		-	-	-	663	12	9	14	13
	N	635	24	36	30	647	30	34	30		-	-	-	664	10	10	16	15
	O	636	22	32	30	648	28	34	28		-	-	-	665	9	11	22	34
	P	637	22	30	30	649	28	32	26		-	-	-	666	8	14	24	38
	Q	638	13	19	22	650	20	24	23		-	-	-	667	6	16	48	40
	R	639	12	21	22	651	14	22	22		-	-	-	668	5	34	-	-
	S	640	12	20	20	652	16	22	20		-	-	-					
	T	641	11	19	20	653	16	24	24	658	20	24	20					
	U	642	13	16	16	654	15	15	18	659	16	18	17					
	V	643	7	9	13	655	8	11	14	660	12	12	14					
	W	644	6	8	10	656	7	8	10	661	8	12	12					
	X	645	6	8	10	657	7	8	11	662	9	9	10					

WARP: 8/4

WEFT		6 EPI				5 EPI				4 EPI				WARP AS WEFT				
		FIG	P	T	B	FIG	P	T	B	FIG	P	T	B	FIG	EPI	P	T	B
	M	705	26	36	32	717	34	-	-		-	-	-	732	10	8	12	12
	N	706	22	32	28	718	32	-	-		-	-	-	733	9	8	17	19
	O	707	22	32	28	719	28	-	-		-	-	-	734	8	9	18	23
	P	708	16	29	29	720	30	-	-		-	-	-	735	6	13	32	32
	Q	709	8	16	24	721	20	30			-	-	-	736	5	26	-	-
	R	710	10	18	22	722	18	24	-		-	-	-	737	4	30	-	-
	S	711	11	20	20	723	18	20	-		-	-	-					
	T	712	15	17	22	724	18	26	-		-	-	-					
	U	713	10	13	16	725	14	20	-		-	-	-					
	V	714	6	8	13	726	8	12	15	729	12	14	16					
	W	715	5	7	9	727	6	9	11	730	8	10	13					
	X	716	6	8	10	728	7	9	10	731	9	9	11					

WARP: 8/5

WEFT		6 EPI				5 EPI				4 EPI				WARP AS WEFT				
		FIG	P	T	B	FIG	P	T	B	FIG	P	T	B	FIG	EPI	P	T	B
	M	762	24	40	-	774	36	-	-		-	-	-	791	9	8	13	12
	N	763	24	37	26	775	24	-	-		-	-	-	792	8	8	15	18
	O	764	24	40	-	776	25	-	-		-	-	-	793	6	11	28	30
	P	765	24	38	-	777	30	-	-		-	-	-	794	5	16	-	-
	Q	766	13	22	23	778	26	-	-		-	-	-	795	4	26	-	-
	R	767	10	20	20	779	18	-	-		-	-	-					
	S	768	10	18	22	780	19	30	-		-	-	-					
	T	769	12	20	21	781	19	30	-	786	25	-	-					
	U	770	10	13	15	782	14	20	-	787	16	-	-					
	V	771	6	9	12	783	7	11	14	788	10	13	14					
	W	772	5	8	10	784	6	9	12	789	8	10	14					
	X	773	5	8	11	785	6	9	11	790	8	8	12					

Index III: Supplemental Wefts With Cotton Warps

Refer to Appendix III for complete information on wefts.

WARP: 24/3   12 EPI

FIG	WEFT	P	T	B	SEE ALSO
796	100	18	26	30	820, 836
797	16	20	30	32	834
798	140	24	34	32	826
799	43	23	36	30	822
800	21	17	20	20	
801	20	48	60	50	810, 823
802	119	22	28	32	824, 839
803	80	26	42	50	809
804	81	16	24	24	842, 876
805	83	14	20	21	812, 828
806	84	15	20	20	837
807	68	15	21	22	827

WARP: 20/3   15 EPI

FIG	WEFT	P	T	B	SEE ALSO
808	118	24	36	52	
809	80	18	26	14	803
810	20	24	40	47	801, 823
811	64	18	25	30	821, 835
812	83	14	18	17	805, 828
813	114	16	25	31	825
814	3	26	28	34	
815	116	26	34	54	818
816	35	26	34	36	817

WARP: 20/3   12 EPI

FIG	WEFT	P	T	B	SEE ALSO
817	35	28	38	32	816
818	116	34	42	56	815
819	36	14	18	26	833

WARP: 10/2   10 EPI

FIG	WEFT	P	T	B	SEE ALSO
820	100	17	26	32	796, 836
821	64	23	38	44	811, 835
822	43	24	34	28	799
823	20	40	40	38	801, 810
824	119	16	20	30	802, 839
825	114	23	34	36	813
826	140	26	37	34	798
827	68	14	16	23	807
828	83	15	22	26	805, 812
829	91	14	19	22	841, 864, 875
830	47	16	20	26	840, 865, 874
831	108	14	19	22	850

WARP: 16/4   6 EPI

FIG	WEFT	P	T	B	SEE ALSO
832	37	22	26	22	905, 917, 928
833	36	32	52	32	819
834	16	40	52	50	797

WARP: 3/2   10 EPI

FIG	WEFT	P	T	B	SEE ALSO
835	64	18	30	44	811, 821
836	100	15	24	35	796, 820
837	84	12	20	30	806
838	85	8	11	11	870, 882, 887, 893, 912
839	119	14	22	30	802, 824
840	47	12	19	26	830, 865, 874
841	91	12	17	24	829, 864, 875
842	81	13	18	30	804, 876
843	82	8	9	9	869
844	128	8	11	14	856, 860
845	86	10	14	17	857, 871, 879, 888, 896, 913, 922, 930
846	67	11	16	21	853
847	34	13	20	28	854, 878
848	103	14	21	28	
849	136	14	21	24	855
850	108	15	19	24	831
851	22	11	17	20	
852	153	7	12	11	

WARP: 3/2   8 EPI

FIG	WEFT	P	T	B	SEE ALSO
853	67	14	21	28	846
854	34	18	34	25	847, 878
855	136	22	23	24	849
856	128	10	14	18	844, 860
857	86	13	16	20	845, 871, 879, 888, 896, 913, 922, 930
858	17	14	18	22	

WARP: 3/2   6 EPI

FIG	WEFT	P	T	B	SEE ALSO
859	92	7	8	12	898, 911, 916, 929
860	128	12	18	20	844, 856
861	129	7	8	9	
862	90	5	6	5	
863	33	11	12	17	885, 890, 899, 906
864	91	30	36	34	829, 841, 875
865	47	26	35	30	830, 840, 874
866	143	9	10	13	884, 900, 910
867	156	12	18	18	881, 886, 892, 915, 924
868	96	26	36	30	877
869	82	9	13	15	843
870	85	13	18	22	838, 882, 887, 893, 912
871	86	13	20	20	845, 857, 879, 888, 896, 913, 922, 930
872	151	11	17	18	
873	150	16	24	24	

Index IV: Supplemental Wefts With Linen Warps

Refer to Appendix III for complete information on wefts.

WARP: 8/2   10 EPI

FIG	WEFT	P	T	B	SEE ALSO
874	47	16	24	28	830, 840, 865
875	91	18	34	42	829, 841, 864
876	81	14	22	34	804, 842
877	96	14	22	30	868
878	34	14	18	33	847, 854
879	86	9	12	20	845, 857, 871, 888, 896, 913, 922, 930
880	25	17	28	28	
881	156	8	12	14	867, 886, 892, 915, 924
882	85	9	13	14	838, 870, 887, 893, 912
883	142	9	12	20	
884	143	8	11	14	866, 900, 910
885	33	8	10	15	863, 890, 899, 906

WARP: 8/2   5 EPI

FIG	WEFT	P	T	B	SEE ALSO
886	156	19	24	23	867, 881, 892, 915, 924
887	85	20	26	23	838, 870, 882, 893, 912
888	86	23	30	24	845, 857, 871, 879, 896, 913, 922, 930
889	8	20	16	20	897
890	33	15	12	16	863, 885, 899, 906
891	12	20	20	20	894

WARP: 8/3   9 EPI

FIG	WEFT	P	T	B	SEE ALSO
892	156	8	12	15	867, 881, 886, 915, 924
893	85	9	13	17	838, 870, 882, 887, 912
894	12	9	12	16	891
895	7	12	23	23	
896	86	9	14	18	845, 857, 871, 879, 888, 913, 922, 930
897	8	9	14	19	889
898	92	7	9	7	859, 911, 916, 929
899	33	7	10	16	863, 885, 890, 906
900	143	8	11	14	866, 884, 910
901	66	6	7	7	909, 923
902	98	6	9	13	908, 919, 937
903	9	6	8	10	904, 921, 925, 933, 934

WARP: 8/3   5 EPI

FIG	WEFT	P	T	B	SEE ALSO
904	9	10	13	12	903, 921, 925, 933, 934
905	37	16	20	20	832, 917, 928
906	33	17	18	16	863, 885, 890, 899
907	135	14	16	17	
908	98	16	18	15	902, 919, 937
909	66	10	12	14	901, 923
910	143	17	15	16	866, 884, 900
911	92	16	20	17	859, 898, 916, 929
912	85	22	26	26	838, 870, 882, 887, 893
913	86	26	34	26	845, 857, 871, 879, 888, 896, 922, 930
914	10	12	16	16	918, 926, 931, 936
915	156	20	30	28	867, 881, 886, 892, 924

WARP: 8/4   8 EPI

FIG	WEFT	P	T	B	SEE ALSO
916	92	7	10	18	859, 898, 911, 929
917	37	10	16	21	832, 905, 928
918	10	7	10	13	914, 926, 931, 936
919	98	6	10	13	902, 908, 937
920	94	5	7	7	927, 938
921	9	6	9	12	903, 904, 925, 933, 934
922	86	9	15	21	845, 857, 871, 879, 888, 896, 913, 930
923	66	6	8	11	901, 909
924	156	7	13	20	867, 881, 886, 892, 915

WARP: 8/4   4 EPI

FIG	WEFT	P	T	B	SEE ALSO
925	9	13	14	13	903, 904, 921, 933, 934
926	10	16	12	14	914, 918, 931, 936
927	94	11	12	12	920, 938

WARP: 8/5   8 EPI

FIG	WEFT	P	T	B	SEE ALSO
928	37	10	18	22	832, 905, 917
929	92	7	12	15	859, 898, 911, 916
930	86	10	16	21	845, 857, 871, 879, 888, 896, 913, 922
931	10	7	12	13	914, 918, 926, 936
932	152	6	9	10	939
933	9	6	10	12	903, 904, 921, 925, 934

WARP: 8/5   5 EPI

FIG	WEFT	P	T	B	SEE ALSO
934	9	12	14	13	903, 904, 921, 925, 933
935	144	10	10	13	
936	10	12	13	13	914, 918, 926, 931
937	98	14	20	20	902, 908, 919
938	94	10	15	16	920, 927
939	152	11	15	16	932